# Be Your Own Hero

Tammy Mariposa

ISBN: 9781549813122


**Independently published by Tammy Mariposa**

Contact via Facebook Group: Be Your Own Hero

# Table of Contents

# Acknowledgements

I dedicate this book with a huge lump in my throat to my beautiful children. Without our experiences this book would not have been possible.

Especially to my beautiful insightful boy who reunited with me and unknowingly assisted me into gaining invaluable insight into the process of Parental Alienation and that the conditioning can eventually be broken, which has helped me to help hundreds of affected parents to cope with this devastating pathology.

His return also gave me the renewed strength to get this information out there to you all.

To the one who taught me to be the lion, and to my two soul sisters, one who's been my constant support and strength and the other who continuously reminded me to look inside and believe in myself.

To my hugely talented illustrator Rosie Alexander for bringing my ideas so beautifully to life.

To my wonderfully supportive family who have been there every step of the way and lastly but by no means least to my soul mate, sounding board and love of my life, without whose unwavering love and support and despite his eye-rolling that "You are always on your I-pad!" this book would never have reached a readable format.

To the many enlightened souls I have met on my journey who were pivotal in my recovery.

To my wonderful therapist and angel on this earth, who I met through Women's Aid and who has helped me see me as others see me and that was a tough call.

In addition I want to thank each and every one of the people I have helped on my journey as I have learned so much from them too.

# Introduction

I write under a pseudonym because I still need to protect my family and friends from the Narcissistic ex.

I must stress that I am not a trained counsellor.

This book is not about naming and shaming. Names, personal details, times and places have been changed so no person or event can easily be traced. Whilst these events are specific to my story I have included those that I think will be generally recognised and seem to be typical of what others go through.

Much of this book comes from articles I have posted on my website and are based on my own experiences at the hands of the malignant narcissist I was married to and it's from this that I share my knowledge, connect with and help other target parents, male and female, who are going through similar ordeals, so for those of you who say all articles should be gender neutral I want to point out at this stage I use my own specific examples in my articles but do understand that NPD affects both genders.

So this isn't just another book recounting the horrors of living through an abusive relationship. Yes I will share my experience of living with a man with a personality disorder and the insidiousness of it all but the focus of this book is how we can move on from that. It's not about surviving, it's about healing to such a point where we can thrive. We can take those messed up experiences and say to ourselves "What are we going to learn from this? How are we going to channel this horror into something positive?"

Well here it is.

How I lived in the darkness of denial pretending everything was ok.

How I escaped the cage he built around me.

How I survived and crawled through the 'Shawshank Redemption Tunnel of Shit' to escape from him finally into clear water and freedom and learned to thrive to the point I could help others.

Throughout the book for clarity, the narcissistic ex will be referred to simply as the Nex and his girlfriend as the O.W the other woman. My children appear as Matty and Chloe and my partner as Joe.

Many people have thanked me and said that I'm responsible for their healing and I say to them that all I've done is reminded them and guided them to find their inner super hero that's always been inside them and when they reach the level of healing I have they too will guide others towards the light.

I encourage each and every one of you to be the best you can be and use your experiences as a learning curve towards your life goals and the beautiful life that's waiting for you once you distance yourself from negativity.

I have friends who shake their heads in disbelief that I'm still standing., but I made it and you can too. This is the trial and error approach to recovering from a malignant Narcissist who stole my children's authentic souls and tried to take every financial asset I had.

# A Little About Me

My career background has been many long years of nursing, both general nursing and with older people. However I had my career ended abruptly because of chronic back pain and eventually because my time was taken up setting up an on-line business.

I have also made myself knowledgeable from my reading and have had extensive counselling following the end of my long marriage to what I then discovered is a malignant narcissist who set out to destroy me by waging a virulent smear campaign against me to assassinate my character and brainwash my teenage children after I divorced him.

I set up a secret healing sanctuary several years ago and have helped hundreds of people to navigate through the trauma of leaving a toxic relationship. I have given huge amounts of my time over the last few years and helped, supported and encouraged those in abusive relationships to leave safely. I have helped many target parents to cope through their heartache and in many cases remain in contact with their children.

During the time I wrote this book I managed to get my son through the fog of parental alienation and back into a warm relationship with me. My daughter is still alienated and brainwashed.

I approached Women's Aid after years of carrying their card at the bottom of my bag.

I knew that one day I would need to call that number.

As I began my frantic search at 3 am googling 'Why is my husband so cruel?' 'Why is he hurting me?' I began to read and study personality disorders particularly Narcissism.

I began to virtually meet beautiful amazing people online who had been through similar experiences. and through Women's Aid I met my counsellor and my angel on this earth.

I finally told my family and friends the truth. Most believed me as they had had dealings with my then husband in the past and had seen his aggressive behaviour first hand. Some were shocked and said "I can't believe he's like that" and I didn't try and convince them otherwise. I developed a thick skin through his never ending smear campaign during which he visited my friends and told them that she might be beautiful but she's mental!

Life was one long nightmare filled with daily solicitors letters and police interviews and documenting every move the Nex made against me.

After he took my children I fell apart and lived from bed to chair in what I can only describe as a brain fog. My online retail business suffered as I couldn't make decisions and I didn't want to live anymore. Through the pain and the dark lonely nights I began to read and read till my eyeballs ached. I studied everything I could get my hands on about personality disorders.

Gradually over the next few months I got mentally stronger and felt able to leave the house alone. I tried to do something to make me feel better every day. I started swimming a little at the pool even though I was plagued with crippling sciatica.

Before long I was pushing myself back to my original fitness level. I started practicing yoga. If the Nex or my children upset me I would shut the world out and practice my breathing and learning various poses. I learned to kickbox and I kickboxed on the toughest days.

Before court I prepared myself mentally and physically like I was going to war, for war was where I was going. A war against evil.

I ate good food when I wasn't hungry. I dragged myself out of bed when I wanted to lie down and die. My counsellor and my family helped me survive but my inner strength was what pulled me through.

We all have this power inside of ourselves when we've been in the depths of hell. Dig really deep even on the bad days and find yours.

# My World Came Crashing Down

My world came crashing down for me one week after celebrating my wedding anniversary. This was 16 years after I met the man that I thought was my soul mate.

He assaulted me for the last time. It really hits home now when you're nearly healed like me. It's taken nearly four years out of that brain fog to heal from such a toxic relationship. I was lucky to find an amazing therapist, to have a great family support who tried hard to understand and a wonderful boyfriend who became my rock and saw me through the toughest times: through the stalking, the parental alienation and into my recovery.

That's why I felt a strong calling to write this book because no one should have to go through this alone. It's the most debilitating, hidden and misunderstood recovery process I have ever come across in my life.

# Loves Young Dream

Rewind back to when I was 21.

I went for my interview to get into nursing college but I immediately warmed to the tutors who interviewed me and it came as no surprise when I got my acceptance letter. I remember walking home in the snow feeling like I wanted to change the world and really make a difference.

Nursing college was daunting at first but I soon made friends and we all studied together. We would go out in the evenings and everyone would head over to my flat first for drinks and dinner ( I was the sensible one saying we must line our stomachs before going out drinking). We would spend time getting dressed up, which was a great part of the fun, and then go out and drink and dance.

I met the Nex in the final year of nursing college. I remember his smile lit up the room and from our first meeting I could sense a chemistry. He showed a confidence that I admired and was always surrounded by young girls hanging onto his every word. I was surprised when he made a bee line for me and was secretly flattered He would say hello and playfully swat me on the leg and I would say "Get Lost!"

We chatted sometimes but I was always with friends and when they told me he had a thing for me I said "Look at him he's surrounded, I wouldn't touch him with a barge pole!" He became more persistent and started ignoring the girls fawning over him.

I know I presented as a challenge to him and it became a game of cat and mouse.

He would smile that winning smile and lock eyes with me before I looked away and talked to my friends.

"Come out with me I don't bite. Well unless you want me to" he joked. I would smile and my cheeks would burn as I walked away saying "In your dreams" under my breath.

He pulled up outside my flat and shouted to me. "Come on come for a drive." I really wanted to but something deep down in my gut stopped me.

However I was lonely and bored having been unattached for over a year and as the weeks wore on his advances and that beautiful smile became harder to resist. I remember sitting in my flat as he sat revving his car under my window and thinking why not! Go on girl live a little! I ran downstairs and said "Ok just a drive." "Get in" he grinned a huge warm smile as I got in  buckled up and he sped off up the street. My heart raced as he began to ask questions. "So are you at nursing college?" I said yes and that I was in my final year and taking my exams in the summer. "Ooh a sexy nurse hey" he said. I giggled and blushed as that was always the reaction from a man when I told him what I did! "There's nothing sexy about nursing you should see what we really do" I said.

He began to tell me about his life in Ireland and how he was going back there soon to work as a Chauffeur for a millionaire his Mum knew. He told me about the cars he had driven and showed me photos and he told me how much he loved Ireland as he loved walking and camping in the country and I told him I was a country girl too and loved to be outside! As we got to know each other I realised that we loved all the same things and a few days later he called for me out of the blue asking me to come with him to see his friends Pyrenean Mountain dogs. "Come and see them they are huge, they stand right up and hug you!"

I remember my red coat getting covered in a swirling snowstorm of fur as they jumped up excitedly. I had skipped home deliriously in lust and phoned my Mum telling her he's different, he's not like all the others. I remember ticking off my list he loves the countryside and he loves animals. We began to hang out more and he told me how he had missed out on life because of his Mum.

It was at that stage that he looked at me with sad brown eyes and told me how difficult his childhood was because his Mum was an alcoholic and he had grown up in care in boarding schools for naughty boys and then after he had failed his exams he had gone to Ireland to get away as he had always known he deserved better.

Over the next few weeks we became inseparable. He would pick me up from the hospital at 10pm and say "I've bought your clothes, let's go camping." I enjoyed this spontaneity as tired as I was but looking back realised he didn't care I had worked all day. We would then drive to the mountains and he would laugh at me as I was always asleep by the time we got there. In the morning he would be cooking me breakfast on an open fire. We often went out to the pubs together from the hospital.

On my days off we stayed in bed and watched movies and ate pizza as he flicked through the auto mart telling me which car he fancied next and telling me the cars he drove in Ireland, his favourite being a Transom Firebird.

We seemed to be a perfect fit and had so much in common and I remember as he lay on my floor in his dusty work clothes as I rushed around making dinner he said out the blue "I'm really falling for you, it's funny because I usually get bored very quickly in a relationship but with you it's different. I just want to be with you all the time."

He jumped up and hugged me running his hands over my body. "You are so sexy. I mean check out that bodywork!" I giggled nervously as I did not feel any of those things about myself, as he went on and told me that I was beautiful and clever too.

He grabbed me round the waist and kissed my neck and declared "You are my Transom Firebird."

As the months went by over cosy lunches and late breakfasts in country pubs, and walks in the hills he began to tell me about his childhood and how he was estranged from his Dad. I listened and tried to help suggesting that he gets in touch with his Dad to hear his side.

I persuaded him to phone his Dad and give him a chance which he did with reluctance and eventually agreed to drive over and visit him and the rest of his family.

When we drove to meet his Dad I instantly warmed to him and we all got along but when his Mum heard about him visiting him she told us both he was an arsehole and asked why would you want to see him?

The long standing feud continued with his Mum after he reunited with his Dad after 14 years of what I now know was a severe case of parental alienation.

He introduced me to his young nieces and nephews and I noticed how much they adored him, running up and hugging him. He was definitely the fun Uncle and seemed to be really good with them, play fighting with them and flinging them in the air. He began to tell me how much he loved children and how his ex had a baby that he had taken on as his own. He told me that she had been pregnant when they started seeing each other and how when they split up because she cheated he had missed her little boy so much. He began to tell me how much he would love to have a baby of his own and say all he wants in the world is to be a family.

I was really freaked out by this and told him I would love to have children but I wasn't ready for that yet and wanted to concentrate on my career first.

Everywhere we went he cooed at babies and when we baby sat for a friend he exclaimed "Look how lovely he is! You're a natural with him, look he loves you."

A few months later it came as no surprise, as loved up as we were, that I found out I was pregnant with our daughter and he was so excited about becoming a father saying it's all he ever wanted. He was so attentive and loving but then over the next few weeks he began to drink heavily.

I would arrive home from work to find him with his eyes glazed over. "Hey nurse sexy come over here, come and have a drink". I told him I couldn't drink being pregnant. Then he would get gradually drunker and drunker and start calling his friends about 10pm arranging for them to meet him as he was bored as I was boring for going to bed early, ready to start my morning shift at five am to get to the hospital for 6am.

I remember him often coming home all fired up and drunk after fighting with grazes and bruised knuckles telling me some guy just started on him in stories where he was always the victim and was defending himself.

I was busy with college especially practical placements and preparing to do my exams in a few months when he suffered a huge shock. We found out that his elder brother had been found dead in a caravan.

He went off the rails then and I spent several weeks trying to help him by getting him a counsellor. He started to get drunk and aggressive in the evenings and began calling me vile names until I was sobbing. He would wake in the morning as I was packing my bags ready to leave him saying things like "Babe I was drunk. I don't remember anything, come back to bed."

Sometimes he was really attentive loving Dad to be and laid his head on my belly talking to his unborn child but every now and again I would get glimpses of a different side of him altogether.

I put his aggressive outbursts down to the stress of losing his brother so suddenly and the stress of impending fatherhood!

I remember he woke me in the night hammering on the door after arriving home drunk from the pub. He was shouting in my face that I could f**k off to my ex if it's a girl as he didn't want it!

I remember shouting back at him slamming the door in his face as I told him our baby was not an 'it' and asked him to leave.

I prepared myself to bring my baby girl up alone.

The following day he told me he loved me and he didn't mean it he's just scared but he had always wanted a boy that's all.

Several weeks later he came home late evening telling me he had had a fight with his step father and had thrown a brick at him. Up to then I hadn't known that he had a step father.

He was fired up and very angry and he punched the mirror and held one of the shards in his hand telling me that he didn't want to live and he was going to slit his wrists with one of the pieces and die here in my arms. He told me "If you go for help I will run off and die somewhere!"

"They should have taken me not Dave. He has children." I put this mental breakdown to grieving badly for his brother and told him he was going to be a father soon too and he had so much to live for and he could talk to a counsellor about it.

He wouldn't let me leave for work and I didn't dare leave him to go to the phone box to call the hospital and the following day I told them I was too sick to get to the phone.

My friends were already teasing me that since I had met him I was never at college.

I never admitted to them what happened that night.

The next evening by way of an apology he bought a beautiful dark brindle staff puppy home to keep me company telling me that now we could be a proper family and I instantly fell in love with him and called him Riley.

I would wake up to him singing to me and loudly playing 'Oasis' Wonderwall, telling me I was going to be the one that saved him.

I was extremely busy at the hospital making up placement days as I had lost clinical time which I couldn't qualify without while I had been arranging counselling for him. But by now he had been given a course of anti depressants and being monitored.

Being pregnant was rough as I had dreadful sickness. I remember one occasion looking after a man who was vomiting and going into his adjoining en -suite bathroom to vomit myself before coming out to care for him again.

I told him I had to study and he started becoming angry and jealous of the time I was spending at college and the Hospital but I told him that would all be over once I finished my exams.

The run up to my final exams were spent cramming with friends and sleeping so I would be mentally fresh.

The evening before I sat my Nursing exam he had a party and kept me up most of the night. Every time I tried to go to bed he would make me feel guilty for leaving. him.

Looking back, he had no empathy and did not seem to care or understand how important it was that I got a decent night's sleep so he played loud music and his friends did not leave until well into the early hours of the morning.

In hindsight I see now that was to be the first time he tried to sabotage my career even before I was qualified.

The day I passed my exams I remember clearly the excitement after we collected our results. Everyone was going to the pub but all I wanted to do was skip home to tell him. I was waiting for him to tell me how proud he was of me. I already had a job lined up and was ready to start earning my first wage.

He wasn't there and he never answered the phone.

I had sensed things weren't right between us over the last few days and I had felt the distance growing between us as I said to myself I must just get through this exam!

I fell asleep cuddled up with Riley on the bed and I can remember him coming in drunk saying "So did you pass then?"

I said "Yes" and he began to kiss me while I lay face down on the bed and as he removed my clothes I cried into the pillow.

There was no well done hug or congratulations.

He then sat on the edge of the bed and confessed he had cheated as I hadn't been there for him, telling me it was my fault as I hadn't given him any attention.

He was sorry and he loved me and wanted me and this baby. He told me again he wanted a family more than anything else in the world.

He told me he didn't know how to be a family as his Dad had never been there.

He promised me he would work really hard and make a go of his building business if I helped him.

He said "Now you're pregnant we should get married."

I told him that I didn't want to marry just because I was pregnant and we should wait and see how things were as he had shaken my trust.

My gut instinct was kicking in to protect me.

I began working full time as a nurse and would fall asleep during the evening.. He stopped helping around the house and stopped cooking. He began to frequently threaten to move out and leave me if I didn't tidy up or clean up when he said, cook him dinner when he walked in the door whether it was six or ten o'clock even if I had just arrived home after a long shift at the hospital.

He did not care that pregnancy was exhausting.

As I got bigger he would shout "Belly do we need any toilet roll" in the middle of the supermarket so everyone turned and stared and if I was taking a bath he would come in shouting "Save the whales!"

At the time I laughed the comments off but as time went on this was just the start of the verbal abusive tongue lashings he was going to deliver.

I remember lying in bed suffering horrendous morning sickness and when I told him he began to tickle me jokingly saying, "So if I tickle you like this will you throw up?" I giggled "Probably!" He tickled me and I asked him to stop but he would not and he thought it was hilarious when I eventually threw up in the waste paper bin.

He spent more time away in the evenings and would come home and demand his tea at various points in the evening. He was bringing very little money home and he told me he hated the flat he had once loved and he couldn't bear to be there.

On one occasion the police arrived looking for him and he made me lie that he wasn't there and then later fabricated a lie to me telling me not to worry as it was a mistake. They weren't looking for him but for his friend.

Over the next few months he settled down and began staying in through the evenings saying that all I need is here. Why would I want to go out. He seemed to stop drinking excessively, reciting his stories of being an out of control teenager with a bad reputation and telling me he wanted to change as he was sick of fighting and getting into trouble.

He kept asking me to marry him and saying persistently "Why won't you marry me?" I told him I wouldn't marry him till he grew up.

We broke up often and I was suspicious he cheated again but never had proof as he told me he was working all day to get me and our baby everything we needed.

He frequently remarked about why would he go out and have a burger when he had steak at home.

I became extremely paranoid about his whereabouts.

Sometimes he stayed out all night and I told him that we were over.

I packed his bags and asked him to leave but he wouldn't leave and told me he loved me over and over again and that he had just fallen asleep at a mates.

When Chloe was born he cried and held my hand and promised he would change. Apologising for everything telling me he had never had a family and he really loved me. He really seemed to settle down and we became a proper family which was everything I had wished for.

Weekends were spent having late breakfasts and roast dinners in country pubs with Chloe or at the sea front or in the mountains walking Riley. I always thought it strange though that he never wanted to be seen pushing the pram.

I thought that he would have been a hands on father after seeing him with his nieces and nephews and hearing him talk so lovingly about his exes baby but he only seemed to be around for the fun stuff leaving me to do all the nights so I was permanently exhausted.

Once Chloe was 6 months old I began to ease my way back into work for a nursing agency and he made a huge effort and told me how hard he was trying.

He would call me "Daisy the cow" as I was breastfeeding Chloe and say to her "Get off my boobs, these are mine!" in what appeared to be a joke and I would laugh and say that this is what boobs were for!

I signed up with a nursing agency and he would drive me to work.

He told me that he was going to start doing up the house as work was quiet.

I would come home shattered from nursing to loud music, smoke, dust, demolished rooms and replastered walls and he would demand that I help clean up after his work as he had been working all day!

The house was a building site and never quiet but I expected once it was done it would settle down.

I used to watch the Nex and Chloe playing together and he would tell me "Wouldn't it be great if Chloe had a brother and he had a son to play football with."

It was during a major football tournament that I found out I was pregnant with Matty.

I cried from happiness when I saw that blue line and I remember walking into the room where the Nex was sitting with his friends watching the football, handing him the test and saying "well you've scored!" He jumped up and hugged me "Really oh wow another baby!" He seemed really excited and settled down for the first few months promising me the world, working extra hours on the house and really making an effort. Chloe would be so excited when his car pulled up and she would run to the door shouting "Daddy, Daddy!" This was all I ever wanted a loving family.

He frequently told me how hard he was trying but the effort didn't last long once Summer came and I was getting bigger once again he began going out to the pubs.

I remember panicking that he never answered his phone and the relief after an hour or two of worry when he finally messaged me.

Sometimes during the day he would get a friend to check on me saying he was busy working.

During that summer as my belly expanded there were always young girls hanging round and he was a terrible flirt and used to play fight with them in front of me telling me that they fancied him but he only has eyes for me. I had refused to play fight with him as he always hurt me. If I was going to over power him he would twist my arm behind my back and say "You're stuck now, aren't you?"

I was constantly paranoid and suspicious but never found any concrete proof he was cheating.

He frequently told me I was lucky he didn't want any of them and all he wanted was me Chloe and the baby.

He fed my insecurities and I began to be completely paranoid checking up on him and second guessing where he was all the time.

I remember begging him one evening not to go out and crying "Please don't leave me".

He knew how vulnerable I was and was beginning to take advantage of that.

He told me I was a mother now and I couldn't wear short skirts or shorts as it was disrespectful and mothers like that look like slags.

He didn't approve of me sitting in the garden in my shorts and a bikini and began to tell me I was lazy and ask me "Why I was sitting there letting everyone look at me?" I would shout incredulously that I was in my own back garden, the house was tidy and I was resting before a long shift.

He would shout things like "if you have time to sit there you can come and strip this f*****g wall!"

He began accusing me of cheating and I would constantly reassure him and tell him I loved him saying "Why would I cheat?"

I remember being heavily pregnant with Matty and he walked in and he spat at me "Who the f**k are you shagging?" I tried to calm him and said "No one, where's all this come from?" He sneered "You're just very clever, aren't you?" I whispered that I loved him so why would I cheat? He grabbed a screwdriver and jabbed it in my face! Those empty black eyes stared through me as he said that he could slash my face so no one would ever fancy me!. I slunk on the floor as the screw driver tip grazed my face. Then he said "F*****g whore" and left me there trembling on the floor crying and worrying I would lose my baby.

A few hours later he returned saying that he'd brought some chicken and was I hungry? I flinched as he came up to me and tried to cuddle me. He said "Look I'm sorry. I just heard some stuff."

Then I found myself explaining again that I loved him so why would I cheat?

When he arrived home I would begin telling him that I had terrible morning sickness, my boobs hurt like hell and Chloe had cried all day as she was unwell and he would stop me mid sentence saying things like "I don't care for your women's lip, all I ask for is a f*****g tidy house and my tea on the f*****g table. If that's too much to ask then I'm leaving!" "It's my way or the highway!" he shouted as he was packing a bag and leaving and "You can bring the children up on your own!" He would scream "It must be what you want or why would you wind me up? Why's my tea not ready? Why's the place look like a shit hole? Why are you not even dressed?"

I would then run round crying with exhaustion trying to put the builders yard that was my house right. There were always huge tools strewn across the kitchen and ladders, paint pots and dust everywhere and he blamed me for it all.

He would often get drunk in the evening and verbally destroy me then fall asleep and by morning in my mind the relationship was over. I would be packing mine and Chloe's things and he would roll over sleepily and say "What's up babe? What did I do?" He would claim to be so drunk he did not remember what he had said. Then he would say let's go out together as a family and expect me to forget it and not ruin the day.

He began to do up the house and we spent days and evenings painting and wallpapering together with Chloe running around. She was so excited about her little brother living in my belly and was very affectionate.

One cold February evening I was sitting in the rocking chair nursing my huge belly. We had tried everything to coax Matty out into the world but two weeks over my due date he was just too warm and comfortable in there. Chloe was cuddled into me kissing my belly and whispering "c'mon baby, baby out!" And she was so excited to be having a little brother to play with. I had to be induced and eventually, after a long overnight labour, Matty arrived like a pale blueberry as the cord had been wrapped around his neck, to cries of "It's ok he's breathing" from the nurses as his little cheeks flushed to a healthy pink! The nurse then exclaimed as she rushed him over to be weighed that he was a big boy at 8lbs 3/4 and was really long. We saw Matty's beautiful long fingers for the first time and he let out a healthy yell!

I felt instant happiness and love as I looked into his perfect little face.

The next few months passed by in an fog of exhaustion, breastfeeding, nappy changing and sleepless nights but I was deliriously happy.

Money was still extremely tight and it was with huge regret that I went back to work part time. When I made this decision based on the fact we were financially struggling Chloe tugged on my uniform and said "Don't be an 'urse Mummy, don't go!" I remember sitting her down and telling her that I was going to look after some people who were sick but I would see her very soon to tuck her in bed and read her a story and tomorrow we would go to get ice-cream, go to the park and buy that teddy bear she wanted.

I was still breastfeeding Matty and spent much of the time at work running to the bathroom to express milk down the sink just to stay comfortable. There were occasions when someone was looking for the nurse in charge knocking on the bathroom door!

One glorious sunny afternoon before a long late shift after taking Chloe and Matty to my Mum's I was sitting in the garden with my eyes closed soaking up the sun and he opened the bedroom window shouting "Oy slag!" and hurled water over me soaking my uniform.

I picked up my bag and ran out the house and started to walk.

The sun dried my uniform as I gulped back the tears.

That was the first time I ran from his aggressive behaviour.

I worked a few days a week and it was great to get back into nursing but I missed my babies. I spent every hour of everyday with them when I wasn't at work.

Several weeks went by before he once again cheated. ( I didn't find this out until after we married as he told me on our wedding night six years later. He told me in a matter of fact way as I removed my hairpins while he rolled a joint for the first time in front of me, that I wasn't around and surely I had realised that one thing led to another when he drove there! He told me everyone knew back then that they were together despite at that time calling me paranoid when I became suspicious. Besides, he went on, it was only because I wasn't around and was always at work! He couldn't resist her as she was easy on the eye and had bigger boobs than me and she changed Matty's nappy).

I remember her vividly. One Summer afternoon we invited the Nex friend and his new girlfriend over for a barbecue and she was pregnant with another man's baby. She was a trashy blonde with dark roots and heavily smoking. She looked uncomfortable in the heat and was complaining she was too hot so I lent her some maternity shorts as having been pregnant myself in the heat I knew how she must feel. I went inside to prepare some salads and I saw her standing too close to the Nex and he was laughing and I began to get paranoid as he had been hanging out with his friend and her a lot recently in the evenings as I stayed home to look after our children.

As I came in the garden she looked me up and down and I heard her say under her breath to her friend "I had no idea she was so f*****g skinny!"

He would brag about me to his friends and say "You wouldn't believe she's had two children" but in private it was a different story and he began to cruelly tease me. "You think you're all that!" "Your bum is so big I suppose that's what happens after you've had a baby!" "Your boobs are not the same. I wonder if they'll go back to how they were!"

I began to feel very self conscious about my changed body even though I had in effect pinged back into shape with all the breastfeeding and running around after two toddlers and returning to a busy hospital ward.

Sometime after Matty was born I got a great job in a local nursing home and by the age of 24 had worked my way up to Matron. The carers used to make jokes that I was most un-matronly. After I got that position the Nex stepped up his campaign to undermine my confidence and once again sabotage my career.

He told me I only got the job because the married manager was screwing me. He refused to look after the children who were now toddling. I would sit and wait for him to collect the children as we had planned but at the very last minute would have to take them to work with me so I wasn't late and from work had to find them a babysitter. Luckily I was friends with many of the carers who willingly helped me out as they loved my children.

With the extra money I was now bringing in I really wanted to learn to drive so the Nex even paid to put me on his insurance and helped me to pay for some lessons with an instructor he had found for me. This man was not a good looking man and I did not see then that he picked him on purpose for this very reason. He did however become a very close friend and confidant following the Nex ranting at me as I used to turn up to my lesson in tears. The Nex used to tell me I was stupid and ridicule me for not being able to drive, cruelly comparing me to the girl he cheated with saying "she's f*****g stupid and she's a cracking driver so I don't know what that makes you!" and then say "Don't kill anyone today will you!" as I left the house in tears. Most of my lesson was then spent trying to calm me down, so because of this the driving instructor who was also having problems in his marriage confided in me so my mind wasn't on reversing round a corner and we would sit and chat and he would say just pay me for half a lesson. I think I saved his marriage but to the detriment of me learning to drive.

The Nex would come out to the car after each lesson and feign concern while chatting to the instructor that unfortunately I wasn't anywhere near ready yet.

He used to proudly tell everyone that I was learning but was a long way off from passing.

Then he broke his leg while out at the pub one night because to quote him "The police had assaulted him" then he insisted I had to drive him everywhere.

It was during this time that unbeknown to me I was to meet an extremely ruthless female narcissist at work.

She was a good 15 years older than me and asked me how I stayed so slim and that I looked amazing considering I have two children. She charmed me from the day she arrived morphing into my friend and confidant. Looking back she was clearly jealous as I appeared to have a perfect life. She fancied the manager and was jealous of our working relationship and banter. Despite him being married to a lovely woman who I had met, she wanted a piece of his business including my job. She was covert and very charming and began ever so subtly to undermine me to my colleagues by handing over all the nasty jobs and during handover make me look incompetent in front of the boss and undermine me in front of the carers. She told the manager she could help out on my days off and he agreed and she took over the rota signing me off for a short holiday. I came back to find her and another colleague who was her flying monkey sedating patients with unprescribed medication. The standard of care was also becoming questionable with patients being left in an uncomfortable state and there had been an increase in preventable pressure sores.

However she even charmed the cleaners to clean her house and had everyone eating out of her hand. I could not cope with the pressure from the Nex or her so I caved under the pressure, took a huge pay cut and left to work in another nursing home.

At the time I blamed myself and felt incompetent but looking back I had begun to lose all my confidence in my ability to do my job as I was dealing with a narcissist at work and home.

The Nex leg was now healed and he told me I didn't need to drive him anymore and we couldn't afford the car insurance now as I lost my job due to my incompetence and he was right as he was ensuring all my money was spent and had insidiously whittled my remaining confidence away.

I had lost all my confidence behind the wheel that I had gained driving him around and actually felt anxious just sitting In the drivers seat. I began to really believe I would kill someone.

Groundhog Day

We had no childcare and juggled them between us. I used to run home from work from a late shift missing them so much. Sometimes I would get home to a lovely dinner and a tidy house and the Nex saying "I don't know why you make it out that it's so difficult. I've tidied up and cooked dinner." Then I would pick Matty up and realise his nappy hadn't been changed for hours. He was soaked in urine and his skin was angry and red. I would chase them around getting them ready for bed and reading them stories and trying to calm them down as the Nex played loud music and got stoned downstairs. I would shout "turn that down, I'm trying to get them to sleep" But he would reply that they'll get used to it. Most occasions I would arrive home to find the house in chaos, the children screaming and unfed and the Nex drinking in the kitchen with his friends quite oblivious to his children's needs. I began to see the inconsistency of his parenting. He rarely put them to bed, instead saying to me that they wouldn't go to bed until I came home. Or on the rare occasions he had put them in bed he would have forgotten to brush their teeth, so I would make them go and brush them and tell them that if you don't brush them the decay monster will come in the night.

So I lived in a Groundhog Day existence of a repeating cycle of work, looking after my precious children and cleaning.

It is from that chapter of my life, from a swirl of memory fog that I remember some, but not all the traumatic events that I recount here.

My therapist told me during this part of my life that because I was nursing at work then coming home and nursing there was no rest and the parameters of normal behaviour got blurred as I was dealing with a lot of confused aggressive EMI patients then coming home to literally keep him normal.

Matty was now nine months old and I was just reaching the stage where I felt I could leave him for a few days with my parents so I could have a break.

The Nex wasn't earning as he had fallen out with his boss and was between jobs.

I scraped enough savings together so we could go to Scotland and arranged for my parents to look after the children. I booked a beautiful log cabin for just the two of us. He told me he didn't want to go at the last minute for why would he want to go to a log cabin in the middle of nowhere. I showed him the brochure and told him how gorgeous it was with a steam room and being huge. In the end, after a huge row, we went and I cooked us a beautiful dinner and he began to relax and kiss me.

Later we went to the bar and he began to flirt with the barman's daughter who was twice my age and twice my size. He was steadily getting drunker and charming everyone at the bar with his anecdotes about working in Ireland and telling jokes and I felt like I wanted to leave as we didn't have much money left and I was tired as it was late. We left the bar and walked hand in hand back to the cabin.

We started to watch a film. He jumped up very drunk by this point as I was dropping on the settee and he hurled a washing bowl of soapy water from the kitchen over me shouting "You're not f*****g asleep!" I was really scared of those black eyes so I got up and began to walk to the bathroom but he grabbed me trying to kiss me and suggested I try shove this bottle up inside me.

He was chasing me around and began to smash the kitchen, head butting cupboards and smashing things with his fists. He started bleeding, then he told me he hated me and I wasn't to go near him and he barricaded himself with chairs in one of the loft bedrooms. I was terrified and I slept fitfully down in the other bedroom with a knife under my pillow.

As soon as it was light I phoned a taxi and he drove me to the nearest cash point. I drew out everything to get me away from him and was planning on going home, I just wanted to be with my babies and away from this madman. He phoned me after he had sobered up and said that he was sorry he had been drunk and please could I come back. I continued on my journey home with tears streaming down my cheeks. He was begging me and pleading with me and telling me that he loved me and how sorry he was. Like a fool I went back and he had cooked breakfast while I cleaned the broken kitchen.
I could not look at any of the people as we drove out and my dark glasses hid my upset and pain.

Little did I know at that time I was dealing with a hidden Psychopathy.

Matty's 2nd birthday.

I was rushing around the local supermarket buying everything for Matty's birthday party. I had made a cake and was buying the things for his tea party with his friends. I had left him with his Dad as I wanted it to be a surprise. I struggled back with two large carrier bags and my phone rang. "Where are you?" the Nex demanded, "I'm just on my way home" I replied. He shouted at me "Who have you been shagging? When I find out!" Then I heard him growl and bang his fist on something. I did not want to go home but Matty and his friends were there waiting so I gritted my teeth and went home. He grabbed me and pushed me up against the wall "You're a f*****g tart. Who are you shagging!" I said "No one. Look it's Matty's birthday and I'm late because we needed all this." I said showing him my bags. I struggled free and holding the tears back walked into the dining room where all the children were. I threw myself into making the best party ever for Matty but my memory of it is tainted forever by his nasty aggressive outburst.

I remember clearly the last time I asked him where he was at night.
He came home at 3am and I asked him where he had been and I told him I had been worried sick and had been ringing him all night. He grabbed me and dragged me up the stairs and threw me like a bag of rubbish into

the corner of the room by the wall to wall mirrored wardrobe. His breath reeked of stale beer, he spat at me "You are not my mother!" I apologised and told him "I was just worried" so he would calm down as he clenched his fist above my head. Then he staggered downstairs and I crouched on the floor not daring to make a sound sobbing quietly, not daring to breathe till I heard the familiar sound of snoring on the settee.
I Never asked him again.

I remember the way he sabotaged my nights out.
I went out for a few drinks with some friends leaving the Nex to look after Chloe and Matty.
He left them in the early evening and came to surprise me, by which time I was on my way home worried about my children. I had no key so I climbed up a ladder through an upstairs window panicking about where they were as he messaged to tell me that he was now in town in the pub where I had been and where the F**k was I?' I told him I was home and screamed at him "Where are the children?" He laughed and said "They're with Andrew down the road!" I slammed the phone down as I realised he had left them with the local drunk and ran down the road to get them as they told me excitedly that Andrew made them pancakes.
That night he stayed out till the following day to punish me for daring to go out.

I remember the handful of times we went out to the pubs together.
The time a bloke had looked at him oddly and he flew across the road and punched him for saying nothing when he said "What you looking at mate?" I ran home followed by him bloodied and aggressive an hour later as I pretended to be asleep so he wouldn't start trouble with me.

I remember his poor excuses and lies for getting into drunken fights.
He arrived home with no trainers and a bust lip once telling me a very convincing story that he had been robbed while waiting for a takeaway and that's why he was late home.

Christmas Memories

The run up to Christmas was always dampened by him. He would sink into a depression from November onwards and we would all make jokes about Scrooge and buy him a bah humbug hat. Poor Dad had a bad childhood and he would tell me that Christmas was like a stiff shit and you'd be glad when it was all over! He revelled in misery and the more we tried to jolly him along the more negative he became.

I made it my mission in life to show him what a loving family Christmas was all about. He wouldn't help with anything so I did it all. I got the tree and the decorations.
I ran around the shops looking for presents and began squirreling away stocking fillers.
I would then begin the arduous task of buying him a Christmas present he would love. He would drop hints and ask me for expensive items I couldn't afford on the family budget. I maxed out my credit card buying gifts for the children and for him, telling him to just get me a few things for my stocking as we would be opening them at Mum's, but not to bother with a present for me as I didn't need anything.

We would arrange to stay over on Christmas Eve at Mum's and have a drink with everyone and get the children to hang their stockings.
He would brew for a fight a few days before picking on me or the children for the mess in the house, or the fact the dinner wasn't ready on time or we were too noisy. He told us all "You've pissed on your chips! Christmas is cancelled!" The children would cry and everything was hugely stressful and he would say "I'm not going. I'm staying here!" Mum would be ringing "When are you coming. Everyone is here." He would be stoned on the sofa or late home. There were times I would ring him and he wouldn't reply for hours.

He would tell me he was round at his exes eating mince pies. I would be upset and ask why he wouldn't eat mince pies with me and the children? He would laugh. He expected me to pack the children's things and his things and any food that I had made and all the presents. He would turn up at the very last minute and shout "Right get in the car and the children would be playing and running around after waiting for him to grace us with his presence for hours. I would be calming everyone down and texting Mum "Yes we're on our way" and "Sorry we are late" We would argue in the car. The Nex was stoned and we were tired and hungry having waited to eat. He would say I'm not doing this any more next year. We're going on holiday and buying nothing for anyone," and I would wearily agree.

We would arrive and he would appear to relax and have a drink. Then he would jump up and serve the roast potatoes and pretend to be the perfect husband. He would grab me in a long cuddle under the mistletoe in front of my parents, despite the fact he hadn't cuddled me all week. He would play the part of the devoted husband and the good father so well and I would say that he was just was stressed and needed to unwind.

Christmas Day he would refuse to get up. He didn't watch his children open their stockings. He never bought me any stocking fillers like I asked. We went to church while he got up.

Then came the moment I had planned the present I had saved for and struggled to buy. Usually an item he had specifically asked for. The children and I waited in excitement while he opened it. It was the wrong size, the wrong colour, he didn't want or need one anymore. There was never a 'thanks' as he looked round the room. I can see now his eyes flashing with envy. Unsatisfied greed on his face sucking the joy out of the room.
We would have a huge dinner and he would drink and take advantage of my Dad's good nature as he poured him another brandy.

The Nex would make small talk with my Dad, joking about setting up a business with him. Once we had had coffee and he was sober enough to drive I would pack everything up and the children would say their goodbyes and he would bark at them to get in the car. They were hyper and excited playing with their presents and he would stand in the hallway picking my dad's brain for money making opportunities and that they should go into business together.

We hugged everyone and said our goodbyes and got into the car. The doors slammed, the seat belts were on, the children were chattering in the back,. fighting over leg space as all the presents were crammed around them. We waved and as we pulled away he changed.
His posture would change. His jaw go rigid. His teeth clench and his eyes blacken as he began to vent on someone. Mostly that person was me. He would tell me how he actually hated the thing I bought or complain how much money had been wasted. Sometimes he would vent on one of the children. He would find a scapegoat and pick, pick, pick on them all the way home. Driving like a mad man, no one questioned him as he jabbed

me with his elbow in the ribs, and the children watched on silently, no one disagreed. Then he would pull up outside our house and me and the children would empty the car and he would say that he was just nipping out and be gone for hours while I packed Christmas away and got the children in bed.

"What's up with Dad?" the children would ask and I would make excuses for him, that Daddy was tired and he had no work at the moment and that they knew how Christmas was a difficult time for him. Then I would tuck our children into bed.

It didn't matter how much I earned. He would spend it as fast as I made it. My wages went out as fast as they went in and were used every month on doing the house up and the mortgage and bills and there was never any left for me.

Several years went by and I thought that was the sacrifice you made for a family. I couldn't even afford a haircut or new clothes when the children were little, I had three breastfeeding shirts that I rotated and I wore black leggings or jeans. I always made sure my children had what they needed and couldn't go shopping without buying something for them.

As the children grew older he began to talk his way into cash jobs, doing up people's houses cheaply and undercutting competitors.

One November when Chloe was 11 and Matty was 9 a traditional family Christmas was planned as usual and the Nex bragged to everyone that he was taking his family away for Christmas so everyone said how lovely. We began to go away every Christmas.

Looking back on holiday he morphed into the false persona he had created for himself. He told everyone he was the boss of a large company with a fleet of vehicles and a successful business.

He would strut around with an air of self importance telling big fish stories, charming everyone and parading his lovely family.

He came across as a really loving family man.

Behind Closed Doors it was a very different story.

Turkey

He texted me "I'm sitting In the travel agents booking us a holiday for next week." so I had to explain to my family we wouldn't be there for our usual traditional celebrations after all only a few weeks before Christmas.

The hotel was beautiful the staff friendly and the food and entertainment were amazing.
One night we were in the bar and we had just watched a fire eating show. This guy was awesome and the children clearly enjoyed it. Afterwards we were sitting in the bar and the Nex began to chat to the fire eater and invited him to sit with us. The children were playing and dancing and I was relaxing finally and drinking Vodka. The fire eater began to chat to me and said to the Nex "Your wife is very beautiful you're very lucky!" The Nex never replied, just smiled and continued to chat and we sat down there for quite a while drinking. I was chatting to some of the female Russian dancers and the children were dancing and having fun.

After we left the Nex was very drunk but as soon as we got out the lift to our room his jovial tone changed. His fists were clenched as he shoved me down into the chair. "You can f*****g stay there! Or I will throw you over the balcony! I saw you down there flirting with him! I tell you what I'm going to f*****g leave you here with him you'd like that wouldn't you? I will leave you all here!" he said pointing at the sleeping children. He grabbed me and told me not to move.
He was staggering around and I was scared  so I instantly sobered up and froze in the chair. Chloe woke up and I said "I'm going to her." I made a mad dash past him and got into bed with her and was so terrified, I clung onto her. He staggered over and smirked "Look at you. You're pathetic hiding behind your children!" He began to verbally destroy me as I cowered in the bed and cuddled into my daughter. Eventually he left and I heard the adjoining door slam shut as he collapsed snoring into our bed in the other room.

When I came back from holiday I began working on the stroke rehabilitation and head injuries unit. It was a high pressure heavy and stressful job but I loved it and I loved most of my colleagues even though we were always short staffed we pulled together as a really good team, despite rarely getting our designated breaks. We survived on coffee, toast, adrenaline and bad jokes! My colleagues were always surprised how strong I was and how I could lift despite only being slim but those years of nursing were now beginning to take their toll and I began to develop really bad sciatica lifting heavy stroke patients and positioning hoists in tiny, badly designed, toilets.

The other staff nurses would ask me to go camping for the weekend or out for drinks after work but I always refused and I'm sure they thought it was because I was stand-offish and didn't want to socialise with them. They stopped asking so I had no social life as I would be too tired after nursing and as soon as I arrived home I was taking care of the children and him.

Weekends were much the same as the week for me unless I was working at the hospital as I would be home looking after the children cooking cleaning and washing and teaching them to tidy their rooms.
The Nex was an incredibly untidy and lazy man but he expected everyone to clean up after his mess. He sat in the kitchen at a unit he had made for himself which had two shelves, one had a small TV and the one below had a laptop that no one was allowed to touch. He would sit there after I had made a big family meal most evenings watching You Tube or chatting to friends and smoking weed. He refused to come and sit to watch a film with me and the children or he would come and sit down and watch till the first break then go back into the kitchen for the remainder of it.
This area where he lived I used to have to clean the day after and I lovingly named it 'shit corner'. It was my first job of the morning cleaning up his cigarette butts, empty food wrappers and empty beer cans. He really was a disgusting pig.
If the kitchen was spotless when I went to bed, by morning it would be a cess pit.

However when he arrived home at any point in the day he would fly into a rage about the mess in the house calling everyone 'lazy scruffs!' He would run upstairs and scream and threaten the children that he was coming to bin everything. If the children were busy doing something and making a mess and he began to rage I would run upstairs and hide everything in my room till he had left. I squirreled all their old drawings and paintings and old toys before he either bagged them up and gave them away to children in the neighbourhood as a charitable gesture or bagged them up  while the children cried and put them in the loft. He threw a lot of sentimental stuff away.

He would empty the contents of the children's things all over the floor and tell them he was going to stamp on them!. We would all be scared and in tears until he left in a temper and we heard the squeal of the van leaving.

An hour or so later, after I had calmed the children and tidied and cleaned everything he had thrown around, binned and destroyed, he would return with peacemaker doughnuts for me and the children, and whoa betide anyone who brought up his previous outburst.

My Last Night Out

I hadn't been out in a year when my good friend persuaded me to get dressed up and go out for a few drinks. I was determined to go despite the Nex usual sabotaging plans with comments to make me feel guilty like "How can you afford it?" "How can you leave the kids?"

Anyway I went out and within an hour he was messaging me "When are you home?" I messaged him back that it was nice to get out and relax. "Who are you with? Don't go to The Royal, there's dickheads in there!" I told him that I would be careful and we would stick to the good pubs.

I had a drink and had a dance and tried to forget about my unhappy life. He rang me and said under his breath "If you don't come home now, me and you are going to fall out big-time!" I sensed the threat in his voice.

"We are on our way home now" I reassured him. My friend came back with me and the Nex was heavily stoned and flirting with her. After she left he turned on me. "Where did you go? You better not have been to the Royal! I will find out you know." I told him I hadn't. "I'll find out what you've been up to you slag!" I tried to run past him up the stairs. "I went out for a drink" I shouted. 'Which further incensed him into ordering me to get back here now. "Who do you think you are talking to" He grabbed me roughly and as I'd sensed the madness in his eyes, my voice softened and locked eyes. I had learned to talk him down. It was like trying to reach a rabid animal.

"Look I went for a drink. I am home now. I'm tired and I'm going to bed." He let go as I scrambled up the stairs.

It became easier after that to just refuse all invitations from well meaning friends.

I became a recluse only leaving the house to go shopping, to see my family or to go to work.

I loved my babies and those were the most precious times coming home from work to spend time with them tucking them in bed after a late shift and reading them stories.
If my shifts allowed I could walk with them to school or we could go to the park.

He was always between jobs.
Holding down a job for a couple of weeks and then coming home and telling me that the boss was an asshole and he had fallen out with him. The stories always featured him being the victim and were never his fault. I began to work more hours to continuously cover the financial shortfall at the end of every month with my credit card just to cover our living costs. We were in so much debt.

One night while he was on the X-box drinking beer we couldn't afford we had a row and he told me that I needed to do more hours and why couldn't I do a couple of nights as well as I was the one earning a decent wage. I told him that I was exhausted.
That night I began browsing bikinis and dreaming of a holiday so I decided to buy ten and sell nine to make a bit of extra money to pay the credit card off.
They sold really fast and my online shop was born. I opened a shop with no retail experience at all apart from a love of lovely things.

Within three months I became a power seller on eBay and I was up past midnight, parcelling items and messaging customers. I began to make more money than I did nursing.
During this time I bought things for the kids and kitted us all out in clothes and began to research what sells and find suppliers.
Suppliers don't come up in Google searches and it took a lot of time and research during which despite having all the money coming in, he complained I was always on the computer.
I was taking parcels to work and storing them in my locker and posting them on my way home from work as he refused to help. Then literally running to the bus to get to school to get the children as I worked in the next town to where we lived.

I began to help him to grow his building company.
On my days off I did the admin for his business including the bookkeeping for both businesses or cleaning as he never lifted a finger round the house.

He would often ring the ward clerk to get hold of me to sort something out for him, generally something he blamed me for like if he lost a customer's address he would start an argument on the phone.

One sunny afternoon I was sitting in the garden before work and he threw water from the bedroom window shouting "Get inside you lazy bitch."
I stopped sitting in the garden and used to leave for work early so I could have my lunch by the canal and gaze wistfully to the pub on the other side where people were sitting in groups chatting and laughing.

Sometimes in the evening he used to wait on the ward for me and watch me rushing around until I had handed over my patients. We often ran over time if there was an emergency.
Mostly I got the bus, arriving home late and the children were running around waiting to be put to bed while he ate pizza and got stoned in the kitchen. It was often ten o'clock before I settled them with a story and tucked them in bed.

He used to crack comments when I came home saying things like "all nurses do is swing their legs on the nursing station" and "So how many Doctors have you had in the linen cupboard today?" "You think you're so clever but I will catch you!"

He hated and despised me when I began to make so much money and began to shout in my face "Some of us have to go out to find f*****g work."

The Nex was short of work and barely in profit, smoking so much weed I had to live upstairs with the children.
The kitchen diner was constantly filled with smoke and the way the house was built the smoke drifted right up the stairs and into the bedrooms and my office.
He would say to me "If you loved me you would sit with me" and I would say back "If you loved me you would stop smoking in the house."

He was constantly on the X-box and passing me on the stairs, as I got up for work he would be heading to bed.

He would make me feel guilty for leaving him at midnight and persuade me to watch a film and make snacks late into the night.

He did not understand the stress I was under and didn't understand or care that I had a duty to care for patients in the morning and I couldn't be tired.

He began to frequently complain he had no friends and I would constantly reassure him that he did and he had me and that I loved him.

He became increasingly aggressive and violent as he began going to outdoor Raves at weekends. He told me that it's something he's always wanted to do and it's just like camping. He felt that raves were unsafe for me as people were taking drugs but he would take me to one that he felt was safe and introduce me to some people that were now his friends.

Going to a rave meant he was out all night. He would do anything to get out the house that night saying he would make it up to me on Sunday when we would all go out for the day. He would become hyper and dance around the house and it was the only time he now really bothered how he looked when he was going out alone.

Sometimes I would get a phone call or a series of texts in the early evening telling me how much he loved me, reassuring me that he was with friends that he would introduce me too. Sometimes I could hear them laughing in the background.

Hours would then go by after I tucked the children in to bed to watch a film with me.

I can't say they were lonely times because times with my children were precious, they were my world. The nights were long when he was out and I spent half the night trying to sleep and the other half staring at the ceiling fighting my gut feelings that he was cheating on me.

Sometimes he would ring me and tell me he was coming home early and not staying out because he missed me too much and then as the evening progressed leave me to realise that he wasn't coming home at all. 2 or 3 am came and went and then I would make excuses to myself that he can't drive because he's had a drink. In the morning he would turn up wasted with bloodshot eyes, stinking of stale beer and weed, admitting that he'd had some pills and danced all night. He then would collapse on the settee and fall asleep. He would be tired and moody all day Sunday which cancelled all the promised family plans and I spent my time trying to keep the children quiet saying Daddy's tired from work. Chloe would climb on top of him and say "Dad did you go to a party and have jelly and ice-cream?" and he would cuddle her and say "Yes and party hats!" If he was dozing he would become very angry if one of the children woke him so we all crept about.

He made me fearful of parties and large groups of people but did take me to a couple of raves and I met some lovely people and sat with him drinking wine listening to the thud of the music resounding round the hills. It was pretty amazing to sit on the hill watching the sun come up at 4am in the morning. People would comment on how fresh I looked as I had never touched drugs up to this point and everyone was wasted. I had my bottle of wine and that was enough for me. I remember those moments only with rose tinted spectacles because they were few and far between.

Most of the time he left me alone with Riley. In retrospect I think we took the dog as he knew I couldn't go very far with him while he went round flirting and getting drunk and dancing. Most of my times at raves were filled with fear and stumbling round with Riley in the dark and helping people who were being sick and handing out water.

If guys came to talk to me my then husband would come from nowhere and glare at them and swat them away like flies, putting a protective arm around me saying that this is my wife. I would ignore his tone and ask if he had met this guy, trying to draw him into a normal conversation. "He has a dog like ours" or "He is a joiner" or something to try and get them to be friends but he would glare at them and they soon got the message that they weren't allowed to talk to me.

The Nex pressured me to drink and take drugs saying they were safe and they will just make me want to dance. I told him I could not and that I was nursing the next day so he would tell me I was boring. Then he used to joke "oh yeah call yourself a nurse and you can't even get drugs!" "Do you know how much money we could make?" Then he would become angry and say "You think you're so f*****g perfect!"

Over that Summer I tried hard to understand why he needed to go there and I began to see it as a huge therapy session full of broken people loving one another.
I even nibbled on a pill on a couple of occasions but I was very wary of drugs.

On Sunday's we would pack up camp and wait till the music generator ran down and we would wait till he was sober enough to drive home then pick the kids up. We were always late picking them up because he never cared if my parents had plans or not then he would crash as soon as we got home leaving me to sort out all the camping stuff and look after the children who were usually hyper and excited because they had missed us both.

He often took Monday and Tuesday off saying he was unwell or tired and boasting to his mates he had been to a rave and you know how it is. They whispered in corners. By Wednesday as he came down off the drugs from the weekend he would be looking for someone to vent on. I remember once handing him a perfect roast dinner and the salt. The lid was loose and all the salt came out into his dinner and he flung the plate across the room in front of the kids so gravy splattered against the wall frightening everyone. Another time he picked up some plates that were stacked by the sink and smashed them on the floor. I never bought new china anymore. He would head butt cupboards. Smash his fists on the work tops and it reached such a pattern that me and Chloe called it black Wednesday! Wednesday after a party I would take the children out before he woke up. and before he had a chance to find someone to vent on.
When he was spoiling for a fight his fists would clench and he would pace as his face became contorted into a rigid set jaw and once his eyes turned black and you knew to get out of the way.
His eyes would flash like a demon had possessed him, his teeth would be gritted and then he would verbally slash up anyone who was around.. It was generally me but sometimes he would verbally abuse the children.

Many times we'd packed bags, many times we'd escaped to my Mum's at the weekends only to return on a Monday to get the children to school or he would phone and talk to the children and say to them that I'm coming to pick you up. I've got KFC.

Over the next year my online business began doing really well and I was still packaging parcels into the night then taking them to the hospital with me the following day so I could post them on my way home before I picked up the children from school.

We continued to row about money as he spent it as fast as I earned it and he persuaded me to take out a personal loan so we could finish the house. He blamed everyone but himself when his business started to slide but his customers used to come up to me in the street and complain that he had not finished their house and they had paid him and ask me when was he coming back?

His Dad lent him money for a new van.

I started seeing friends and decided to re join the gym so I would fit a run in on the treadmill before work.

As I became more independent and tried to have a bit of a social life he became increasingly jealous.

Up until that point he had always given me his old phone when he bought his new one, so he could say that it was his and pick it up and use it or scroll through it anytime he wanted. Despite the fact I ran an online business he had the best phone and laptop that no one was allowed to touch. When I bought my own new phone and laptop in a deal he flew into a rage "Why did you go behind my back wasting money?" so I told him "I could afford it through my business" and he said "Really I don't want to hear about you playing post offices! When I married you, you were a f*****g nurse. Now you sell stuff online! I'm not proud of you anymore! Have you thought about how that makes me look!"

A few days later he charged in the house and threw my phone at me because I hadn't answered it immediately. It was exactly three minutes after he rang and I was going to ring him back. I was busy in the office. He bruised my hand as I dodged out the way but he broke the screen.

The next day he went out and bought himself a second hand phone nearly as good as mine.

I made a huge decision backed by my parents to quit nursing so I could be home for the children and not tired all the time.

The matron got me a counsellor to persuade me to stay on at least as an agency nurse but I wasn't eating or sleeping and had incredible sciatica. I was told at the hospital after extensive physio through the summer holidays (during which he accused me of cheating with the young physio) that there was nothing more they could do for me. I would have to have spinal injections to get rid of the pain.

This was the decision to change my life as I began to speak to the counsellor and explain about how my home life was. but little did I know how difficult things were going to become between me and the Nex once I told him I was going to quit nursing for good as soon as I knew it was financially safe to do so. I had given up relying on any money from him and was lucky if he bought a packet of bacon at the market or food for the dog.
He told me he was going to leave me if I quit nursing and I told him I didn't care.
He didn't care I was crippled with sciatica or I was continuously run down and stressed.

I later discovered this was the year where he met a Social Worker Manager while building her a patio and began a seven year affair with her while she financed his lifestyle.

One evening after a particularly busy period at the hospital; knockout sales in my online business; rowing with him over how we were going to waste our money on Christmas, buying everyone else presents (his way of driving a wedge between me and my family as he was trying to separate me from family related events); I decided to avoid the stress of it all and paid outright for a five star luxury two week holiday after begging for the time off work where we were continuously short staffed.
.
I booked Egypt after a particularly busy Halloween in my shop selling costumes and bikinis I had shipped in from the USA. I paid for the whole holiday outright one evening. We hadn't been away for a long time and I booked for a fortnight over Christmas! I will never forget Matty's face when he said "So we are going to find Nemo Mummy?" Chloe was so excited when I told her we could ride a camel on the beach and maybe go and see the pyramids.

Egypt was as amazing as my dreams. I will never forget arriving in the dark to our beautiful hotel. There was sumptuous marble reception area and huge glass chandeliers. This was 5 star luxury and I had worked hard in the stroke rehabilitation unit for this. My back was very painful and I thought we all deserved a really good break and it would give me and the Nex some much needed time together.

I remember waking in a beautiful bedroom with excruciating back pain and pulling aside the huge blackout curtains to reveal bright sunshine palm trees and a turquoise sea, a huge contrast to the cold windy England we had left behind. This was paradise.

The sea was amazing, clear and blue and as soon as you stepped in brightly coloured fish zipped past your feet. I was a keen swimmer and had snorkelled my way all around Cornwall in my childhood so was keen to go and look at the fish. I left Matty with another adult and me the Nex and Chloe who was a good swimmer swam out over the coral. It was like another world but as soon as I put my head under the water and breathed through the snorkel I was scared. I heard my breathing like Darth Vader and I panicked, I had to get out to the jetty as I felt unsafe with the Nex there. I watched him swim out with Chloe as I swam back to my son. I was angry at myself but struggling to breathe having a full on panic attack.

As soon as I got back I composed myself and hugged my son. Matty was a nervous swimmer and had taken a long while to learn as his Dad's idea of teaching him was to throw him in the water. This put him off learning for several years. I had taught him only the Summer before when I had joined the gym with the children through the holidays.

I spent the rest of the holiday swimming with Matty and looking at the fish at the shore while the Nex told me angrily I was pathetic and him and Chloe went right out to feed huge fish boiled eggs from lunch.

It took me years to realise I feared and did not feel safe with the Nex and that's what caused my panic attack.

We rode camels along the beach. We walked hand in hand to the town. We ate seafood platters and rice dishes and omelettes for breakfast.

The staff were so friendly, making swans from the towels and teaching me and Chloe how to do it and the evening entertainment was fabulous.

Then an attractive older woman arrived with her children, saying that her husband who was in the army would be arriving later. The Nex immediately began flirting and chatting with her like I wasn't there.

"You're a bit of a wide boy aren't you?" she said.

We became friends but I didn't trust her. As couples we met up on the beach and in the bars for karaoke.

The Nex became loud and drunk and began to fall out with all the husbands in the group. That night we all went to the local club. He was falling out with me and chatting to her. I returned from the ladies to find the Nex and this woman all over each other dirty dancing and grinding each other.

They didn't care my children or me saw. I said "What the hell?" He grinned at me and innocently said "What? We are dancing!" I said "How do you think you would feel?"

I spent the remaining week sober keeping an eye on them as until her husband arrived she was continuously trying to get him alone.

It ruined the second week of my holiday and seriously made me think about the future of my marriage.


When we returned after a somewhat relaxing holiday we arrived home to a nightmare! The front window had been broken after someone had thrown a brick through it and there was no explanation as I thought we got on well with all the neighbours.

I kept asking the Nex "What have we done? Why are they behaving this way?"

He played the victim so well telling me and my family that they were threatening to burn our house down and shoot him on the doorstep.

He told me everyone on our street was jealous of us going on holiday and having a big house.

Thus became the hate campaign of the Nex and the neighbours.


I broke friends with my closest neighbour who was trying to protect me from him.

He told me if I spoke to her again he was going to leave me.

The hate campaign with the neighbours was unbearable as my friend turned on me as I was too scared to report him.

This woman had her own issues and began to then bully me and she enlisted the help of the local children who were previously my friends.

They threw things at my windows and yelled "You are a f*****g slag" as I walked down my driveway till I became frightened to leave the house.

This woman let them play in her back garden adjoining to mine and they screamed shouted and teased my dog through the door and then denied it.

I could not understand why they were being so hateful towards me (I found out later he had threatened one of the neighbours and put his hands round her throat)

I began to break down at work and have to leave the main ward to cry in the sluice. I tried to talk to the Sister on my ward. She took me to see the Matron where I cried and all the hell I had been living through tumbled out and she arranged for me to see the counsellor.

He Began To Show His True Colours

When we returned from Egypt I told him I was leaving my nursing career for good.
He kicked me hard in the back and told me to "Get up you f*****g lazy bitch, its a bit of backache! I suffer back ache every f*****g day." I was crippled and could not lift my head without shooting burning agony in my leg and bottom.
I knelt at the computer to run my online shop as it was too painful to sit and I would wake in the night with a feeling like a red hot poker burning down my sciatic nerve.

At this point, once the comfy lifestyle that I funded was threatened, I began to see the true him. He screamed at me things like "What use are you to me? Go to your f*****g Mums Even the dog has a purpose. He shuts the door and guards the house! You do f**k all for me you've never done f**k all for me, you sciatic old bag."
I began to see him for the cold heartless cruel bully that he is. He was attacking me now I was weak and vulnerable.

These incidences are in a swirl of memory fog as I only remember snippets.
Him coming in the house and me running into the bedroom as he chased me and grabbed me shouting blaming and swearing. I would scream "Leave me alone" and he would get even angrier as he said "Oh yes you want everyone to hear, don't you!" Our dog would often be cowering next to me and he would kick him and tell him to get out! He would whimper and the Nex would say "I never even touched you!" He would grab my face and hit me on the head or push me down on the bed face down and slap me saying "Why can't you just do as you're told? We could be really happy if you just did as you're told!"

I remember a violent episode where he grabbed me and threw me across the room and spat in my face and called me names and told me I was a liar so I would escape out the house to a neighbours. Once he followed me with a tea towel and flicked me in the face with it shouting "get home now" as my then friend stood between us saying "Go home leave her alone!"

My friend stood between us as he threatened me "She's not coming with you, leave her alone!" She tried to get me to report the violent incidences and helped me take pictures of my injuries and accompanied me to the Domestic Violence unit. I would not press charges as I was too scared and each time he assaulted me I minimised the abuse and rationalised his behaviour. He told me she made him angry and before she came along we were ok. That I didn't see how jealous she was of me and did not see how much she fancied him. He would scream that I was blind to all this. He enlisted another neighbour to talk some sense into me and to tell me how much he loved me. This man sat with me and told me that he was always telling him how much he loved me. The Nex told me that if I didn't break friends with this woman he would really fall out with me. Was I going to let another jealous woman destroy what we had? So I refused to speak to her again and tried to patch things up with him.

The violence was escalating, first from a push and a shove to throwing me forcefully across the kitchen. He would pin me to the sink pushing his body weight against me grabbing my chin, gritting his teeth, snarling and hitting me on the head with his other hand saying "Maybe this will knock some sense in!" Or he would come up behind me as I was washing up and grab me roughly and shout in my ear till it rang shouting "F*****g listen!" I began to flinch when he came near me and he smirked as I did so and said "What you silly bitch, I haven't touched you! You're lucky, if you were a man I would knock you out! But you're not worth the jail time!"

If we were downstairs and he realised I was escaping upstairs, he would block me at the top and tell me he was going to throw me down the stairs or throw me through the window if I didn't listen to him. I would be running round gathering my phone and putting my shoes on ready to escape his violent rage.

Then this mood passed over, life settled down again and he made an effort to show me how much he loved me.

Until a month later it returned and he threw me across the room once again.

At this point I had a very close and trusting relationship with my teenage daughter and we texted and spoke on the phone regularly throughout the day. She was rarely late home and was a very respectful lovely girl to be around and we hung out a lot together.

I tried to hide the way her Dad treated me but she would come home from school and I would be standing with my back to her at the sink and muster a cheerful "Hello how was your day?" while drying my eyes. She would say "What's he done Mum?" I would say "Nothing I'm fine" and she would say "You're not. What's he done, tell me?" while I burst into fresh tears. In this way we became allies that united to keep him from raging and on a level of pleasant. Between us we had learned to spot the signs before his temper escalated and would ask "Shall I make you a sandwich?" Or we would jump up and help him look for his keys, praying we found them before he exploded!
He would sit on the toilet with the door open and hurl shoes at me or keys down the stairs.

As Chloe reached puberty she was a stunning looking girl and became visibly wary of her Dad as he began to change towards her, teasing her and making frequent rude comments about her appearance.
Chloe began to put a little weight on but she was eating healthy meals and snacks and I knew it was just part of her developing into a woman. As she physically changed he began to verbally attack her.
"You don't have the body for leggings" he smirked. A friend of hers later told me she cried all day at school over that remark alone. He used to say "You know your Mum keeps you fat so she gets all the attention?" Of course I told him how ridiculous that was and argued that I feed the children healthy meals and perhaps it was the pizza and chocolates that you shared with them after tea that needed to stop but he did not listen and continued to blame me.

She would say in defence "you're the fatty and you have a grey hair. I can see it there"
As she teased him back, he became more vindictive and began to tell her that she will grow up and have children with three different men and live

on a council estate. That she will be a slag like her Mum and we will leave him and be pushing prams round together.

Chloe would be left in tears sobbing into my lap "It's like he hates me, Mum" she would say.

I often stepped between them saying "Wow stop it you two!"

I would say that he didn't hate her but it was just that she wasn't a little girl anymore and he was having a hard time with that.

Of course not knowing then what I know now, he was losing control and we were seeing glimpses of narcissistic rage as he lost control of her.

Chloe was beautiful and fun to be around and was popular with the boys and he could not stand to see her developing close relationships with them.

He would say "You don't need a boyfriend Chloe, you've got a loving Dad".

She had girlfriends over for sleepovers and we all used to bake together. The Nex would walk in the kitchen and literally snarl at me and say "Why are they in here!" then turn round sweetly and say "Hi" to everyone and flirt with Chloe's friend.

He began to step up his controlling campaign demanding to see Chloe's phone and read her messages and he trampled every healthy boundary she had. She began to lock her phone.

So then he enlisted a young lad, the son of one of his exes to befriend her and spy on her. He told me and we had a huge row as tears rolled down my cheeks and I said "She's a good girl, Why don't you trust her?"

He snarled at me banging his fist on the breakfast bar telling me "You know f**k all about raising kids! You can do this on your f*****g own" then he would storm off shouting and drive away.

I would then run to Chloe's room calming her down saying "It's ok he's gone now."

She would sit on my knee saying between sobs "I hate him! I wish he would be run over! Why doesn't Dad trust me? I don't go out to parties. I do my school work and I come home when you say so, why doesn't he trust me? Why does he think I'm taking drugs? Why it's like he hates me!"

The following day he came home telling me she can't be trusted shouting "I know where she was and I know she was doing drugs the other day!" Chloe was sobbing upstairs and came to the top of the stairs to listen running down in a fit of anger into the kitchen shouting "Why would I do drugs Dad, Why would I want to end up like you?"

He ran after her shouting "I know you better than you know yourself! Don't lie to me!"

Then I heard him say to her "You know she keeps you fat so she is the slim one!"

I ran after him and tried to calm him down and he threatened me through gritted teeth that he was going to throw me through the window and that I knew "F**k all" about teenagers.

He confiscated her phone and hid it threatening "Don't you dare look for it. I'm going to check it when I get home!"

Chloe and me waited till we heard the screech of tyres disappear into the night as she whispered "Mum if he looks on my phone he's going to see I kissed someone!"

I went to get the phone and we went through it together in so much shaking fear while she erased all the excited messages about her new boyfriend to her best friend Angela.

Ten minutes went by and the Nex rang and screamed at me "Why do you have to get involved? I wasn't falling out with you. I was angry with Chloe." I told him through tears that he can't treat her like that and I wouldn't have it. I could take it but I wouldn't have her hurt like that.

At this point we were in the middle of decorating Chloe's bedroom and then he refused to do anymore as he wasn't speaking to her.

I had ordered her new curtains and a chandelier and he refused to help.

The following morning as the sun streamed in and woke her up he wouldn't let me hang the curtains saying "We have to teach Chloe a lesson." I bought all the extras for her room and finished it myself one evening while he was out.

During this chaos I was stripping and painting all the rooms as I just wanted the house finished. He watched me finish the children's rooms and then a final feature wall in the bathroom as a contrast to the black tiling and units. I did this extremely carefully with the edging brush and he grabbed a sanding block and scraped the words 'shit' all over it in the wet paint! He said "This is shit, do it again!" and locked me in the bathroom while I sat and cried through the night.

He told the children "Me and your Mum are finishing this house, selling it and moving abroad" He told me that they didn't respect him as they didn't even make a birthday card for him but they did for me. That we should throw Chloe out as she was rude and turning into a slag.

He began to tell me that we should have another or maybe adopt one because they paid you loads of money to look after them.

The children were understandably upset and I told them I would never ever leave them and if he was going to go abroad he would be going alone.

I began to realise he was insane.

I told him he needed help. I told him he wasn't right in the head and he was a bully.

He sneered at me that he knew I was paddling my canoe in a different direction to all of them. We all know you are the crazy one. He began to tell the children they would always be a unit and nothing would separate them and he told me that if I ever took his children away from him he would growl and bang his fist on the breakfast bar so that I flinched.

My Light Bulb Moment

It was at this time as trapped as I was that I knew I had to get me and the children far away from him.

I know to this day when my light bulb moment was, the day I saw with renewed clarity that I was trapped by a bully.

I was washing up at the sink as usual with my shoes and mobile phone close by listening for the sound of the transit van roaring up into the cul-de-sac. The house was filled with the aroma of the beef casserole that bubbled in the slow cooker. The children were watching TV as a treat for doing all their homework.

As I washed up my heart quickened and I tried to slow my breathing but I was panicking trying to get it all done before he came home.

Chloe shouted "Mum Dad's on his way". I stopped what I was doing and went into the lounge.

Matty ran upstairs and went to his bedroom and Chloe rushed around the lounge straightening cushions and picking up after herself.

I ran back into the kitchen putting things away, getting the table laid and checking the casserole.

My stomach lurched as I heard the roar of his van driving on the lower road as Patch barked excitedly.

I heard him pull up and park and slam the door then he entered the house.

He stormed in slamming the door munching on a piece of fried chicken.

"What the f**k have you done all day? This place is a shithole!" he sneered.

As usual I found myself explaining the children had made cakes, the dinner was on and they'd both done their homework.

"I don't care. I go out and work my fingers to the bone and I come back to this!" He pointed at two plates stacked by the sink waiting to be washed up.

Then he walked over to the sink and swept the offending china on the floor where it shattered in tiny bits.

I didn't even flinch anymore just dutifully bent down and started picking it up.

"Look do you want me to make you a coffee? I'm sorry it's just been a busy day" I reasoned. "I made £200 today'" I carried on brightly.

He snarled and replied "Yeah but that's not profit is it? I don't care about you playing post offices!"

"You can f*****g get rid of that business or I'm leaving!"

We had this argument frequently and I would reply that if I shut my business how exactly did we pay the mortgage and bills?


The Nex was an unqualified builder and despite bragging to everyone about his fleet of vehicles (he had on finance) and how much he made, by the time all his materials and labourers had been paid in cash he barely turned over a profit.

I knew the truth as I had the horrible task of his bookkeeping.

Having never been to business school, I learned the rudiments one afternoon from my sister did the accounts for her husbands company.

Anything I didn't know I would ask the accountant and every six months or so my Dad would sit down with me and help me put both our businesses on spreadsheets and get ready to be checked by the accountant.

The stress of doing his books was phenomenal because he never kept receipts and it never balanced as he hid most of his cash in his sock drawer.

He lived beyond the law in every respect and assaulted me the day I declared his business to the tax office as I didn't want him to get in trouble for tax evasion.

He threatened me upstairs after sending me to get documents to hide what he was doing as the tax investigator sat downstairs.

He continued to shout at me.
"So c'mon tell me exactly what you've been doing today?" he would sneer.
"I've cleaned all upstairs. put the casserole on, posted my parcels, done a food shop and nipped to the gym for an hour and then home to help with homework."
"Oh the gym, so who you shagging down there?" He would grab me roughly against the sink, pinching my chin and hitting me on the head with his free hand. "No one, because I love you" I would state as his eyes went cold and crazy.
"Why can't you just do what you're told?" he spat at me.
Chloe came into the room and he turned round to face her smiling sweetly "Hey sweetie how was your day?"
I ran upstairs where Patch was cowering behind the bed and caught a glimpse of my tear stained face in the mirror.

"Who is this woman? I sure as hell don't recognise her anymore" I whispered to the drained gaunt reflection.
After he left and I heard the roar of the van fading I sat in a daze. "I just can't do this anymore" I shouted.
It was a moment of revelation as I stared into those sad eyes and I admitted it finally to myself. I lived with a bully. I then said the words out loud "I live with a bully. He's getting worse!" Yes, he had a bad childhood and yes, he is insecure but why should I take this anymore!"
"I'm keeping the family together for whom? My children? But he's abusing them now. I've got to get us out."

My children knew what he did to me as towards the end when I was getting stronger he got careless. His anger was less in check and the children saw, so instead of telling them "Hey your Mum needs milk from the shop" and calmly sending them out so he could abuse me he did it so they could see and they stood between us shouting "Leave Mum alone!"

I was deeply saddened as my beautiful once confidant teenage daughter became insecure listening to her Dad's constant put downs and criticisms.

50

I told him to leave and for the first time ever he packed a bag shouting "I had it all, a beautiful wife, beautiful children and a beautiful house." "Oh well," he shrugged his shoulders and smirked as he slammed the front door.

Life settled down as I started to rest and get some sleep and I began to feel much better. I went to the hairdresser and started regularly swimming at the gym. Friends started to comment on how well I was looking. I threw myself into my new business and began to meet up with friends for coffee. I was getting over him and I felt Ok and strangely relieved. He began visiting the children and taking them out and he would often say "Give this to your Mum" or bring me something and I really believed we could all be friends.

Idealization and Love bombing

He told me at this point that he was living in a bedsit with a friend in the next town. He began to compliment me and tell me how well I looked. Sometimes he would try to cuddle me just as friends. He told me he was seeing a counsellor and working on his anger issues. We went out to eat and to walk the dog on several occasions to discuss the children as he told me they never respected him and we should give up with them and have another. I told him I would never bring another child into this.

He told me he was going to live with his Dad several hours away and work with him for a while. ( I later found out he was seeing a girl down there) but at the time he was chatting to me on Facebook and texting me and it was then he suggested, ten months after our initial separation, that he hadn't fallen out with me but had been angry at Chloe as she did not respect him.

He told me he missed me and thought we should try again. He told me how much he loved me and that I would never find someone who loves me like he does and said "Let's be a family again."

I suggested we wait until after he had finished the counselling. He would come round after the counselling sessions, telling me his counsellor said that he would make a great counsellor. We discussed him working with children again which is something he wanted to do but could not because of his criminal record for kicking a police officer in the face 8 years earlier.

Blame Shifting

He called me constantly and asked if we could meet up on the sea front for lunch and just to talk. I eventually agreed to this as I still had feelings for him and hoped we could make it work once his anger issues were resolved through the counselling. He parked and we chatted in the sun but it wasn't long before he began to blame me for everything, so I made my excuses and left saying we are going round in circles. I cannot deal with this anymore.

Several weeks went by and he began to get letters to our address from the parking company of an unresolved parking ticket that he had refused to pay from parking illegally that day when he had met up with me.
He phoned me and said that it had been my fault as if he hadn't met up with me he wouldn't have a ticket and he was so angry. I told him that I would try and email and sort it out. This had been my role throughout our relationship, taking the blame for his messes and taking responsibility and sorting them simply so as not to see his rage.
I emailed them via his email and I told him they would be in touch soon. He ignored all their emails. Usually I would have alerted him to them but he wasn't living with me at the time.

Several months went by and I received a hand delivered threatening letter from the bailiffs for £400 as this ticket had escalated over the months of not being paid.
I contacted him and he told me he was on his way round. He ran into the house and chased me up the stairs grabbing me roughly and gritting his teeth "You f*****g bitch, you've been withholding my mail this is your fault" he raged. He threw me across the room and I hit my shoulder on the mirror. He edged closer towards me his eyes burning with madness. "Don't think they are taking anything of mine!" Then he threw me on the bed where I cowered and left shouting "You better f*****g sort this out. Give them your f*****g laptop. It's your fault! If hadn't met you on the beach!" He ran down the stairs and I heard the door slam and the squeal of brakes as I sat and sobbed. I composed myself,locked all the doors and windows and phoned the bailiffs who were very understanding once I explained the situation. I then phoned my Dad to bail us out and he brought me the cash straight over.

Those weeks he behaved unpredictably to love bomb me and sometimes to be aggressive. Shouting at me, grabbing me roughly saying that we should be sleeping in that bed! We should be together and be a family! He would get angry and shout "Why should we live here in this big house when I have nothing, I live in a bedsit!" Later I realised that he was actually he was living with the OW quite comfortably. I put his mood swings down to the fact he was working through some pretty rough counselling sessions. He would come round unannounced, chat and want to get physically close to me. Sometimes we would cry and hold each other.

I was so confused and I loved and hated the person that he was.

Future Faking

He told me he was going to finish the house and buy me an eternity ring. He told me if I didn't believe how much he loved me he would run round the block naked to prove it.

A few more months and he had morphed back into the charming happy go lucky guy I fell in love with those many years ago as he got down on his knees and begged tugged my sleeve imploringly and said in an audible whisper "I miss you sexy blue eyes!" and crying that he just wants his wife back.

I wouldn't go out with him in the car but he begged me and said we could just talk.

He had chicken pieces and bread and wine and said "We're going for a picnic. Are you hungry?" This was the kind of spontaneous thing he used to do when we first got together.

We drove miles and we talked and we laughed and listened to music and he reached for my hand. We stopped by some fields and it was muddy by the side of the car so he put the picnic bag on one arm and grabbed me on his shoulders with the other as I squealed.

He had transported me back to the earliest months in our relationship and there and then all that mattered was me and him. He carried me on his shoulders over the mud then we ate and we drank and chatted. Then he leaned in and kissed me tenderly.

I only realised once we got back to the car after I had been intimate with him how duped I had been.

We were driving home and he began to verbally blame me for everything that was wrong in our relationship. Then he sneered and said "I'm surprised you couldn't taste my girlfriend." I asked what was he saying and he told me that his girlfriend had been where you were just then! I wanted to throw up as I got out the car.

That night I got a text saying he's sorry he was just so lonely, that she meant nothing to him, he just wanted his wife back and it was lovely to spend time with "sexy blue eyes." We texted through the night as I told him I couldn't do this anymore, he was making me ill and I could not eat, I could not sleep and I wanted a divorce.

I told him to go to her we were done.

He arrived the following day and barged in the house upstairs to the bedroom. I was lying on the bed on the laptop and I hurriedly sat up as he sneered "Oh yes what are you up to? You slag?" I told him I wasn't up to anything and I was still married. He said "Bullshit. You're shagging around. That's why you want me out!" I said that I still loved him but I couldn't do this anymore. He again grabbed my sleeve and begged me to give him another chance saying that he couldn't live without me and he was going to throw himself in the canal.

I repeated that I couldn't do this anymore wanted a divorce.

He grabbed the laptop and threatened to throw it as I said "You have a girlfriend. We are finished!"

I was so upset and frustrated incredulously explaining to him that he has a girlfriend!

He screamed at me, gritting his teeth. "If you don't tell me your Facebook password right now I'm going to my girlfriend" and I screamed right back "Go then. You made your bed go lie in it!" I don't know where the strength came from. I think it was driven from fear and anger and a feeling that I just didn't care anymore. I just wanted him to leave.

I was so angry as he remained in the room and I said "Did you tell her about yesterday?"

He flew into a rage and grabbed me as I stood by the window and put his arm around my shoulder looked me in the eye and said "I could hurt you if I wanted to, you know?" and just as casually put his hands round my neck enough to make me scared but not enough to leave a mark then he turned to me with gritted teeth and flashing demon eyes and said "I don't do divorce, I married you for life! If you leave me you will have nothing. I will take everything and I will show my children a real mother!"

"You watch!" He snarled then he left me in a sobbing heap.

My Splitaversary

The day I got the guts to tell Matty to call my parents and get them to call the police.

I shudder recounting the memories of that day.

I was in the garden planting tomatoes and he arrived home and began yelling at me because I stopped Matty playing an over 18 computer game he had given him. "You always take the things I give him" he shouted across the garden. Of course I tried to reason with him that I didn't want him playing it as it was not suitable with prostitutes in it and killing lots of people. Matty was only 14. He picked up a metal bucket of water and launched it at me across the garden soaking me and hitting me with the bucket. "That'll calm you down, you silly bitch" he screamed and then smirked as I squealed as the cold water winded me. I tried to breathe and to run back into the house and he put his foot across the door so I couldn't run past him into the kitchen. I was panicking and freezing and Matty came running in and said "I'm disgusted at you Dad!" My daughter helped me to come back into the house and she got me a sweatshirt and put a towel around me.

The raging Nex walked in while I was sat on the sofa and my daughter stood between us and physically blocked him from me shouting "Leave Mum alone!" Matty was scared and said "Shall I call Nanna?"

I was in shock and scared at the unpredictability of his rage until the Nex said "You are an asshole" and turned like the coward he is and stormed off and drove off in the car.

Mum and Dad arrived and we discussed what to do. Woman's Aid was shut by then so we decided to ask the Police, just for advice, but they thought it serious enough to send an officer over.

The Nex returned with peacemaker doughnuts for us all and argued with my Dad that he had only thrown water over me as otherwise he might have hit me. What was he to do as he couldn't control either his wife or his daughter? Then a Police Officer arrived and arrested him as soon as he came in the house. As he was led away he snarled at us all through gritted teeth and said that we had all betrayed him. "You watch what happens now!"

That was the end of my marriage, seven days after we had celebrated our wedding anniversary.

I watched him cry and begging me on his knees to take him back saying that he couldn't live without me (while he was living with someone else!) This didn't work and I started putting his stuff in the garage so he turned on me. "You've destroyed my life! Now I'm going to take everything and destroy yours! You watch, you will have nothing!"

That evening Chloe wrote a message to my elder sister telling her what had happened and that her Dad was mental and Mum needed to leave him, which was fortunate, because, some while later Chloe told me that Dad had said you stabbed him with a garden fork and that's why he threw a bit of water at you! "He cried, Mum, and I held him like a baby. Don't deny it, as I even saw the wound on his leg."

She would not listen when I tried to explain that I would not do that and she had been shown an old work injury on her Dad's leg. This was really the first occasion she started to believe his alternative versions of reality but, even during the times she refused to speak to me she would not testify in court against me.

He harassed me through the Summer and told me I was teasing him because when he turned up in the house I was always wearing shorts.

He looked me in the eye and said "Look at you! You are much sexier than her but she doesn't make me insecure like you do!" "You know you're beautiful, I can't live without you!"

He followed me into the gardening store and watched me picking up flowers, came over and handed me some money "Get yourself some flowers" he said so I took the money and spent it on a Chinese for me and the children. I was not going to take him back again. In my head we were done!

The follow up to his arrest was that he was charged with battery and received a one year conditional discharge and this assault was later used to apply for an injunction and a non molestation order so he wasn't allowed near me for a year.

It was Autumn 2011 and the leaves were just beginning to fall when I began divorce proceedings against him on the grounds of unreasonable behaviour. My solicitor informed me it would be much quicker than getting the evidence together to prove adultery.

My solicitor stated in a letter to the Nex "You have recently subjected her to physical and verbal abuse. This has resulted in the Police becoming involved and we strongly advise you to stay away from her." Then she clearly stated "If you do not take heed of this advice then we have instructions to make an urgent application to the Court for an injunction/ occupation Order."

Last night the Nex began harassing me and my family.

They received texts and missed calls and messages basically telling lies about me.

It all came to a head when the Nex messaged my sister pleading,

"What am I supposed to do when my daughter comes crying to me saying her mother punched kicked and hit her."

This followed with an answering machine message on my Mum's phone saying something similar.

Following this he sent a message to my younger sister that he would be going to the police about this.

I tried to stop shaking and calm myself down and dialled the police myself and told them what he had said and they told me he hadn't called them but they would log it as an incident.

He's upset the truth about his true behaviour has come out.

I was in a brain fog and had just began studying NPD.

I knew he was being difficult about the children but did not understand the pathology I was now fighting.

Little did I know at this stage this was the beginning of a huge smear campaign to blacken my reputation as a mother and assassinate my character.

The day the children left was traumatic so I have pieced it together from solicitors letters and police reports and messages to my sister.

Several months after he was charged for battery and left the marital home he started inviting Chloe and Matty for barbecues and shopping trips so they could get to know the OW.

He had told me several weeks earlier she was a Social Worker Manager in children's care who was ten years older than me and he bragged "I will never want for money again, she earns loads and she's taking us on holiday, she also bought me some canoes and a van!"

I encouraged this as I thought that now the Nex had a girlfriend he would leave me alone. I fully supported my children spending time with their Dad even though it hurt at the time as I was still very lonely.

I began to worry over the next few weeks that the OW was apparently very wary of me according to Matty and they weren't allowed to tell me where she lived but came back every weekend telling me they had had a barbecue or had been shopping. If I then asked for normal details like "What did you eat?" they would clam up and snap "I'm not telling you Mum!"

The Nex had also taken Patch as he slept with Chloe every night.

I remember that Mum and Dad came over to see us all as they'd just returned from holiday with gifts for Matty and Chloe as they always did but the children didn't turn up from school as the Nex picked them up deliberately to stop my parents seeing them. I was sick with worry and had no way of contacting them.

They arrived with no warning with the Nex who waited impatiently outside revving his engine. They were under instruction to collect their stuff saying they were leaving.

I cried and begged for an explanation as they rushed around grabbing things while he beeped his horn impatiently! Chloe shouted at Matty "Hurry up we're going!" then she looked over her shoulder as our eyes connected briefly and she said "Bye Mother! "They scrambled out the house slamming the door.

Time stood still till I heard the jeep roll into life and squeal down the hill. Then they were gone. I bolted the door and sank to the floor and sobbed.

I texted Chloe and received a rude reply. He had twisted her mind!

Matty had no phone and no way of contacting me and did as his Dad and sister asked him to.

The following week Chloe was still responding to my messages abusively.

I spoke to Matty's counsellor at school the following day and explained everything. They were appalled and told me I could see him at school and they would help me.

The link counsellors were all onboard with me and trying to help in any way they could.

It was a difficult meeting as Matty had been brainwashed with lies but over the hour he came around and listened to me. He was very angry and confused.

I thought if all goes well I would be picking him up from school for the weekend and hopefully me and my family could undo some of the psychological damage done to him but he never responded to any of my messages.

I lived from bed to chair didn't eat and couldn't work.
Several weeks passed in a haze of memory fog.
My children  eventually got in touch and told me Dad was going away with the OW so they could stay over that night.
They began to have regular weekly visits.

Divorce papers were issued at the County Court.  My solicitor informed me "It is likely that they will take approximately 2 weeks to process the documentation and send a copy to him."
Today I wrote a letter to my solicitor expressing my worry that the Nex would further upset me when he receives the divorce papers.
I was told to contact the police if there is a further incident where I fear for my safety and if the harassment continues my solicitor reminded me we can apply for an Occupation Order, which up to this point I was too scared to go through with.

Made progress with Chloe and we were now texting and it came to light that she'd heard lots of lies but she knew her Mum. He was trying hard to break our bond. I was staying at my parents house as I did not feel safe to go home alone.
The warning letter has been delivered to the Nex.

I approached Women's Aid and they told me they could come as part of the Sanctuary scheme for abused women  and  make my house safer by adding security lighting and changing the locks.

I just took up kickboxing with my sister at the local gym and she is dragging me there telling me it will do you good.

September 2011

The Nex came up to the house to get Patch's dog food.
He parked outside and waited in the car and let Matty out to come in the house.

Matty came in and hugged me, told me he missed me and said Mum "I've come for dog food."

I hugged him and told him "I'd missed him" and he clung onto me.

He then said "Can I come and stay today Mum? I will just ask Dad."

He ran out and gave his Dad the bag of food and discussed it through the window.

His Dad got out the car and I could tell from his stance and the way Matty was behaving that they were arguing.

Ten minutes later without hugging his Dad he came back in the house.

His Dad sped off.

I stopped painting his room and spent the rest of the day with him.

He stayed over and cuddled me all night.

The following day we spent a lot of time together.

At about 3pm the Nex again drove up and parked outside the house.

Chloe got out the car and came to the house.

She said to Matty, "We're going to Chester now you have to come."

Matty came in and said to me "I don't want to, I want to stay here with you."

I said "You can choose what you want to do."

He went outside and spoke with his Dad, not admitting he wanted to see me saying he missed the cat and he felt ill.

Some ten minutes later the Nex and Chloe drove off.

Matty is being heavily influenced by his sister and Dad.

I then told him I was going away on Thursday (While the injunction was served) and would he like to come and stay over on Wednesday evening before I go.

He looked uncomfortable and said "I don't know if I can Mum."

I said to him "If you want to it is your choice."

They came back for him later that evening.

He had no school things no glasses and everything's been taken there from my house.

so sadly he had to go back.

I told him I would message him everyday on Facebook and to check everyday.

I messaged him on Facebook last night and he hasn't replied.

This morning I phoned the school counsellor and arranged through school to pick him up on Wednesday evening.

I feel like Chloe has been yearning for her fathers approval all her life.

All he has done is put her down and criticise her.

Now she is clinging on to this super Dad who is pulling out all the stops for her.

She is hating me for his approval I think.

The Nex visited again about 1pm and sat outside my house revving his engine while his mate tried the door which was bolted.

The children are at school and he has the dog so there was no need reason for him to come here.

For the last few months I have been chatting to Stuart who is in the RAF. Finally I have agreed for him to drive over and take me out for dinner.

This evening he drove over and parked on the road below my house and I was planning on walking down to meet him then we were going to go for a drive out and have dinner. He was getting a bunch of flowers out the car to give to me.

When I went up to the bedroom to finish getting ready there was a huge valentines card from the Nex that he had written a year ago declaring how much he loved me! It was open in the centre of the bed. He expected me to go to the bedroom with Stuart and it would then sabotage our night.

It spooked me that he had been in the house as I knew he had been watching me and had got in the house while I had been out shopping earlier that afternoon.

As I was sat In the kitchen texting Stuart and telling him about this and how scared I was the Nex came flying in through the back door with Patch and another lad grabbing hold of me roughly shouting "If you have any man in this house I'm going to break his legs.". He snatched the back door key slamming the door behind him and ran through the house and out the front door then ran down to the lower road where he got in his car which he had parked behind Stuarts car.

I had just time to ring and quickly forewarn Stuart to leave so the Nex then chased him driving alongside him and shaking his fists all the way 6 miles to the next town.

I had to call the police and they advised me not to stay the night there as I wasn't safe as the Nex has the back door key so could return.

Me and Stuart met up later that evening for dinner and he told me that he wasn't scared as the Nex was a terrible driver and he had flown over the enemy over Basra so it took more than that idiot to scare him. We had a drink and after I had calmed down we had a good chuckle over him!

After this incident however I was really scared so moved in with my sister until the injunction and a non molestation order was served on him.

I was only going home to feed my cat once a day. He was upset being left alone and after the injunction was in place and I moved back home he went off for long periods by himself.

During this time my sister found a little kitten and rescued him from the side of the road. She already had a cat of her own so I said I would look after him until we found the owner. We put up posters and posted on the local lost and found pet sites and no one came forward to claim him. He got on really well with my other cat so I decided to keep him and called him Tiger.

A few weeks later my other cat came back with wet paws and I dried him and thought nothing of it. The following morning he couldn't walk and I took him to the vets and they told me he had been poisoned with anti freeze. I was told that because he's long haired he had licked his paws clean and ingested enough to poison him. I had to have him put to sleep which was devastating.

So now it was just me and Tiger.

I remember saying to him "I'm so glad we found each other" and soaking his fur in tears.

I am awaiting a return call from Louise at Women's Aid re: making house safe so he can't get in.

I had to go up to the court with my solicitor and face the Nex who was sat with the OW and the judge told him "You were arrested for battering your ex wife so will not be allowed to go anywhere near her or to the marital home for a year." The Nex argued that his tools were in the garage and he would need to go and visit daily to collect them for work and the OW complained and said she had nowhere to store his tools.

The judge told him therefore he had to organise his own lock up facility and he would be allowed to visit once only to collect them. Then he told him he was to be served with a one year injunction and non molestation order.

It was then arranged that he was only allowed to come as far as the road below my house to collect the children and if he came any closer he would be arrested.

October 2011

Matty hadn't answered any of my Facebook messages and still did not have a phone last week despite telling me "Dad says he's going to get me one soon."
I had to contact school again to ask Matty to talk to me when I got back after my trip away.

Matty messaged me on Facebook that he would be coming for the whole weekend by his own choice.
Finally he seemed like he was starting to stand up for himself.

He arrived on Friday however as we arranged in his school uniform with no clothes to change into.
I really believe if he had gone to his Dad's to change he would've been stopped from coming to see me.
He was very upset and said that "Staying over during the week can't happen Mum because I have no books or stuff."
He also told me "Dad cries when I come here," so is suffering being emotional blackmailed.
We had a lovely calm weekend.
I texted Chloe asking if she had a good weekend and saying how I would love to see her but she was rude and also explained how if she had her way Matty wouldn't be seeing me either.
She said I had lied in court.
She is in total denial. It's like she doesn't want to believe the abuse happened.
She would rather believe I caused her Dad to be angry and that he's all better now.
She was angry that I had texted her friend (who I know well) to see if she was okay.
In the end after heated texts I had to say "I don't deserve to be treated like this!"
I got the response "It is your loss not mine."

Matty asked to phone Chloe as he wanted to stay longer and told me "I would stay over If I had my books Mum."

Chloe told him you have to be ready on the street at 6pm I'm not coming up for you and he didn't argue with her and is completely under her thumb.

She also sent frequent texts to him saying "C'mon Matty we miss you you've been gone ages" over the whole weekend putting pressure on him to return.

He told me he would love to stay on Mondays if it could be arranged.

I told him we can arrange that.

I then emailed my solicitor to ask if we can arrange him to stay with me half the week so he has his things.

Maybe Friday to Monday because I know this is what he wants but is struggling to stand up to everyone especially his sister.

My parents also visited on Sunday and he hugged them and told them he loved them.

We have arranged to go out with my family next Saturday when he is over.


Matty has been coming on Fridays and staying over till Sunday evening. He has been fine and his behaviour has been fairly normal under the circumstances.

Chloe doesn't respond to any of my messages and now hasn't been in touch for weeks.

I am exhausted and tearful today.


I wrote my daughter a letter

"I do not deserve to be treated like this Chloe. I love you and I always will love you but If you cast your mind back to what you, Matty and I have been through and do it with honesty you will realize that you have no right to judge me nor to treat me badly."


I got the usual curt hurtful response.

"We will be waiting for Matty at 6 make sure he's there. Bye."


A week later Chloe texted to say she was coming for tea!

I expected her to be in touch as she is going to a music concert and expected me to pay for it.

However due to her disrespectful rude behaviour I have not.

I sent her a text,

"I know over the last few months I haven't been there for you and I'm truly sorry for that and for thinking of what I was going through and not about you and Matty.

I love you and always will and just want you to be happy.

I really look forward to seeing you on Friday with Matty Please bring Patch as it would be lovely to see him and the cat pines for him."

She replied rudely and abruptly,

"I don't need your life story, So will you have the money then?"

So I responded "No I will not reward your disrespectful rude behaviour. You were not brought up to speak to me like that."

My solicitor contacted me after putting a formal contact proposal together from Friday evenings to Tuesday mornings as Matty had requested. We thought once this was arranged then he wouldn't feel pressured by the Nex as it would be out of his hands.

My solicitor contacted me and said ,The Nex has stated he does not agree with your abuse allegations but he does not wish to defend the same. We are therefore able to apply for your Decree Nisi which is the interim divorce.

Matty turned up at my house after school on Friday.

He stayed through till Sunday evening.

Chloe just phoned and told him he was being picked up.

He said he didn't want to go and wished to stay over another night.

She said "You have to come" and then said she wanted to see him.

"You are staying at Mum's Tuesday and Wednesday because we are going out" she told him.

No one had informed me of this.

I was simply being used as a babysitting service.

When I said on the loudspeaker Chloe Matty can choose to do what he wants in a pleasant way she was verbally abusive to me then she put the phone down.

I felt like Matty was being bullied to go there and if it was his decision he would've come home.

He told me he had fallen out with the OW last week and was rude to her.

He was clearly very confused and upset at that moment.

A few days later Chloe rang at tea time and said they were coming for him.

Again no one had informed me of this and I was expecting Matty to stay for tea.

Matty said he had to go so I said "You have a choice."

He said "I don't I used it yesterday."

Chloe came to the house for him and spoke to him in an agitated state "Hurry up Matty."

I broke down and went upstairs as Matty was packing and Chloe was outside and said "Why Matty? Why is she like this? What have I done to her?"

He said "I don't know Mum" as he was going out the house.

I said "When are you back?" and he said "Maybe tomorrow."

He has no credit for his phone and wouldn't let me buy any as the Nex promised him they would.

He has no means of contacting me and I'm beginning to feel like this has been done on purpose to sabotage our relationship.

Chloe said as she was leaving "It's great how you can afford new flooring and not my concert you're an evil bitch!"

I told her "I love you and miss you but will not reward your rude disrespectful behaviour."

Then I bolted the door and heard the car drive away, then I crumpled in tears on the floor as I felt my heart break.

Matty hasn't turned up tonight as we arranged.

I have sent him a message on Facebook.

I have texted and rang his phone which doesn't answer.

He still has no credit and no way of contacting me.

I do not have the home phone no and if I did do not feel able to contact him this way.

I now have no way of contacting Matty.

I have sent Matty a message on Facebook.

I have texted and rang his phone which doesn't answer.

He still has no credit and no way of contacting me.

I found out from a friends Facebook that Chloe had written 'Shopping in Chester' this morning.

I can only assume that Matty has gone too and that once again plans were changed at the last minute so he wouldn't come to me.

I really feel that the Nex has put everything in place to stop me developing a good close relationship with my son.

I am continuing with the counselling sessions through Women's Aid to help me come to terms with this and understand why my daughter is behaving in this way.

Late October 2011

Again I was unable to contact Matty via any method.

Yesterday was the first Halloween I have ever spent without them.

We always went trick or treating and had a party on Halloween, usually without their Dad as he showed no interest in it.

At about 3pm Matty rang from a call box with just enough money to say he was coming over.

The beeps went and I had to ring back on the payphone and explain I was not home but the decorator is in so he can go home.

Matty has a mobile phone and last time I saw him I again offered to buy him credit but he refused saying his Dad was sorting it.

His Dad hasn't paid for credit for his phone for weeks and I feel this is deliberate to prevent him talking to me and texting on a daily basis and building a relationship, especially over the holidays.

While I was in town I had to buy food for his tea not knowing whether he's staying or not.

When I arrived home he said he was and he would be staying Saturday night and he doesn't know about Sunday.

I don't know if I'm coming or going, cannot make any plans of my own and feel I am just used for babysitting purposes having the last say in any arrangements as I cannot contact Matty.

There have been further developments with Chloe over the last week.

She was upset our family cat had to be put to sleep and contacted me to ask if I was okay via text.

Several texts followed and she began to communicate briefly.

Following on from this she was doing her mock exams and contacted me to say she would like to meet up with me for a smoothie in the local coffee shop.

It surprised me to find that Chloe was very affectionate and very keen to tell me everything that has happened to her over the time she hasn't communicated.

She did not discuss why she had behaved appallingly towards me and I did not bring the subject up following my counsellors advice.

She began to talk freely revealing the fact she has a boyfriend a year older than her and that her father knows nothing of this but is suspicious.

However her Dad introduced her to this lad as he worked for him and Chloe told me that her Dad had taken him aside and put a knife to his throat threatening him not to touch his daughter or he will hurt him and threatening him not to tell my daughter of this incident.

I was pleased that Chloe had confided in me and told her everything will be okay he can't just go round threatening people and she has a choice of who she goes out with.

I am now concerned that her Dad will find out and there will be further incident.

She is very keen that I meet her new boyfriend this weekend.

She has expressed a wish to come and stay with me when Matty comes this weekend.

She asked to come back to the house following this meeting and was very impressed at the house being finally finished and the rooms being so lovely.

She concerned me by telling me that her father now smokes in the house and takes drugs in front of her.

She concerned me by telling me that she often has to parent Matty getting him up for school, and that her father and the OW go out late on a school night and expect Matty to get himself to bed.

On one occasion her father came and shouted at Chloe after he came in late and blamed her for not getting Matty in bed.

I explained to Chloe that she is not a parent and this isn't her responsibility.

I am generally concerned with the lack of parenting going on, the threats of violence towards her boyfriend and the smoking and drugs around my children over which I have no control.

November 2011

The weekend with the children was a great success.

I had my friends over and their sons had a sleepover with Matty.

Over the weekend Chloe opened up to me about her feelings towards her

Dad saying "The cracks are starting to appear."

She said her Dad is very needy and says "Don't leave me" and he cries in her arms so is emotionally blackmailing them.

She is fed up with the OW as she is very unpleasant about me and says "I have taken their Dad's house" so I explained that I bought the house myself and put him on the deeds and it is therefore jointly owned and she said "I know Mum."

The OW told Chloe that she cannot take Patch up to see me as I have Dad's house and I don't deserve to see him which has greatly upset me.

Chloe also told me her Dad is very rude and personal about me and I am discussed regularly and she tries to defend me.

They usually come for Matty at 6pm but this weekend Chloe rang her Dad and said she was staying with me for tea.

Matty was his usual loving self.

Ten minutes before the Nex picked them up Chloe became agitated and upset saying "Hurry up Matty you know what Dad's like."

I tried to reassure them both helping them get their stuff together but Chloe said "He blames you if we're late and I don't want him blaming you."

I was angry and upset as they were leaving and said "I don't care if he blames me he has blamed me for 15 years! The only thing that matters is you and Matty."

I hate what he is doing to my children and feel they are living in a very emotionally unhealthy environment of bitterness.

Following this weekend Chloe isn't responding as much to my texts suggesting that she is being further manipulated.

December 2011

I am deeply concerned following spending the day with Chloe & Matty.

I have got much closer to Chloe and had an opportunity to ask her if she would like to move back home pointing out the advantages to her.

I can tell that she would like to do this immediately from her behaviour. However she said "Mum it's not an option, at all."

I said "Why darling, you can tell me."

She said hugging my shoulders, "There are things you don't know and I can't tell you."

I believe they are being manipulated to stop them moving back in with me.

Chloe has become increasingly protective towards me over the last few weeks.

When I asked Matty he just said "It's awkward" suggesting Chloe hasn't told him everything.

January 2012

The children are still living with the Nex but coming on Fridays through to Sunday as before.

They are more relaxed and things are as normal as expected under these circumstances.

However the Nex clicks his fingers and Chloe's personality changes.

She becomes agitated and upset shouting at her brother to get a move on, "C'mon you know what Dad's like" she says.

I did manage for a few weeks prior to Christmas to get Chloe to a counsellor once a week for her insecurity and lack of confidence issues.

This was difficult as she had to lie to her Dad and Matty saying she was going to the Doctor.

She told me after Christmas that this was impossible and she didn't want to see the counsellor anymore.

I am having to handle this very carefully as she is showing a lot of anger, which of course is all directed at me.

I have spoken to her counsellor who has said she needs to go and will come to the house to see her if needs be.

Over Christmas her Dad has showered her with huge gifts and caused a further rift between me and the children saying "I don't care that's why she bought you f**k all."

I am paying all the divorce costs which are high due to the domestic violence.

I have had to pay thousands in bills and the mortgage to keep the family home running and have the children at the weekend when they want to do things and It's really hard with no child allowance.

I am too stressed to work and in a permanent state of tearfulness.

I have lost weight rapidly and feel unwell.

I have discussed on several occasions with the children that I think it would be beneficial that they should come Friday and Saturday and then leave Sunday evening before school and they did agree to this.

Chloe would've been able to continue with the counselling and I would be able to keep in touch with school and homework.

I have been upset to find Matty often doesn't do his homework and gets detentions.

The school no longer inform me of this and I only found out by looking in Matty's schoolbag for crumpled notes.

Matty complained they still eat late and "No one cares when I go to bed."

I believe Chloe parents Matty and does a large number of chores in the household.

I am very unhappy about this but now when I mention coming to me on extra days they tell me "We can't you know what Dad's like."

He is emotionally blackmailing them and bribing them with gifts.

They listen to all the derogatory words their Dad and the OW says about me and repeat them.

They defend their Dad to the end of the earth.

Their Dad is doing a super brainwashing job on them and I feel like I am literally good fighting evil.

Very upset as Chloe has confessed her Dad is bullying her just like he did me. Shouting at her and swearing and recently confessing he threw a laptop charger at her and hit her in the face.

You can imagine how angry and upset I am. I just want to storm over there and rescue them both but I can't.

I phoned her at the weekend to check what time they were coming for tea and she was in her room crying but couldn't talk and was whispering down the phone between tears.

"Whatever it is tell me" I said "I'm sending a taxi straight over" and she said "'I've not spoken to him all day as he's picking on me."

Over the weekend Chloe took me aside without telling Matty and told me how the OW knows nothing about how Dad really is and he is always nice to her and doesn't even swear in front of her.

She told me he even washes up and unpacks the dishwasher when the OW is there.

He has to vent his anger somewhere and he's acting round the OW.

I am shocked he's managed to keep it up so long and this is why my daughter is getting the brunt of his bad temper.

I can't rest now thinking about this and have informed my solicitor and Chloe's counsellor but I'm treading extremely carefully.
I now do not feel my children are safe.
It disgusts me how well he's duping the OW who is a Social Worker in Children's Care.

Unfortunately Chloe's Dad's manipulation is strong.
Chloe is anxious coming up to the end of a visit with me and she begins shouting at her brother to "Hurry up you know what Dads like."
The Nex always arrives early or late honking his horn and phoning them and we all have to drop what we are doing even if I'm serving Dinner.
Matty runs round like a frightened rabbit collecting his things.

We had to pretend Chloe had the Doctors then me and Matty would leave her in the house to chat to her counsellor undisturbed while I took him out for tea.
Chloe has had two counselling sessions now and has begun to reveal some disturbing things.

My injunction states that the Nex isn't allowed to have any one on his behalf come to my house.
Chloe has told me that he regularly sends two lads in the evening onto my street and they copy car no plates outside my house and report back to him.
I do not feel that any man is safe coming to my house.
They also have the only set of keys to my garage and come to collect materials from the garage for work despite the judge forbidding it.
I do not feel safe as they can gain access to the back of my house and garden with these.
I do not feel safe as one of the men was the same one who came in the house through the back door when he was pretending to take the dog back and threatened to break any man's legs who came in my house months ago.

Chloe is also very upset because her Dad gets her boyfriend to work, buys him lunch and doesn't pay him properly.

Chloe stated that her Dad has begun to shout and swear at the OW stating that she was ill in bed and he was shouting at her down the phone "I ask you to do one simple f*****g thing for me and its too much trouble."

This sent chills down my spine because he often shouted that at me when I was busy or ill and couldn't do something immediately.

She has also said "To be honest Mum I don't think she feels she can do any better than Dad."

I'm so upset and knew that despite my feelings towards the OW I feel sorry for her that she is in the devalue stage of the relationship being abused as I was.

The Court application paperwork for a Residence order for Chloe and Matty are ready to be filled in so my application can be issued.


The situation with the children has changed dramatically in my favour and I no longer wish to sell the family home.

My children are now by choice coming three days a week over the weekend.

I feel they are now in a position to return to me although this is going to take time still.

They are both unhappy with the current situation.

I feel they are only there at their Dads through pressure love bombing and bullying.

I know now as Chloe opens up to me after every counselling session the pressure she is under from her Dad.

She has told me that she thought the OW was cleverer and stronger but is now letting him bully her shouting and swearing at her a lot.

She has also told me he has said she can't stay with me longer than two days or she (me) will get to keep the house for another five years.

He's told everyone including the O.W. that I will be out of the house in a month and he's going to buy me out and rent it out.

While the OW finances everything expecting to be paid back.

Chloe's boyfriend who has been coming every weekend has also told me he is frightened of him and doesn't want to work for him but has no money so has no choice than to work for him.

I am trying to help him seek alternative employment and support him.

I am discussing the possibility of college with him.

My children are more themselves especially Matty who is now calling me beautiful Mummy and not being rude.

The household my children are being brought up in is far from stable and very emotionally unhealthy.

I feel as I always have that they need to live with me as I can provide the love stability and support they need as teenagers and I can meet their emotional needs.

February 2012

During a very fun relaxed time with my family while me Chloe & Matty were staying over I heard Chloe sobbing down the phone in her room to her boyfriend.

It became apparent that he was trying to persuade her to go home to live with me and she was explaining she could not.

I heard the following:

"I can't move out He's held a knife to your throat."

"He hasn't done that to me but he emotionally bullies me though."

He says "I will move away with Patch and you will never see me again!"'

'He says "He'll take everything from me."

She was getting angry with her boyfriend and saying "You don't understand."

"Before I had these bad relationships and my Dad started getting at me I want to remember who I was!"

"If I leave he will pursue me and Matty and then Mum too."

I heard all this in horror but knew if I confronted her as I had done before she would deny everything.

I tried to talk to her the following day and ask her if she wants to come home but she said she is happy at her Dads.

I feel completely powerless against his brainwashing campaign and I feel like no one can help me to keep my children safe.

A week later I was travelling back home from London on the train and sending Matty pictures of Big Ben and he began to send me messages on Kik messenger (now our only method of communication) saying he was ill.

He typed "I'm really ill and feel like I'm going to vomit.

I have really bad earache and can't hear out of one ear."

So I wrote back "I love you and want to take care of you.

You might need to see the Dr."

I asked him if Chloe was there and told him to "Go and tell someone he was ill."

He replied "Everyone is busy."

I gave him advice about keeping warm and drinking fluids.

I said "Go and ask someone to help you."

I know he wanted to come to me.

He said "I can't" and went to bed.

When I finally got Chloe to pick up the phone she became sarcastic and said "He's locked under the stairs on bread and water."

This is one of a series of instances where my son is being kept from me when he needs his Mum.

I had to ring the school today to find out if he was off sick and the only contact I have with my son is via Kik messenger.

I feel so helpless and powerless.

Matty was still very ill and was pyrexial when he arrived unannounced at my house last night.

It has now been several weeks of him being unwell and I do not feel Matty was being cared for adequately where he is living.

Also living in a smoky environment has been detrimental to him.

I have taken him to the Doctor this morning and he has been given antibiotics.

I have told Matty he will be staying with me until he is better and the tablets are finished.

This was to be the start of a child protection issue from the police against the Nex, and the continuation of his huge smear campaign against me to deflect the heat from his behaviour.

I felt unsafe and Matty was ill so we went to stay with my parents for the weekend.

The Nex drove over and banged on the door and handed his phone through the letterbox to my Mum as she had refused to answer the door. There was a police woman on the line who he had told he had full custody and he was shouting to me "To give him his son!" I took the phone and explained that we shared custody and Matty was ill so he was staying with me until he was better.

The Nex chased Matty the full length of the house hammering on the windows while he stood like a frightened rabbit whispering "What do I do now Mum?" I moved him to a safe place away from the Nex and spoke to the policewoman who told me she understood about the injunction and told me she would send an officer out immediately They quickly sent an officer out who interviewed me and the Nex was asked to leave. The police told me it was now out of my hands and was a child protection issue against the Nex and I would be interviewed shortly.
I never heard anymore until five months later when I was interviewed by a social worker.

I wish to put the property on the market as soon as possible as I do not feel safe from the Nex stalking behaviour despite the injunction.
I also wish to make an application to the court to resolve matters with my children.
I now have Chloe's boyfriend expressing his wishes that she moves home he says he constantly worries about her living with her Dad.
He said "If he harms a hair on her head he will harm him."
I then discussed the Nex threatening behaviour i.e. holding a knife to his throat.
That he must not retaliate in any way but come immediately and discuss this with me and my family and talk to the police who will keep him safe.
I do feel now that Chloe's boyfriend trusts and believes me and is beginning to realize that the Nex version of past events are lies.

I have now reached the stage where I can discuss why Matty won't move back home.
He said "Mum do you know how much trouble it would cause and he'd take all my stuff."
He said "It's just stuff I know but it is mine."
I said to him "If he stops you taking things from the house I will buy you everything new.
I'm not going to stop you seeing your Dad its important you see both of us."
Chloe's boyfriend also begs her to come home too and I think once she is 16 he wants to move in with her here.

I've said this is possible if they are still serious about each other in April when she turns 16.
Both my children said they discuss moving home all the time.

My solicitor informed me today that if the Courts agree that the CAFCASS service needs to be involved to speak to your children i.e. file wishes and feelings report then the CAFCASS service will have access to the Court application form prior to meeting the children now we have applied for joint custody.

Matty's 14th birthday today so we surprised him with a new Rainbow Tiger Bearded Dragon as he loved them when we visited the reptile zoo. His cousins all gave him hand drawn cards and all the family including Chloe's boyfriend met up for a lovely Chinese banquet together.
Had a very memorable relaxing night.
He told me he loved his birthday and his new pet was his favourite present.

My solicitor informed me that "In relation to your Children Act application this is ready to be sent to the Court but unfortunately the Public Funding situation has still not been resolved. I will therefore not be able to issue your Children Act application until I have received notification from the Legal Services Commission that a substantive Public Funding Certificate has been granted on your behalf."

March 2012

Chloe was whispering and crying down the phone on Sunday evening and asking if her boyfriend could come and stay the night with me as he had no where to go after a fight with his Mum.
I phoned him immediately and asked him to come to the house as he was very upset.
Anyway it transpired that he was having personal issues with his Mum.
He explained he couldn't cope with this.
I said he could stay the night in Chloe's room after Dinner which he was happy about.
I arranged for Chloe's counsellor to come and see him to arrange a counsellor for him.
He was in agreement with this and filled the referral form in.
I am encouraging him to sort things out with his Mum but have told him

he can stay in the meantime as he has nowhere else to go.

I have helped him find clients to set up on his own as a painter/decorator and assisted him in applying for college.

Chloe is in full agreement with this.

Chloe is concerned that her Dad will "kick off" if he hears about her relationship with him.

April 2012

Life has settled down now the year injunction and non molestation order are in force.

However after some well deserved breathing space the Nex has begun to harass me again.

For the first time since Chloe was born I never saw her on her birthday so a few days later I arranged a lovely garden party as the weather was beautiful.

I decorated the garden and bought new furniture as I wanted everything to be perfect. We sat outside and had a lovely meal and a cake and the Nex began revving his engine on the street below. He rang Chloe and she told me "Dad's getting someone to bring us a pizza!" she whispered with her hand over the phone! She paused and composed herself to reply "No Dad, Mums done me a birthday meal!"

A few minutes went by and he rang again. "He's asking me who's painting the fence Mum and who's here! He said, "No one better paint his fence!" He rang off then rang back 15 minutes later! Chloe was crying and ran in the house and went to her bedroom and got into bed. I went up after her and she told me she was scared and her tummy hurt.

He tried hard to sabotage her belated birthday party.

The following day I arranged for her to see the Doctor as she had constant tummy pains and he prescribed antispasmodics for stress.

July 2012

Sunday afternoon. I received an urgent message on Facebook from Chloe. "Mum are you there?"

"He's thrown me out, I've got no phone credit I don't know what to do!"

I composed myself and wrote back "I'm here where are you? I love you."

She replied "My phone is dead, I'm in the lakes camping, he's thrown me out will you come and get me?"

"Ok where are you? What are you looking at? Is there a hotel nearby? What's it called? Walk to the nearest hotel" I hastily replied as I was so worried that we'd lose connection.

We drove there within a few hours and she was so angry and upset! "Mum I thought he was coming back for me after he threw me out the car.

He drove back slowed down and wound the window down but he was just shouting at me again then drove off again!"

It became apparent that the OW and her were cleaning up the caravan and he was calling her lazy then Chloe fell out with him over her boyfriend.

We arrived home and Chloe's Prom was just a few short weeks away with her final exams the week after.

Chloe came to me in a panic, "Proms ruined Mum! I have no dress and no shoes I can't go!"

I tried to calm her down "Chloe do you remember when we watched Sweet Sixteen and you cried and said no one would do that for me and I said when prom comes round I would make sure you got the prom of your dreams?" "Yes" she sniffed. "Well it's not too late. We've got a few weeks. Is anything organised?"

"No" she replied sobbing.

I told her "Right I'm going to ring round some Limo companies.

Are there any others that don't have transport?" She said "Yes" so I said "Ok well we will talk to them too."

We cuddled up on the sofa and I contacted all the local Limo companies and her friends.

"Right we will wait till they get back to us. What about your dress now? I said consolingly.

She dried her eyes "I just wanted to look like Nikki Minaj Mum."

I typed 'Nikki Minaj' into eBay and as if by some miracle there was her powder blue dress!

Worn for prom already that Summer and up for auction so I messaged the seller and asked if we could buy it now and deliver it for tomorrow, luckily they wanted a quick sale!

I was so excited! "Chloe this is perfect! It's a bit big for you but Im going to buy it! Tomorrow we need to go and look for shoes." The next day I checked the bank and the mortgage had gone out that day! I pulled the remaining £40 out the bank before anyone else claimed it! We bought a beautiful pair of diamante shoes and she told me we could share them. Tomorrow I would ring the gas and electric company and plead poverty!

The following morning Chloe was very angry and shouted "I'm going to fail all my exams I've got no revision books!
I hate that controlling bastard I never want to see him again" she screamed.
"He told me if I ever leave I can't go back for my stuff."
I stifled my anger and my tears and ran Chloe a bath and tried to calm her down.
"Mum I just want to get in the bath and slip away I can't do this! I don't know any Spanish!"
I cuddled her and laughed saying
"Then we will revise Spanish all weekend until you can" I said!
"What you can't even speak it, you can't pronounce it!" No but you're going to revise by teaching me!" She laughed at my shocking pronunciation as we crammed GCSE level Spanish into the weekend!
The OW eventually sent the study books round before her Maths exam.

Chloe is living with me and seems to be very happy and I am trying my best to protect her from her fathers manipulative bullying behaviour.
He has pulled up in the car on the street below on several occasions and she rushes out for a chat only to return half an hour later with a tear stained face but won't discuss anything he has said to her with me.
She has collected some of her things in one visit but hasn't been back since and refuses to collect her stuff and states "Mum it's just awkward."
She has had to share my shoes and I have had to buy her all new clothes.
Matty sadly still lives there as he says "I have no reason to leave Mum" it is still very awkward and no one helps him remember his clothes and essential items.
However he stays with me from Friday to Sunday most weekends despite his father trying to stop it happening.

Chloe's perfect prom dress arrived as promised to her squeals of delight!
It was slightly too big and she had to be sewn into it so it fit snugly but she looked beautiful in it.
Her Dad had upset her telling her he wouldn't be attending prom but he would send a photographer.

The day of the prom arrived and my hairdresser curled Chloe's hair and we helped her get into her dress.

The limo came to pick all the girls up and one of them said "I wish you were my Mum I can't believe you sorted this limo out!"

Prom turned out to be the magical fairytale it should have been despite everything.

The Nex took Matty away for the day to an outdoor festival so he could not attend.

The Nex friend came to take photos and then I got an excited text from Chloe late on that evening saying "Mum It's ok I don't need a lift Dad's just arrived with Matty he says I look beautiful and he brought me flowers and twenty quid and he's bringing me home."

He wasn't allowed on the street so he used the fact Chloe's feet were hurting to drop her off right outside on my street and broke the injunction. I did not report it.

Prom brought me and Chloe closer together again and she encouraged me to date again.

We had always shared a love of make up and fashion and now she was at beauty college she promised me as she manicured my nails that "After everything you have done for me I will give you a free treatment every week."

She helped me do my hair and lent me a handbag and helped me get ready for my dinner dates over the next few weeks.

I met up with a couple of guys I had been chatting to on the dating site for dinner and after the second dinner date I was quite depressed.

August 2012

I had already begun talking to Joe for a couple of weeks and I messaged him to complain about my disaster date on the dating site when he asked how I was.

I told him how this man had basically lied about his looks, his height and the person he was. He was a lot shorter than he had said. How he had texted me ten minutes before to ask how tall I was. I told Joe how I had turned up and seen him and was about to leave but he had spotted me. This man had chatted to me for several weeks telling me how much he loved the countryside and going for walks and going out for dinner but when we got chatting in person a very different person emerged he told me he liked to be at home with his kindle and I soon realised we had nothing in common. He told me he drove but had arrived on the train! So many lies.

He suggested we go for a drink so I told him it was such a lovely day and said "Why don't we go for ice-cream and a walk". I got Chloe to rescue me by telling him I had a parcel to collect urgently and had to sign for it! I was so miserable on the way home and needed something to pass the time so went to see a fortune telling gypsy on the seafront. She did my tarot cards telling me I thought I had met my soul mate but I hadn't I was however going to meet him very soon. She told me I must look after myself as I could have a breakdown. I cried all the way home.

A few weeks had passed and Joe told me he would come and buy me an ice-cream and make up for the disaster date.

As we chatted over the next few weeks the ice-cream turned into hurried dinner plans. When we met that evening the restaurant we had both chosen was shut as we hadn't pre booked and it all seemed to be a bad omen. However when we did eventually sit down to a delicious Thai banquet I quickly realised how comfortable I was with him. I barely drink alcohol so found myself getting very drunk very quickly as we ordered a second bottle of wine and swapped stories and I held his hand and told him you have a beautiful soul.

Over the next few weeks as I got to know Joe and he had cooked us all dinner me and Chloe were clearing up the kitchen and she hugged me and told me "I really like him" and said "I can see he makes you happy and I can see you being together for a long time Mum."

It was very important my children liked Joe.


Chloe's boyfriend had recently confessed to me that her Dad was planning on lying in wait to jump Joe after he left my house to go to work and this was logged with the police.

Chloe's boyfriend confided in me he was very scared of the Nex and both of them were too frightened to be seen in public together.

Chloe would say "Mum I just want to go on a proper date to get pizza or something!"

I suggested while her Dad was stalking around the house that I help her prepare a date night in the house for them.

I helped her find a pretty dress and to cook a three course dinner and then disappeared upstairs.

I just wanted things to be as normal as possible for them but knew that the Nex would cause trouble if he saw them out together.

Chloe's boyfriend would ask me to lock him in my house if I nipped out to the shop and when I returned he would be stood by the window hiding just out of view whispering "I think he's down there revving his engine!" He wasn't allowed any closer to the house or he would be arrested for breaching the injunction.

Over the next month or so Chloe and her boyfriend began to get the confidence to go out in public and spent some time on the beach and were dating normally.

Me and my sister were having coffee at Costa on the promenade and the Nex drove past and stuck two fingers up at her and we ignored him.

A few days later Chloe found out her Dad was in hospital having his appendix out as it had burst so I reassured them it was a routine operation and once it was out he would be fine. Both the children were understandably upset and I encouraged them to see him.

Chloe returned from her visit and told me how he was emotionally bullying her to come home saying with his hand on his heart "One day I pray my little girl comes home to her Daddy."

As he was recovering Chloe's boyfriend told me how he was gritting his teeth saying "he's biding his time" waiting for the injunction to end.

Yesterday was a beautiful sunny day and me my Mum my sister & Chloe were sat outside Costa having coffee and the Nex drove past staring at us. He never did or said anything. We later realized this was because the OW was with him so he was behaving well.

Me & Chloe were walking through the shopping centre later and The Nex turned up with the OW and shouted after me.

I turned round to face him and told him for the first time in my life calmly "Leave me alone you nasty piece of work."

Then I turned round and walked out of the shopping centre.

Chloe followed her Dad clearly upset and angry and refused to talk to me. I ran to my friends house as my legs shook and my heart was beating so fast I couldn't breathe as I was so scared. I never expected him to talk to me as it's clearly a breach of his injunction and I don't know where the strength came from to speak to him like that.

I was fuelled with adrenaline.

I logged this incident with the police and they told me it was then out of my hands and they would have to charge him for breaching the injunction but when they tried there was no CCTV evidence.

I told them as usual I didn't want any further action as it just upsets the children and I wasn't prepared for Chloe to be interrogated and put on the spot about it.

Chloe calmed down later and went on to have a lovely date out with her boyfriend.

I am still scared of him & only feel safe in this town because of the injunction.


Matty continues to live with his father who continues to feed him lies about my personal life saying I have slept with all his friends.

Matty told me I may be seeing Joe but "I know you have friends with benefits you're a slag Mum just admit it you know you are!"

I sat him down and told him "I was only in a relationship with Joe" and asked him what a slag was? He said someone who sleeps around. I said "Yes and I only sleep with Joe!"

I was so upset and angry that his father was filling his head with lies because I was finally happy and I wanted my children to like him and finally see me in a normal loving relationship.

This is further damaging my relationship with my children which is his bitter intention.


My friends meanwhile are telling me that the Nex is saying "He can't understand why I divorced him as he threw water at me as a joke" and the statement written on the Nex behalf by the OW states I was aggressive and shouting and he threw water at me and wet one half of my body only.


In actual fact he soaked me through and wouldn't let me back in the house to change

Chloe had to get me a sweatshirt to wear and shield me from her Dad as he was aggressive and physically threatening after I came back in the house.

He did this in front of Matty and Matty said "I'm disgusted at you Dad." That night Chloe messaged her Aunty saying her Dad was crazy and Mum needs to get rid of him.

My relationship with Matty is very close now provided his father is not mentioned in any shape or form.

Even relating to good memories from the past in which his father was a part makes both my children angry and bitterly defensive.

Joe worked away and we met up once a week and as the relationship progressed I began to go and visit him also once I felt Chloe and her boyfriend were safe and happy in the house.
Chloe's Dads visits to the lower road were becoming more frequent and she returned brightly one day and told me Dad's okay about me having a boyfriend and he's even offered him some work.

The Nex continues to abuse me through the children on the phone on hands free by screaming at me through it while they are in the house.
When this happens I walk away to another room and shut the door.
Through the door I can hear him shouting and threatening the children using them to try to get me to sign over the house I paid for over the last 15 years for 20k.
They continue, through his manipulation to take his side telling me "Just take it Mum its a good offer."
Matty is increasingly verbally rude and is developing a very chauvinistic view to women from living with his father.

I had to tell Matty he wasn't welcome in my house if he's going to be disrespectful and rude and got the response "sound."

The Child Protection Follow up Interview

This was to be the first time I heard about the child protection issue the police had raised from five months earlier in the Winter during the incident when Matty was ill.
I hadn't heard anything so thought it had been dropped and was happy about that as I knew it would cause the Nex to rage and further upset the children.
My relationship with Chloe was becoming strained at this point as she told me "I was trying to get her Daddy into trouble with the police" and Matty parroted "I was trying to take them away from their loving Dad and send him to prison."

Prior to the initial visit from the social worker Chloe became increasingly hostile and verbally and physically abusive and me and my Mum had to tell her she had to leave with her boyfriend and go to her Dads if she was going to bully me.

She broke down in tears and I told her I will not accept bullying behaviour in my house. She chose to stay.

Our relationship is better but strained with her phoning her Dad and reporting back to him.

Miss Fowles interviewed me, my Mum and Chloe and I expressed my concerns regarding Matty's welfare and problems with funding from Legal Aid.

She was appalled the children were still not sorted out in an amicable way.

However she said there was nothing she could do to speed this process up mentioning her own divorce had not been sorted and it has taken years.

She took my hand and said "You all just need to move on."

I felt patronised and reminded her I had begun divorce proceedings against a violent man I had a years injunction and non molestation order against because of him assaulting me and that my house had been flagged up by the police for the last 3 years.

It was clear at that point that her view was biased and she had been influenced to believe the OW and my daughter who told her I was obsessed with the Nex.

Chloe's Dad gave her a form for me to sign from the bank to shut our joint bank account.

I refused to do this or let her be a go between and told her to tell him everything will get sorted in court and I don't want to discuss it. The joint bank account contained the evidence he left me in thousands of debt.

Chloe responded saying Dad's being really nice and helpful as he always drops her & Matty off if they want to come here.

They have no empathy for my current financial situation that their father has left me in believing all his lies.

Over that Summer Chloe and I began to fallout if I asked her to tidy her room or lay the table.

She became increasingly disrespectful and rude.

I began to see she was in a toxic relationship with her boyfriend as he showed signs of insecurity, jealousy and warning bells went off in my head. I gave Chloe a beautiful maxi dress as it was a bright sunny day instead of the usual leggings she had started wearing every day.

She looked stunning in the floor length dress with her hair down, Jackie O glasses and flat sandals.

We arrived home from the shops and his behaviour triggered me, We were greeted with the all too familiar set jaw and the silent treatment as he ran upstairs. Chloe ran after him and I could hear him shouting then she returned to the kitchen with a tear stained face and told me she didn't want the dress as it made her look fat.

This was the point I realised that this lovely charming boy was in fact as toxic as her Dad and she was stuck in a trauma bond with him.

He would pick a fight with her and she would come downstairs and tell me and ask for advice then when I told her he was disrespectful she would turn on me with him and say stop interfering.

One day when I arrived home from visiting Joe she told me she had moved out while I was away to live with Dad.

"I will still come and see you Mum but we're not getting along" she said.

September 2012

Today my solicitor wrote a letter to the Nex as a last ditch attempt to arrange a formal contact arrangement with my children pointing out the facts that the children don't know they're coming or going and how much distress this is causing everyone concerned.

We proposed contact with the children alternate weekends and requested to share the school holidays in a flexible way and if this was not forthcoming then we would have no other option but to make an application to the Court.

In response we received a letter written by the OW on behalf of the Nex saying the children don't wish for a formal arrangement since I am an incongruous unreliable parent and couldn't be trusted to be there when they turned up to stay.

The reasons for this follow

He brought them when there was no arrangement so I wasn't there so they were hammering on the door and If I then arrived I had no Dinner planned as I had just been away.

I then rushed to the supermarket to buy emergency food and my daughter swore at me down the phone telling me to get home now!

On another occasion they stated the OW had brought emergency food round as there was no food for Chloe and her boyfriend one weekend and this they listed for my solicitor.

Despite me going away and leaving a roast chicken and an apple pie for their dinner that night.

I was made to look like a neglectful Mum this way.

The OW letter stated the children are old enough to decide as and when they want contact and indeed if they want contact.

There was no formal arrangement in place which caused me and the children huge amounts of stress.

If I bought Chloe and Matty new clothes they went home wearing them and then I never saw those clothes again.

So I was constantly buying new items.

I had to say enough and make them change before they left my house after visits.

There was no arrangement in place regarding times of pick up so he would turn up as I was cooking Dinner saying "Hey let's go for KFC."

If I told the children we were having a takeaway at the weekend and they had told their Dad they would arrive telling me they had one yesterday.

Chloe would receive a phone call at any point in the day and start shouting and ordering Matty around, "Quick get your things Dads here. "

He picked them up early or late and I would be dishing out the Dinner or we would be eating.

I never knew who to cook for and I was housebound as him and the OW would tell them I didn't care if I wasn't there when they arrived.

He used me as a babysitting service if he went away with the OW.

Following his breaching of the occupation order and regular harassment a letter was also sent to the Nex from my solicitor.

Stating "We have recently been contacted by our client who informs us that you are contacting her on a regular basis.

Our client does not wish to have any communication with you whatsoever and we are therefore asking you to refrain from contacting our client in any way.

If you wish to discuss matters with us in relation to the children or financial matters then please divert your correspondence to ourselves and we will obtain our client's instructions.

If you do not adhere to our request then we will advise our client in relation to the possible options she has to prevent you from contacting her.
We strongly advise you to seek independent legal advice."

October 2012

Since not being able to prove the Nex breaching the injunction and subsequent harassment this is no longer in place.
The Nex has stepped up his bullying campaign to frighten and intimidate me to the point where I no longer feel safe in my house.
Banging on the windows and waving when he picks the children up.
Waiting outside for me to come out to say goodbye to the children.
So goodbyes are hurried as I cannot wait to bolt the door after them.
The children laugh at his behaviour and say he never abused me.
They ridicule me and say I'm just a silly victim and want attention.
I have been having counselling through this and realise the children are in denial and want to believe their Dad's normal now.

I am happy to move things on as quickly as possible and I want to move out the house and rent somewhere as I no longer feel safe.
I fear that now the injunction is no longer in place he can just walk in my house.
I fear the children will let him in when I'm out one day so never leave them alone in the house so am housebound if and when they turn up to stay.
The children still never know when they are staying over with me until a day or so before and are always picked up an hour early or late.
There is no organisation in place and I can't plan anything.
I can't work and can't do anything I'm just an emotional mess again.

I went out with my boyfriend and my parents and returned to find a huge builders bag of mouldy gravel in the middle of what was a clear driveway.
I see this as his reminder that he's still watching me and is jealous of my new boyfriend.

The children say he is just cross as he wants to come in the house to finish jobs on it.

I told them I have done more jobs on the house since he left in the last year including finishing the front and back garden which is why he put the builders bag there because the driveway looks lovely now.

Today a neighbour informs me that the Nex has threatened them and is going round threatening and intimidating anyone who is trying to be supportive of me.
This is logged with the police.

After many weeks of looking for a house to rent while I was being bullied out of and fighting for my own house in court I was feeling very fed up and depressed.
Then I stumbled upon the perfect house and couldn't wait to inbox Chloe and Matty.
I arranged to view it and invited them to come along as it was important that they loved it as much as me.
As soon as we entered the front door I felt at home and Chloe squealed as she saw the size. There was a huge master bedroom downstairs with wall to wall fitted units for me and Joe and a huge Lounge Diner perfect for entertaining, A huge kitchen that backed onto a huge conservatory and a decked area and garden.
As we were shown upstairs Chloe squealed in delight as she saw her bedroom. "Mum there's even spotlights round where my bed will go" she said. Opposite was a lovely bedroom for Joe and a shared en suite bathroom.
Every room had the wow factor and both the children were tugging at me shouting "Mum you've got to have this one!" as Chloe was running round the garden.

I was going to decorate and turn the huge conservatory into a nail studio for Chloe who was at beauty college so she could take clients in there and practice her beauty skills.

They both hugged and kissed me and returned to their Dads and I continued to text them in excitement.
Then I got a very short text from Chloe, saying "Why was I moving closer to Dad and still obsessed with him?" and I replied "Your Dad was complaining in court about having to drive you over to my house so I

have moved closer so you can walk to my new house and its also closer to college and school and your friends."

Matty said "So there's no reason for Dad to come here Mum?" I said "No" as it was in the other direction of town and not a road he would ever have to drive down.

"Don't worry Mum I won't let him anywhere near you again" texted Matty.

Later on that evening I heard from a very reliable source that the Nex was smashing up the OW's kitchen building a conservatory!

November 2012

I went out in the afternoon to visit my friend & returned a couple of hours later to find my front door lock tampered with.

On speaking to a neighbour it was found to be glued so the key would not turn.

The police were due to come out to see me to take a statement regarding the Nex alleged threats to my boyfriend that afternoon.

I called the police & explained I was going to have to break into my house.

This I did with the help of a neighbour and then we had to buy a new front panel & barrel.

Logged these incidents with the police but told them I didn't want them to do anything further as the children would be upset.

This incident traumatised me as I knew the Nex was watching me all the time.

Everything was organised for a big family get together for Mums birthday. The Nex had no way of contacting me as I had blocked him on everything but he left a rant on Mum and Dads answer phone which was now flagged up to recognise nuisance calls from the Nex and record them.

"Don't think they are coming to your birthday!" the Nex ranted, "They don't want to and don't want to see any of you!"

To my surprise the children came round for their weekly visit and I asked them if they wanted to come to their Nanna's birthday and they both said "Why would we want to go to that?"

So we had to plan it without them as we knew the Nex would sabotage it. That night as we left on the motorway a neighbour rang me.

"He's breaking into your house! He's kicking the door in!" she told me.

Mum and Dad said "right we need to go back!" I said "No this is what he wants."

I rang the police and explained the situation to them and they told me they would go straight round to stop him.

I then received a further message from my neighbour stating they had gone around the back & were now in the house and going upstairs.

An officer attended the property almost immediately and spoke to the Nex asking him to leave without removing anything.

I had told the police that previous to the injunction being served he had been asked by the Judge to remove all his belongings & there was nothing left in the house that was actually his.

We did not break our journey we continued to the hotel.

The police and my neighbour soon let me know he was removed from the property.

My boyfriend came straight from work and we went on to have a really lovely weekend with all the relatives we hadn't seen in years.

Matty even phoned his Nanna to wish her happy birthday on the morning but made an excuse for Chloe saying she was too busy.

Apart from me arriving at the hotel a bit shaken up and tear stained from the stress of dealing with him on the journey we did not let him sabotage our plans.

However on returning to the property I felt very unsafe.

Chloe blamed me for her father & boyfriends near arrest & would not understand .

Chloe and Matty both became hostile again saying "Why I had nearly got their father arrested?"

I tried to explain the situation to them to no avail as the Nex had used this incident to further get Chloe's boyfriend back on board & alienate my children again.

Since this incident apart from trying to text my children they have been very uncommunicative.

A message was left on my Mum and Dads answering machine appealing to me not to take him to court & saying it will cause everyone ill health. Please can I move out and can he have his house back so him and his children could move on!

This upset my parents as the Nex has not contributed to the mortgage or bills for many years.

The Nex left a new message on my parents answer phone stating he had to get in the house as he was concerned about Matty's animals especially his bearded dragon.
I never let the children know when I would be moving to my new address to avoid harassment from their father.
My children's pets were being well cared for during this time & I texted Matty to tell him so.

I returned home from my parents to find the lock tampered with again so I could not enter my house so I arranged for a removal company to come the following day and after breaking in to my house again my parents stayed overnight with me and helped me pack the remaining boxes.
The Nex and Chloe's boyfriend came that night and terrorised us all by staring in the windows.
We called the police but they could not find them so this was logged as another incident.

I had refused to tell Matty and Chloe the exact moving date as I was scared that the Nex would cause trouble.
This caused problems for Matty as he was clearly being grilled about it.
He sent me messages saying "What kind of Mum moves house without telling their kids?"

Matty blocked me after weeks of saying "Why can't you f**k off and just move away with Joe?" The Nex had told him I had moved on and never cared about him and he wrote on Facebook he doesn't have a mother as she doesn't care about him. He also told him I had left his beloved pets unattended.
The Nex was furious he had not been able to cause trouble on moving day.

After I moved house the Nex really stepped up the alienation process.

Chloe's boyfriend texted me on several occasions to apologise for giving the Nex the key to the house but I told Chloe he was not welcome at the new house for betraying me as I could no longer trust him.

The Nex sent him round to my house during the injunction to rant at me and I did not engage with him.

December 2012

I have not seen the children for weeks due to his behaviour and it was lovely to see them.

The children tell me the Nex is taking part in charity fund raising for a local hospice.

No doubt to appear an upstanding member of the community & to smokescreen his true behaviour.

He kept them busy all day knowing it was my birthday & all the family were over for a special celebration. Both the children were dropped off late in the afternoon despite being invited for lunch.

Chloe came in and went straight into the kitchen and began rifling through my kitchen cupboards to see what there was in a very disrespectful way and Matty followed pulling out crisps and cereal and saying "Is this all the biscuits you have, we have five different types and we have chocolate cereal."

"She buys us everything we want" Chloe said smugly.

Chloe was not herself & very upset about everything she thinks I have done including move house without telling her because I do not care.

I have told her the circumstances in which I moved & that this is not the case. She spent the entire visit curled up on the sofa texting either her Dad or her new boyfriend.

I got a lukewarm hug at the door and a "Bye Mum."

Matty turned up with a lovely girl friend & was his usual loving self and played as usual with his cousins & interacted well with my family until ten minutes after their father called when he became submissive & left with his girlfriend when Chloe asked him to.

Matty was planning on coming after school to stay over in the new house for the first time. He was so excited as he was going to play on his new Ps4 that me and Joe had bought him for Christmas.

I left him to settle in his new room and told him that Joe was looking forward to playing a game with him and he was going to make us all a lovely dinner.

I received a phone call while he was in his room from my ex sister in law telling me that the Nex father, his Granddad had died after a long term illness and then Matty told me that he had got a phone call from his sister and she was upset but he didn't know why and was worried about her.

I knew Matty would be distraught as his Granddad had cancer and no one had prepared him or given him a chance to spend time with him. So I wanted to be there for him and tell him I was also very fond of Granddad and that he will be at peace now.

I sat him down and put my arm around him and told him why she was upset and that sadly his Granddad had died then I cuddled him and said he must go to his sister and Dad as they need you .
He told me he would be back for dinner soon.
Several minutes passed and I received a text from the Nex saying "You nasty vindictive bitch!"
An hour or so later Chloe hammered on my door and as I opened it I was met with a tirade of abuse as she screamed at me "I was nothing to do with her family and how dare I tell Matty his Granddad had died!"
After attempting to explain to Chloe that "I am your Mum and I was doing what any Mum would do, be there for her son and that I also was very fond of Granddad."
Chloe screamed at me "You see that man in there well soon he's going to realise you're an arsehole and leave you too!"
I had to physically push Chloe out my house as she is bigger than me and was out of control and I felt threatened. As I did so I noticed her boyfriend standing there smirking.

After I bolted the door I ran back in the house sobbing as Joe got up I collapsed on him! He said "It's ok calm down, I heard everything, I love you so much. "I said "No please don't love me, I don't want you to love me look at me I'm a mess." He said 'It's too late I've already fallen in love with you!" as I collapsed and sobbed in his arms! "I love you too!" I sobbed.

I then received an angry text from Matty saying "He's not staying over and to give him his stuff back as it's not yours!"
I responded that "I was sorry if he felt I did the wrong thing by telling him his Granddad had died and I will leave his school things for him to collect" and I asked him "Why do you think I would keep your stuff?" Only assuming his Dad had told him I wouldn't give him his things back.

I received no response until an hour later when I received another angry text saying "Why was I lying about the ps4" and "Why didn't I admit it was Joe's and it wasn't his?" He told me he never wants to play it again.

I responded and explained that the ps4 was his Christmas present and that I loved him very much but he never replied.
I texted him the day of his Granddads' funeral and he sent me a loving text back but Chloe ignored all my attempts to communicate with her.

After that incident Matty never stayed again for a long time.
The OW sent a series of nasty texts to my parents that any communication should be through her as I was upsetting their family life!

I requested again via my solicitor to be left alone and to send a letter to the Nex telling him not to contact me in any shape or form, especially through our children who he has upset time & time again. Since moving to my new house I have actually started my business up again with a new name.
I am also seeing my Women's Aid counsellor to help me through this.
My old neighbours tell me that he is doing extensive work in our house & telling people he plans to move back in at the end of January.
He also has three lads that he has moved into my house which I believe is a breach of our mortgage agreement.
Chloe is in agreement with this & Matty is being kept in the dark & appears to know nothing of his fathers plans.
My neighbours are also very wary of him as they saw & heard the abuse he put me through.

He has been upsetting & hassling my friends & accusing my friends boyfriend of carrying out work in his house which is untrue.
This he has done many things to upset and unsettle my friends and cause them to fall out with me.
I am so weary of all this & just want what is legally mine so I can continue to live my life & see my children in peace.

After meeting Kate Matty's girlfriend at my birthday she began to keep in touch on messenger and I persuaded her to come out with Matty for a Carvery dinner as Matty was being uncommunicative again.

We had a lovely dinner in the local pub and Matty was very relaxed and laughing and joking until his Dad phoned and asked him where he was and he said "I'm with Mum having dinner." After this he ran outside to talk with his Dad as me and Kate attacked the chocolate fudge cake. Matty was kept on the phone for the whole of pudding.

I chatted to Kate and smiled at Matty through the window as I could see he was very upset.

We went home and me and Kate decorated the Christmas tree.

We started watching films and then there was a loud knock on the door so I got up to answer and asked "Who is it?" There was no reply, so I began to think it may be Chloe so I asked "Is that you Chloe?" Still there was no reply so I braced myself and opened the door to the O.W who said crossly "I know he's here! Where is he? He's turned his phone off!"

I shut the door in her face and shouted through the door, "How dare you come here pretending so I answer the door!"

I had not clapped eyes on this woman since seeing her in court the day I went to get an injunction against the Nex and the shock had winded me as I sunk to the floor and could not breathe.

Matty cuddled me once I recovered and said "I'm sorry Mum I will tell her not to come here." I said "All the time you have lived with your Dad and I have never ever been to your house. She could have texted to ask where you were."

The Nex was still texting me despite being warned not to by my solicitor. "I know Mum I'm sorry," Matty replied as I cuddled him and told him it wasn't his fault.

I calmed down and told him to text his Dad and tell him he was ok.

Chloe then rang him and told him he had to get home now and feed the dogs and he argued with her and put the phone down.

We had a lovely Chinese dinner then we all did the can can round the house!

It was so lovely to see Matty so relaxed with Kate.

He stayed over that night and I promised to make them pancakes in the morning but had to run out early for some syrup. I arrived home a few minutes later to find Matty leaving saying he had to go home now. I gave him a hurried hug at the door not knowing that would be the last time we would hug for the next few years.

I phoned Matty the following day and he was being distant and I asked him if he was ok he said the words I will never forget "Dads staring at me it's really weird I've got to go" I heard the Nex growl in the background "That's the last time you're staying over there!" I heard a click as the phone went down and crumpled into tears but little did I know that that was the last time we would talk to each other for the next two and a half years.

I was in a fog and just beginning to get my head around the fact that my then husband had a mental disorder. At this point in time I felt broken and alone. He had done everything he set out to achieve and ripped out my heart by taking my children.
Little did I know at that stage he didn't just want to control me but he actually planned on completely destroying my close bond with my children and wiping me out of their lives.

January 2013

My children are now completely alienated.
I am broken.

February 2013

Following the child protection case flagged up by the police when Matty had been ill last year, it was several months before social services contacted me to answer questions and make a statement. As knowing how this incident would make the Nex rage and because at the time I had a good relationship with both my teens and didn't want to rock the boat I answered their questions very generally.

When they interviewed me I did not want to get Social Services involved as Chloe lived with me and had been repeatedly told by her Dad that I'm just trying to lose the OW her job. I felt at the time that the truth would have alienated Chloe who at that time I shared a close loving relationship with. Unfortunately to this point there had only been his side.
Social Services knew the Nex was convicted of domestic violence and also of the resulting injunction that was put in place to keep me safe.

The OW had sent a letter on behalf of the Nex to my solicitor the previous Summer stating I am mentally ill and I should re visit the Doctor if I needed further support I had not visited the Doctor only a Domestic

Violence Counsellor at Women's Aid. The letter stated "I was therefore having counselling to deal with my marriage breakup as I could not cope and was still obsessed with the Nex" even though I initiated the divorce proceedings.

The OW stated on behalf of the Nex that "I was an inconsistent mother in need of parenting classes." She also refused to discuss my children with me or work with family services in her social worker capacity for 'the best interests of the children' seeing their Mother stating "She needs no help with parenting my children."

The family support worker had been instructed to work with me through a parenting plan and said "All we need to do is prove to the OW you are a good Mum" but as we began to chat and fill it in she looked at me and said "I have no concerns about your parenting" and told me "I did not need to complete it."

The OW seems to thoroughly be brainwashed into his lies so has been very effective in her social worker capacity at protecting my children from me.

Interestingly the Nex rudely declined being interviewed by the family support worker and stated he doesn't want the children interviewing either. In fact the family support worker stated that she experienced him verbally twisting what she had said as he tried to take control of the situation.

The OW has also convinced Matty's school of this which explains why despite many attempts to communicate with them I have been effectively fobbed off. The family support worker is contacting Matty's school on my behalf as they have effectively ignored all communications with me since the OW has become involved. She has arranged to see me again to discuss the way forward.

Meanwhile my relationship with my children began to deteriorate to such a point that my solicitor, who was trying to arrange formal contact at the time, as the Nex was severely limiting and messing up contact, told me not to go ahead because the children were too brainwashed.

Their phone numbers were changed and I received a text message from the OW saying if I wanted to speak to my children I would have to do it through her as I was upsetting them. She would vet the messages and pass them on. I was apparently upsetting their family life.

Then followed a vile letter saying I needed parenting classes according to the OW which I chose to ignore.

Six months had now passed and I thought nothing more of the child protection referral.

My children still refused to see me and I could not contact them.

When a family support worker contacted me six months later out the blue regarding my children having been assessed and carrying out the CIN plan finally interviewed me I broke down and explained that I wasn't mentally ill and had never visited a Doctor but the Nex was an abuser. She listened in horror as tears rolled down my cheeks and was very reluctant to give me a copy of the report. I was told it would upset me, but I insisted she email me the report right away and bring me a hard copy.

In my naivety I had thought that nipping the child protection case against him in the bud at the initial assessment would mean my children wouldn't be upset but in retrospect now knowing how evil he was I would have made a stronger case of the child protection issue that the police referred to social services.

The family support worker told me that the police had insisted a social worker had to open the case following the child protection case against the Nex.

I was incensed about the way children's social services had conducted themselves both in the manner of the investigation and the sheer length of time it had taken. I also felt that social services incompetence now played a major role in alienating my teens from me.

Ethel Mould who carried out the initial assessment went off sick shortly after this investigation started.

Mr Damian Pain just left the report on his desk and was transferred to another office without dealing with it after I had been told in a letter that I would receive it shortly.

They don't seem to care how much this is messing with my life and it screams incompetence.

By this time the Nex had alienated my children from me completely.

Having nothing further to lose I now made a formal complaint against children's social services.

At the first stage their initial response from them in answer to my complaint was they would add that the mother states she isn't mentally ill and they tried to drop the case.
I proceeded to take the complaint to stage 2 and an outside investigator was brought in who was a retired social worker and he decided I had grounds for a formal investigation.

Once under investigation social services admitted they could not produce notes for either my interview or the Nex. I never received any information regarding the assessment but it later came to light that the interviewer had entirely taken on my Nex side of things and there was a complete fabrication that I was in fact mentally ill.
Unbeknown to me during this time social services produced children in need assessments which did not mention domestic violence but said the reason for the child protection referral was due to my mental illness.

I of course never heard anything about this and was busy fighting the Nex hate campaign during which my children wanted to tag me on Facebook as a basket case and told me I was crazy. This report was apparently only sent to him and we later discovered their policy is to only send it to parents that ask to see it.
This was something he clearly knew about only because the OW was a social worker.

We agreed a list of complaints of 7 elements including the OW a social worker in children's care manager had a part to play in the children's alienation.
At the end of the investigation the investigators report was sent to Children's Social Services where they failed again to meet the timescale by over six weeks. Their only explanation being the manager dealing with my complaint had gone to another job and left it on his desk only to be alerted by the investigating officer after I contacted him to find out what was happening.
The investigating officer immediately asked them to send it to me.

On reading the report It turned out that 5 of the 7 elements had been upheld, but they had no hard evidence to suggest his OW was assisting him.

I got a long list of grovelling apologies and promises that they would retrain the staff responsible to prevent this happening to anyone else.

They stated "I can also confirm that the suite of leaflets with regards assessment information for both parents and children are in for being printed. Guidance will also be drafted and shared across the County. This will reiterate the importance and the need for social work staff to gather parental views when completing assessment. It is anticipated that this work will be completed by the end of February."

The report was amended thus, "I can confirm that we have added to the social care record in relation to your children that you do not have a mental health problem and that you felt that your 'depression' was linked to your experience of domestic violence. It is also now noted that your ex-husband was the perpetrator of this domestic violence towards you. "

I would also like to reassure you that the learning from your complaint will be discussed with the staff involved via supervision process as part of their learning and development with a particular emphasis on recording practice.

Despite reassurance that all these things were carried out to this day I have never seen any hard evidence of this.

Ironically enough the department was inspected by Ofsted several months following this utter shambles and deemed unsatisfactory highlighting the very issues that I raised with the department. I gave up asking for hard evidence and decided to approach the cabinet minister of children's services to assure me that everything had been carried out. He promptly sent it straight on to the head of social services who effectively told me that everything had been carried out but there was still no evidence of this.

One of the elements of the complaint was that social services had helped alienate my children and I asked them that now my complaint had been upheld that the misunderstandings about my so called mental illness would be addressed and they would help me re establish contact with my children.

Their response was that "Due to the length of time the investigation took to complete they told me there was nothing they could do as the children were effectively brainwashed!" I told them I was very unhappy about this and told them I wanted the original family support worker to talk to my children and tell them I was not and never have been mentally ill and discuss their Dad being abusive.

Social services arranged this after several complaining phone calls from me by which time my daughter was 18 and so refused to speak with the family support worker so she remains alienated.
The family support worker did speak to my son and he agreed that Dad was abusive and that was the reason we divorced. He was also told I was not and never have been mentally ill.
He still refused to speak to me and It was to be another nine months of alienation before he approached me.

Yesterday afternoon I messaged Matty's girlfriends Mum and she told me she couldn't understand why the Nex has custody. I told her this is not the case as we have never been to court and we have joint custody of the children still. I then realised that he is telling people he has sole custody to give more weight to his lies.
Matty's girlfriend's mum listened to me for an hour in shock and revealed that my son is round at her house nearly every night after school and he eats there and doesn't leave till late most evenings. She said "He has even started coming out with us at weekends and is a lovely boy and makes everyone laugh." She said "I think if he had a choice he would live with you but he's too scared" then she reassured me that she will try and do some fishing but he doesn't talk about home life at all.
I thanked her for taking care of my son and she said she would help and is just a phone call away.

Everyone who knows the truth sees what is happening everyone sees the man behind the mask except my children and the OW.

Today with the assistance of the family support worker we have a meeting with Matty's school. They listened and told me they would talk to Matty and try and get him to meet with me in a café. He agreed to meet me as long as the family support worker was present.

Over the weekend he changed his mind and the school told me there was nothing further they could do if he refused to meet with me. The school refused to take Matty's birthday parcel to him.

I'm struggling to cope not seeing the children and being constantly verbally and mentally bashed by the Nex and his accomplice. I have shown my family support worker a letter from my counsellor stating she supported me after the long term effects of domestic violence and not due to the breakdown of my relationship as the OW wishes to believe.

March 2013

It's Easter Day today and I am really going to try and make an effort to be happy for everyone.
I feel so sad inside and I miss Chloe and Matty. I wonder what they are doing right now?
I went to church and prayed for them today remembering all the years we had been together there as they collected their chocolate eggs from the vicar, such happy times. I try to concentrate on what the vicars saying but it's too painful as I force back the tears and making my excuses I squeeze through the pew to escape.
I can hear my heels clacking on the wooden floor and the vicars voice fades as I step outside into the church yard and let the tears fall. "Why is this happening? I'm a good Mum! All I've ever done is love my children. Why is he doing this?" I asked God as I stood in the bright sunlight blotting my eyes carefully trying to avoid the smudged panda look so I could hide the fact I've been crying.
Mum came out to look for me and we walked through the gravestones, me with my dark glasses on now trying to gulp back the tears. I had to get out I had to leave. I was married in that church. Everything happened in that church the children went to Sunday school, I sobbed.
My Mum hugged me and said "I know it's not fair lets go home.". We arrived home to the beautiful aroma of roast lamb and soon were joined by the rest of the family.
As we had our Easter lunch my stomach lurched as I heard the all too familiar sound of his jeep revving up the road. "It's him" I whispered as my face paled.
Mum said "It can't be!" There was a knock on the door and my Mum looked startled "It's Chloe and Matty" she whispered. Mum leapt up and

threw open the front door "Oh hello" she said in as normal a voice as she could muster, "Come in Happy Easter!' Chloe replied coldly "Why would we want to come in?" Nanna said "Well can I have a hug then?' Matty looked most uncomfortable as Chloe said "Why would we hug any of you after everything you've done to Dad? We've only come to see our cousins. Their cousins ran out and they hugged and said "Hello" and took the Easter eggs.

I heard the Nex revving the jeep impatiently across the road. Matty looked miserable Chloe looked angry as the Nex barked "Right kids get in the car!" Mum went out and said "Look this is ridiculous all we want is a fair settlement you're being most unreasonable! You've got to stop this!". He wound down the window as the children got in hurriedly "She's not getting a f****** penny from me!" I watched in horror through the window as I clung onto my Dad as the Nex sped off in a horrible rage.

I had to calm myself down I wasn't going to let him do this!

This wasn't about delivering Easter eggs this was about sabotaging Easter lunch. Under the guise of being a good person. He wanted that fight! I was so angry and upset but determined not to let him ruin Easter Day.


Summer 2013


The Nex continues his drive by slow down and stare routine on a regular basis.

Mostly he drives by alone, he waits to see if I am alone then parks up revving his engine and flashing his headlights into my window. Sometimes he has one of my children in the passenger seat beside him and they drive by slowly and you can see by the look on their faces the shock as they realise they are outside my house. They only see my shock, fear response before they look away.


The Nex has also followed me home on several occasions and each incident is logged with the police.


There has been no improvement in relation to contact with my children.


As Summer ended after much negotiating my solicitor has backed the Nex into a corner a few days before court and he is now agreeable to buy me out this means the property will be transferred into his sole name, and I will receive a lump sum.

Winter 2013

A couple of months ago I became pregnant, although I have since had an early miscarriage.

I've just received some very disturbing news recently from someone connected to the Nex's family. I was visited by the community midwife and had a positive test done. Following this despite updating the midwife's records with my change of address and explaining the circumstances that the address must be updated the hospital database was not so the clinic used my old address and the midwife called there and encountered the Nex who quizzed her intensely although she didn't explain why she was calling on me. In addition the clinic sent my test there as well.

Although the Nex has said that they always return any mail for me to sender (itself rather petty as they could forward it straight to me) the report has not been returned. Now I find that his family "know" that I am pregnant so it appears that he opened this private letter addressed to me.

In addition I have been told that the OW has been digging around in my medical records, which she probably can access being a social work manager. I don't know if this is because of the believed pregnancy or to do with this complaint, as one of my reasons was that the initial Social Services reports had said that their interest in me was my 'mental illness' and the first stage response was to say that "I asserted " that that was untrue.

I don't know if she has been taken to task by Social Services and is trying to prove that I have been mentally ill.

February 2014

Eleanor, the family support worker has been to see Matty and had a fairly successful meeting with him. She stated "It's clear that he loves you and can't see you." She also took the opportunity to tell Matty that I'm not mentally ill but was depressed due to his fathers abusive behaviour.

She is trying to arrange to see Chloe to meet for coffee in town.

I think this is a long road but feel hopeful now Eleanor is involved again.

The Nex continues to harass me on my Facebook business page.

The police were informed the first couple of times as he wrote personal comments on his own wall with a link to my business page.

However he went one step further writing a vile review telling people lies about me to damage my business.

My friend screen shot the messages

A friend of mine replied and Chloe replied 'Vindictive exes' and a long nasty rant so my friend replied with kisses and a smiley to Chloe.

An hour later his nasty review was removed.

Today I have finally been released from the mortgage on my house as it has been transferred into the OW'S name.

I am amused because the mortgage company refused to transfer it to him due to lack of funds so it has taken some time to release me from this.

March 2014

The Nex's ongoing harassment has escalated to the point where I had to get him formally warned by the police.

I'm exhausted of his slow down and stare drive by's and him honking the horn,

Verbally harassing members of my family,

Writing bad reviews on my business page.

This has meant I have been extremely stressed again and unable to go out.

The police are all on board with me and told me they do not think he will stop unless they issue him with a formal warning.

I reluctantly agreed to this knowing that he would retaliate.

Unfortunately as a result of getting the Nex formally warned he has sent the police round to me saying I'm harassing my daughter.

This follows the last few months as Chloe and Matty have successfully been receiving a few gifts letters and cards at Chloe's workplace from my family and I but he has now found out.

This has escalated the situation as my daughter has now issued a statement saying she wants me and our family to stay away. We had a meeting with the police and they are finally beginning to understand how the Nex is alienating the children and they agree that leaving presents when she's not there is not harassment.

As a result of all this I'm planning on moving ten miles away.

You cannot get a jeep down the road where I am moving so hopefully I will be able to get on with my life and feel safer.

No one not even Matty's school will be informed of my secret location. I just want to move away so he can't harass me anymore.

It was Mothers Day and I was grieving for my children.
Me and my counsellor were sitting in the conservatory and we heard a knock on the glass and a neighbour asked "do you have a stripy cat?" My counsellor got up and ran out down the road and scooped up a lifeless Tiger and walking back up the road she shook her head and I crumpled onto the floor. He had been run over. I lost control and 1 was screaming "No I can't lose him, not Tiger no I can't lose anything elsc!"
My counsellor poured me some of my Dads port to calm me down as I sat rocking my cat.
My sister came over to pick me up and we buried him in the garden.
It was a mothers day I would never forget.

The Nex had been given a final warning by the police to stop stalking me and I moved to a secret location where I began to run an abuse group and write this book for other survivors.

"You have to sink right down into the depths of despair to find that little voice inside that whispers then shouts 'Get up and fight you are not done yet!' There is a superhero inside all of us you've just got to find her."

One day in the not so distant past I had a family two beautiful children a lovely dog who I had since he was eight weeks old and a three bed semi and two cars, I worked as a nurse and ran a clothing business.

I lost every single thing that was mine and during this devastation and grieving for my children rattling round in the former marital home broken and alone that I wrote for myself.

I Owed Myself A Thousand Joys

I know brighter days are coming.

For every evil negative cruel experience I shared with the Nex, I swapped for a positive experience. For every place he hurt or upset me, every room in my house where he attacked me, I replaced with positive happy memories of people who loved me, and the laughter of children.

The kitchen which was my prison, became filled with people, music laughter and the smell of fresh baking. I learned new recipes and cooked for people who appreciated my efforts.

Every day out that he sabotaged I replaced with new amazing people and experiences.

I learned to decorate, I learned to run a website so I could run my online business single-handed. I danced and sang again. I joined the gym and swam and kick-boxed and practiced hours of calming yoga.

I looked after my nieces and nephews and let the sound of their excited voices and laughter, wash my grief away and heal my heart.

When I was upset I walked in my neighbourhood where I had previously scurried to the shops with my head down, and I began to smell every rose.

I began to notice the little birds tweeting in the trees and watch the cats blissfully sunbathing across driveways.

Time began to pass more slowly as I watched the fluffy clouds float across the sky.

Every sense in my body became alive and yearning for new experiences. After I left the Nex's toxic soul, my black and white life became beautiful again, like I was suddenly seeing for the first time in glorious colour.

"Let go of anything toxic in your life. Partners, friends and family members, a dead end job, and other negative life experiences. Remove anything that no longer serves your soul and you will see huge positive changes in life."

"Me too!" became the most healing words to my ears when I began to find fellow sufferers online after leaving the abuse.
Our abusers keep us in the dark and kept us believing that they behaved as they did because of us.
The validation that we are not crazy, is a momentous discovery, and from that point on we can move forwards into recovery.

As I began my healing journey, as the brain fog began to lift I felt my way through, what I now recognised as what I can only describe as an underworld of evil that is all around us.
I began therapy and also meeting survivors on the internet, in support groups and helping those who were a little further back than me.
Their tears and pain mingled with mine, as they told me "I can't get out of bed, I'm stuck, I can't go on."
I began to write for them and for me, from my heart to theirs and the words eased their pain and mine somewhat.
I would wake through the night typing my thoughts and messaging others that cried out for help. I knew I wanted to help others negotiate their way through this maze of darkness towards the light that I could now see.
I saw people asking. "Why did he or she do that, I thought they loved me? How could they be so cruel?" and I would message them back. "I've been through this, I understand."
Sometimes my own pain and panic attacks and tears, would overwhelm me and I would put my notes to one side, promising myself that I would pick up my writing again, when I felt stronger, and more in control.
The Nex smear campaign was in full force and he was stalking me and had taken my teens and turned them against me.
I was taking him to court to get a fair settlement on my house and so I kept a daily diary of detailed notes for my solicitor.
Friends and family said "You must write a book" and I nodded and smiled wearily "Yes I know one day, when I am not being stalked, when I feel safe and when I am healed, I will write a book to help others going through this."

I do consider myself to be healed to this point now. where I can live a normal life. I have moved on emotionally and am happy with myself and in my relationship.

Experts predict it takes approximately a year of healing for every five years of narc abuse, so in my case this was accurate as I began to feel better after three years (just under 16 years of living with him).

When you're nearly healed like me the best revenge is no revenge and moving forwards and despite everything living a good life and being finally happy.
This is something I work towards everyday. I have grieved for my children, but there is a huge open wound in my life that can only be closed when I have my children in my arms again and I know they are both safe from abuse.

How I Started the Chrysalis to Butterfly Healing Sanctuary

I began to develop the healing sanctuary following my own horrific experiences of getting out of a long term narcissistic relationship and suffering the after effects of a malignant narcissist destroying my close bond with my children. As many of you know I have given huge amounts of my time and supported those going through abuse to encourage them to leave an abusive partner to go on to live amazing lives.
I wanted to show and encourage each and every one of you, to be the best you can be and use the abuse as a learning curve towards your life goals, so you will begin as a chrysalis and emerge as a beautiful butterfly.
Covering the science stuff and helping with your questions in a friendly environment where you can lick your wounds safely, heal and grow with us. We can be serious and empathetic but also we have a good giggle because that's the best healing therapy of all.

The beautiful butterfly represents us, our light, our love and going forwards from a changing chrysalis as, we work on our inner wounds, to a new enlightened 'us' emerging. Brighter stronger wiser butterflies going out into the world, with our new knowledge to spread our happiness.

I have split the information into manageable bite size 'Chrysalis to Butterfly Healing blogs.' These are all handwritten by me over my recovery and many have been shared with other survivors on my 'Chrysalis to Butterfly Healing Sanctuary' page.

Designed to be read In order, chunk by chunk in your recovery but also in titled sections, so you can easily refer back to them quickly if you need to.

I know when we eventually get away from the toxic person our brain is shot to pieces. We suffer from brain fog and there's plenty of good reasons for that too which I will explain shortly.

All I will tell you at this stage is your brain fog will gradually lift and your memory will sharpen as you get further into healing.

So find yourself somewhere comfortable make yourself a cuppa and grab some of your favourite biscuits and come heal with me.

## My Journey and the People I've Met

"I have met people on my journey I would call earth angels because they've been there at my darkest hour. Maybe we are angels because we go to the depths of hell to become strong enough to drag others to the light with us."

The older we get I do believe that it is not a coincidence when we meet people in these groups. Since my abuse experiences I have learned so much from many I have never met. and then simply pass the messages on to those who need that's the beautiful way these groups work, no one is alone once they find us.

Life is just a steep learning curve shaping us into who we are going to be. so whether we are just starting out or have already begun our healing journey we really are just one big healing family helping each other.

## What Is Abuse

"Abuse creeps up in intensity and it's incomprehensible that you learn to live with it and as the abuse escalates in severity and I'm here to tell you it does, you don't admit to yourself you are in fact dancing with the devil!"

Do you recognise this as your relationship?
Are you walking on eggshells?

"I wouldn't be consciously aware but as tea time approached I would get this flutter of excitement because I hadn't seen him all day. Sometimes he was fun and really over the top like a bit manic but I would get this sense of foreboding.

I would check where my phone and shoes were. I could sense from the way he drove up the road and his footsteps into the house whether I needed to stay or grab my stuff and get out.

He would stomp in raging like a caged animal looking for someone to vent on. Sometimes I doubted my intuition and I would carry on washing up and making the tea, going through the motions with a calm voice and talking him down once he had arrived home, much like one of my patients at the hospital, but if he was brewing a big fight as he slammed his fist on the kitchen worktop then I used to chastise myself for not guessing right and plan my escape."

"For all those who are not sure they are in an abusive relationship. I am here to support you. I won't judge you if you don't leave. It's a process. I will hold your hand till you are free. I know how tough it is to make those final steps to freedom."

There Are 7 Types of Abuse.

Physical Abuse is intimidation, isolation restraint, aggression and endangerment.

Mental abuse is gas-lighting, silence, manipulation and victimization.

Verbal abuse is screaming, bullying, name-calling, berating and blaming.

Sexual abuse is jealous rages, coercion, sexual withdrawal, rape and degrading acts.

Emotional abuse is intense anxiety, guilt confusion, shame, anger, hostility, rejection and fear.

Economic abuse is stealing, destroying assets, hiding resources, refusing access, falsifying records, and interfering with work environments.

Spiritual abuse is dichotomous thinking, prejudice, elitist beliefs, demanding submission, excommunication and estrangement.

If your partner says "If only you would behave I would not have to hurt you, You make me so mad, If you wouldn't just wind me up! Why can't you just do as you are told? There is no one who makes me as angry as you. Why are you doing this to me? Why would you want to make me angry?

Me and you are really going to fall out if you go out with your friends! You know how I worry about you, When you wear shorts you just look like a whore. Do you want everyone thinking you're a whore? I know you are cheating on me. I don't know why you bother to lie to me. You are a liar and a cheater. You're lucky I put up with you."
Or the Nex favourite "If you were a man I would knock you out."

THIS IS NOT YOUR FAULT...it is called 'PROJECTION'
Where they accuse you of what they are doing.
Where they threaten you verbally or physically to get you to alter your behaviour to comply.
This is not love. This is abuse and is only about them controlling you.

So abuse is about CONTROL.

Teetering On the Edge Of The Relationship Knowing Something is Wrong

For those still teetering on the edge of a relationship with a disordered person knowing something isn't right. In fact something is almost definitely wrong. In that brain fog of denial we all get blinded by lies again and again because they are master manipulators. We want to believe that this wonderful person exists. The one that's love bombing us back with the words we've yearned to hear and gifts and promises of a rosy future.

This is a fictitious false mask they wear.
The more you educate yourself on the way Narcs tick and how to handle them it all becomes clearer.
I won't judge you for returning to your abuser.
In fact I can explain why we do it over and over and how to break that toxic cycle when you are emotionally strong enough and how to finally get free.

Panic? You don't want to be free from him? You can't live with him and can't live without him?
I will explain the physiological and other reasons for that incredible hold they have over us and how over time we can break free.

## Imagine Waking to No Drama and Chaos

For those of you who haven't quite made it out yet. Close your eyes and just imagine waking in the morning without that feeling of dread as to what today will bring.
Imagine getting out of bed and not listening to their ranting voice.
Imagine going downstairs and fixing your own breakfast in peace without having to pander to their every whim, and worrying that you might slip up on those emotional egg shells.
Imagine a life that was filled with darkness and chaos and confusion being replaced with a life filled with joy love and peace.
Now imagine this doesn't have to be a dream.

## Take My Hand

If you feel alone right now feeling unsure and bewildered by everything. I want you to know thousands of women and men have been where you are right now.
Some of us are just a little further down the healing road than you.
There's a beautiful peaceful happy place waiting for you when you take your life back.
Come take my hand and join us.
"Ssshhh". Don't tell anyone. Pretend everything is okay. Practice the smile and the tight lipped "Yes I'm fine!"
Abusers abuse because they have your silence. Once the silence is broken you take back your power!

## Shame and Embarrassment

Your feelings that it's your fault keep you stuck. It's not your fault. This is not about you at all. Its projection from a mentally disordered person that cannot look in the mirror at their own faults so blames you. You have to leave it won't get better. You can't help them. It gets worse. The mental and physical abuse gets worse. The threat is real. You must go 'no contact ' now and concentrate on you and your recovery. Life is beautiful out here. You have to dig deep and find the hero inside.
Reach out for help. If you are down a hole nobody knows unless you shout.
Peace love and light and strength to you.

Narcs Isolate Their Victim

Narcs isolate you and surround you with people who are on their side, so there is no one that you can discuss it with. The times that you have tried to perhaps open other people's eyes to what is going on have been met with disdain, disbelief, and dismissal.

Maybe you've even been accused of being crazy, until you begin to wonder if it is true. You may well feel like you are going crazy, that's what living in the reality created by a Narc can do to a sane mind.

As you move away from his or her toxic fog you will see it isn't you.


Escape Plan

Action Plan for leaving your abuser when your head's in a muddle.
   1  Visualise the outcome you want,
   2  Make a list in a safe place of how to get there. You can do this on a locked phone or on paper left at a friend's house.
      Where could I go? How can I  get there? How much will it cost?. Who will help? Especially Who can I trust?
   3  Call a local Women's shelter for help and support with your plan,
   4  Save up a get away fund or find out through the shelter about local financial resources and pack clothes and personal items and store in a garage or unused room. Perhaps pack stuff like you're doing a garage sale so if it's found you can say that.
   5  Only tell people who are helping you escape, be very careful who you trust.
   6  You're nearly there...BREATHE!
   7  Wait if there's children involved, to organise new schools etc.
      This paperwork could be found by your abuser. It's best not to even tell young children until after the escape time and then tell them you're going on an adventure/holiday.
   8  Leave no clues around the house, cancel all social networks and block your abuser. Do not write anything about leaving on there.
   9  Leave safely at a time when you know your abuser isn't around as this is the most dangerous time and when they are most likely to rage at losing narcissistic supply in you.
   10  Never look back.
      You are on the road to FREEEDOM!

If you are being stalked by the Nex

If your intuition tells you that you feel unsafe listen to it and put every protective measure in place. The Nex stepped up his stalking campaign once the non molestation order was over and I had a boyfriend.

If a Narcissist feels threatened that they are going to lose you as supply for good then they will rage and display unpredictable aggressive behaviour. Keep an accurate record of times, dates and incidents including any witnesses and log this with the police.

Ensure your neighbours know your situation so they could be a place you can run to and as a precaution never leave the house alone if you think he's in the vicinity.

Tell friends where you are and get them to check on you.

Keep a charged phone with you at all times, secure your house your locks windows etc and put up suitable lighting and install CCTV as you can use the video footage to provide evidence. It's better to be over cautious and safe.

Initiating 'No Contact'

At this stage you can scroll down to the section 'What is a Narc' but if your brain's too muddled for that at the moment I've used the more simple analogy of cat and mouse for now and you can read the pathology at play when you're mentally stronger.

When you watch a cat play with a mouse it's similar to the way a Narc, once we end the relationship plays with us, taunting us and teasing us and being downright cruel while taking chunks out of us and watching the life slowly drain out of us. If you are that mouse then playing dead is the only way to survive. You are not fun anymore if you act dead and offer no reaction.

This is when you make your escape as they find more live prey.

So Why Do I Feel Physically Ill?

Why Do I Still Want and Miss Them?

The Trauma Bond

"Healthy relationships don't cause you pain make you cry and make you fearful. If your relationship looks like this it is nothing to do with Love. It is about control"

I'm sorry you are going through this.
There is a trauma bond that attaches you to them. The lover and the abuser. I know it feels like a physical pain because that's exactly how it is. Your body is addicted to the pain they cause and the drips of love they give you. It will get easier the more you understand and I will be there to support you through it.
Hang in there sisters and brothers!

Leaving a narc and initiating 'no contact' is exactly like weaning yourself off a drug and going cold turkey.

Why?

If we don't recognise abuse as abuse we make excuses for it. They were tired they was hungry or they were stressed. We try to 'love' back the man or the woman we thought he or she was during the love bombing stage. ( the false mask) It's not enough for people to shout "leave him he's a jerk! He treats you so badly!" There is so much more at play here! Understanding abuse is far more complex and you need to get to grips with the psychology the physiology Stockholm Syndrome, The role of Oxytocin etc and why you feel unworthy ( even though you think that's normal too because that's how you have always felt) enough to accept emotional and or physical abuse. Only then can you leave them never to return when you are stronger wiser and feel worthy of love.

Understanding Abuse

1. Stockholme Syndrome,
2. We are addicted to pain peptides after narc abuse,
3. The role of Oxytocin.
   the cuddle hormone that binds you to an abuser. This will explain why the pain is physical.
4. We are going through a grief response.

No contact does gradually get easier.
Stick with it and I will show you how.

What Is Stockholm Syndrome?

A psychological phenomenon derived from a 1973 bank robbery in Stockholm, Sweden, where four hostages were held for six days.

At the time of their imprisonment, during which they were threatened and abused the hostages expressed empathy and sympathy and had positive feelings toward their captors, to the point of defending them even resisting the governments efforts to rescue them.

Months after their ordeal had ended, the hostages continued to show loyalty to their captors and refused to testify against them.

In their media interviews, it was clear that they supported their captors and actually feared law enforcement personnel who came to their rescue. The hostages had begun to feel the captors were actually protecting them from the police. One woman later became engaged to one of the criminals and another developed a legal defence fund to aid in their criminal defence fees. Clearly, the hostages had bonded emotionally with their captors.

Hostages in similar circumstances experienced the same sympathetic, supportive bonding with their captors.

The researchers determined that such behaviour was very common in these situations.

Emotionally bonding with an abuser is actually a strategy for survival for victims of abuse and intimidation in a situation where they no longer have any control over their fate, feel intense fear of physical harm and believe all control is in the hands of their abuser.

In a domestic violence situation:

The victim expresses positive feelings towards the abuser and defends him.

The victim expresses negative feelings toward family, friends, and authorities making rescuing them very difficult.

If you're in a controlling and abusive relationship you may have said, "I know what he's done to me, but I still love him, I don't know why, but I want them back" or "I know it sounds crazy, but I miss her.".

What Is This Deep Pain?

So why is it so hard to let go and move on?

Okay so what's the science behind our addiction to trauma?
Pain Peptides made simple.

Here's The Science Bit.

We are addicted to pain peptides during and after an abusive relationship. Pain peptides manufactured in the brain in the hypothalamus are distributed via the blood circulation and received by the cells of your body. Our cells become addicted to these powerful doses of neuro peptides which the narcissist continuously triggers us with so we become addicted to them.

If you have been in a long term negative and toxic environment and as a result have a victim mentality and feel despondent, angry or depressed about the way the Nex treated you the neural peptides that are released and feed the cells of your body are related to these feelings of victimization. The cells in your body are addicted to this particular peptide and literally summon your brain for this specific powerful chemical thus creating that yearning to be close to the Nex and to need them. This is a vicious circle as when this happens you start feeling even more despondent and depressed and you start thinking about why you are feeling this way and your brain then secretes more 'victim' peptides. You may be just as addicted to negativity and sadness and pain as a heroine addict is to heroine. Our neuro-peptides are just as powerful and addictive as synthetic drugs.

So how are we going to release our addiction to pain peptides?
Learn to laugh in the face of adversity!

Rewiring a Happy Brain

We literally have to do a lot of work to undo the damage and rewire our brains.
The brain is actually wired anyway to pay more attention to negative experiences. It's a self-protective characteristic. We are scanning for threats from when we used to be hunters and gatherers in the stone age and this is especially apparent after the brain's been exposed to an abusive dangerous situation.

So what can we do?

We can re-wire the brain by building new positive neural pathways by doing anything that makes us 'Soul Happy.'

These new positive thoughts create peptides that emit positive hormones which create wonderful feelings and emotions throughout our bodies.

How do we do this?

Little by little by being kind to ourselves day by day.

Scheduling something in our daily routine to make us Soul Happy.

Why No Contact Makes Us Physically Sick

The Role Of Oxytocin

Oxytocin is the cuddle hormone and has a lot to answer for in the narc empath relationship. This beautiful hormone is released during breastfeeding and bonds us to our babies so we love and protect them. Oxytocin is produced in the hypothalamus in the brain and promotes a strong connection. This same hormone is released during kissing cuddling and sex so you can guess which way this goes during the love bombing stage in a relationship with a Narc because they mirror our strongest sexual desires, this produces an electrifying sexual bond we mistake for love. Yes this pesky hormone bonds us to them making us feel safe and protected when we in fact are not. Quite the opposite in fact. This is the beginning of the trauma bond' that is created that makes us miss our abuser and crave their touch. It all makes horrible sense, doesn't it?

The Grief Response

It is so important in our recovery to allow ourselves to grieve. Grieve the person we loved under the fake mask. One of the worst things you can do is bottle up all those feelings and go out on the verge of tears pretending you are ok. So before you go allow yourself to feel those emotions deeply! Yes it will hurt. Put on a song, have a cry and grieve. Ladies put your make up on do your hair and feel fabulous. Go out with only people who get you try avoiding exes and your old haunts but if you're triggered while you are out that's ok.

You can concentrate on your breathing slow and deep and get away from that trigger. Go and throw yourself back into living. When you get home rest. Psychological stress is very draining and socialising is something we have to rebuild on slowly. This is a new skill. You may find you need a reclusive day or two after being around lots of people and crowds. Tune yourself into how you feel and do what you need to do to feel better.

Processing Feelings After Initiating No Contact

Initiating no contact. It's that whole push pull thing. We love them and we hate them. We want to feel them close yet we want them so far away as they make our skin crawl. Remember all the things at play here. The trauma bond, the addiction to pain peptides. Fighting co dependency as they made sure you were dependant on them and took every ounce of your independence. Fight it, fight it all and maintain no contact and ever so gradually through the pain and education you will start to feel less panicky, less like you can't face the world.
Take baby steps day by day until one day you will feel the intense peace of freedom.

If you have just started no contact you are processing so many feelings right now. The main one being grief for the person you fell in love with. They will never be accountable for any of the problems in the relationship and blame you for everything, but you know the truth.
You need to be so gentle and kind to yourself right now and not apologise for how you feel. There really is a lot going on now psychologically and physiologically to explain why you feel so empty sad and devastated.
As you move forward with continued no contact away from their toxicity you will begin to feel better and the sadness and brain fog will lift.
Hang in there I've been where you are. I know it sucks but I know you can get through it and feel better.

Narcs can't cope with not being the centre of your world anymore because they lost control of you! Block, block, block!

Once We Initiate No Contact

So you've gone 'No Contact'. Boy they hate losing control of you, but despite love bombing texts at 3am you have ignored them.
What next? Be prepared for the love bombing to get a little desperate then angry.

Do you see their true colours now?
Insulting accusing trying to lure you back to explain yourself.
Keep going this is the tough part and you've got this.
You know exactly what you are dealing with right now.

Once we start no contact the ex narc will do anything and say anything to reel you back in to their web of lies and chaotic world so they can maintain you as narcissistic supply so they will say phrases such as "I can't live without you" often with fake tears and "I'm going to do myself in. I can't go on!" Using children to get to you playing on your pity and guilty feelings.

Grand gestures called 'Future Faking' such as I was going to do this for you or that for you. or buy you this or that. Often a ring or a promise of some sort. Asking you to lunch just to talk or a more brazen approach "you know you want me". using sweet talk sexting, using new supply to make you jealous are common place.
They use whatever triggers worked on you in the past. These changing tactics might go on for several weeks or months while you do not respond. If you maintain unwavering no contact this becomes anger and the mask comes off and the real Narc is there before you: angry and irrational.
Aren't you glad you went 'no contact' now?
Hang in there brave sisters and brothers.

I Left My Abuser But I Feel Sorry For Him.

You have a real live beating heart! Dang it, that's what got us all into this mess to start with. It's normal to feel caring feelings and feel sorry for them.
Acknowledge it because you are a loving person. Then remember what they did to you. Write it down if you need to, incident by incident and tell yourself you do NOT deserve their abuse and you will not fall for their lies to be sucked back in to more abuse.
Hang in there keep strong maintain no contact!

They Love To Play Cat and Mouse

Narcs want you to occupy every waking (and the ones where you should be sleeping) moment thinking about them and doing their bidding. They love to play cat and mouse where you chase them, panicking they will meet someone else,(look up triangulation) they are in an accident, they got into trouble with the law. They don't care what attention it is as long as you never stop focusing on them.

You chase them trying to lavish love on the poor messed up boy or girl who had a bad childhood then when you stop and say "no more" they stay away (the silent treatment) with no contact longer and longer to punish you as you are trying to move forwards. Drips of love (love bombing) to keep you engaged. All part of their twisted messed up game. The only solution to save your sanity is no Contact, none at all!

So You're Close To Breaking No Contact!

It's all part of the healing process to fall and trip on your face. I remember how I felt when I was where you are. I would just crave to see, feel or touch him or hear his voice. Your feelings of love were real and still are despite you finding out painfully theirs weren't and as I did the relationship and closeness you felt were fictitious. It's times when you think about and act on breaking no contact that you must actively allow yourself to grieve and allow yourself to be sad or angry.

Find a smaller stick to beat yourself with. It's not because you are stupid that you fell for their lies. It's because you are a loving giving empathetic human being and because of this they took advantage of you.

Stay away from them you deserve so much more. You need to connect with a counsellor and work on your self esteem and self worth. You need to study everything on NPD and you will see that this wasn't about you.

You have so much life to live and love to give. You need to start caring for yourself and a total detox from them and you will discover that life is beautiful because the further you get away from their toxicity the better you will feel and you will find wonderful people and opportunities will be attracted to you.

You've got this!

Are You Kidding Yourself You Went 'No Contact'?

The situation can never change if the Nex keeps texting you and you allow them to poison your life. Waiting for the next text to ignore. Are you still looking on their social networking sites trying to 'over think' their loved up pictures with their new victim ( yes victim)

Are you secretly hoping you will bump into them by visiting your old haunts? Are you upsetting yourself on a daily basis? Be honest now. You need to dig really deep right now. Pick a time when you are feeling strong and empowered and block them from your phone.

You cannot function like this and need time to heal from their chaos. This isn't no contact.

Who is Important here? Them or you? You have chosen them unwittingly of course as you are devoting your energy to worrying about their next text. Their next update on social media and exhausting yourself analysing it all! FOCUS on you and your healing and find your inner strength.

You really need to put a wall between the toxic person like they no longer exist and you will slowly feel a shift but right now NOTHING can change.

Grey Rock Explanation If Co Parenting

If you have children with the Nex then going no contact is incredibly difficult so try using the Grey Rock Method for dealing with psychopaths. 'Grey Rock' technique is a way of training the narc to view you as an unsatisfying pursuit. You bore them and they can't stand boredom. Grey Rock is primarily a way of encouraging a narcissist , a stalker or other emotionally unbalanced person, to lose interest in you.

It differs from 'No Contact' in that you don't overtly try to avoid contact with these emotional vampires. Instead you allow contact but only give boring contact.

How I learned to 'Grey Rock' the Stalker Nex.

When the Nex pulled up outside and flashed on his headlights the first time he stared in at me I was like a frightened rabbit running away. The second time was the same as he always did it when I wasn't expecting it. Thereafter I got control of my breathing never looked directly out the window and learned to act. He would stare in and I would pick up my phone laugh into the phone as if I was chatting to someone and casually get up and draw the curtains like I was thoroughly engrossed in my conversation.

I became very good at this and it annoyed the hell out of him and gave me my power back!

Hoovering

Will they now leave me alone?
Maybe yes maybe no, depends whether they have supply or not.
When a narcissist comes back after a long period of silence, which could be anything from a few weeks, months or even years we call this 'hoovering.'

Why Do Narcissists Hoover?

The answer is simply because narcissists are empty souls. They need narcissistic supply to emotionally exist as they do not feel in the same way as a normal person so they have to steal a soul.
They feed on causing drama and need to know that they are affecting or upsetting their previous target. They need to feel secure in the knowledge that you aren't over them and you could be hooked back in if required as a future feed if their current one dries up.
Narcissists keep multiple sources of supply including their current main one that they groom and love bomb intermittently to ensure a steady uninterrupted supply.

Watch Out The Nex Doesn't Try and Hoover You Back!

The narcissistic abuse cycle continues as long as the victim allows it.
The Nex will try and recycle previous supply if he or she is running low or the new supply isn't as compliant any more because they themselves have caught onto his or her games or caught them cheating and called time on the relationship. This is when the Nex may come and rubbish the new supply to you telling you they have made a huge mistake! "They're crazy, I had to leave them as I couldn't forget you" and loudly proclaiming "You and me are soul mates we're meant to be together!"
This future faking is music to our ears and what we have always wanted to hear during the relationship.
It makes sense to have an old source of supply that accepts them unconditionally than to go to the extreme expense and effort of cultivating a new one.

When they come back for a spot of hoovering and realise the love bombing triggers aren't working and you begin to see their real true vulgar evilness berating you with nasty words, telling you "you're no good, you're ugly, your bums too big." Whatever they can to provoke a reaction from you so they can feed off your pain.

Once you have seen it in all it's glory remember that is truly who they are. Chin up head held high and walk away, because you know at that moment you are worth so much more and the only loser is the one you're walking from.

Don't forget a bum wiggle on the way out!


Minimising Emotional Abuse

For those of you who have recently left King or Queen Narc do not risk being hoovered back in because of rose tinted spectacles of good times. Pick up a pen and write down every little thing he or she did to you.

Do not minimise the emotional abuse.

Top of the page

It is not okay that they ignored me for several hours,

It is not okay that they swore at me and called me vile names,

It is not okay that they pushed me or grabbed me,

It is not ok that they hit me or slapped me.

When you are done keep it for weak moments and re read it.

Stay 'No Contact' from this toxic person.


Surround Yourself With A Human Shield Of Good People

As you move away from the Nex and their entourage's toxic cloud of chaos and destruction you allow space for good happy positive people to come into your life. People the Nex repelled. Remember those?

This is why it is imperative you escape, go NO CONTACT with NO exceptions so you can close that chapter of your life shut and seal it.

Then fully in control you can pick up your pen and begin to write your new life how YOU want it.

Once you surround yourself with a human shield of good people and positivity the evil will bounce right off.


Okay You're Still With Me?


You Are enough Out of the Brain Fog To Ask What is a Narcissist?

Narcs Have No or Little Empathy Or Insight into their behaviour.

So you meet this charming man who tells you how unlucky he is in love. He left a crazy ex who got drunk and hit him. He really wants to meet that special woman. He looks at you with puppy dog eyes tinged with sadness. He just wants to be loved. Your heart goes out to him and you try to help as a friend to fix him. He says his mother messed him up. Maybe he needs to connect with her again? He hasn't seen his Dad in years. You suggest that he tries to contact him as you know boys without fathers often grow up to be delinquents. Yet here hc is holding down a job. sociable and the centre of attention. Well if people like him he must be okay. You admire his confidence and the way he works the room. You're told he will do anything for anyone.

He love bombs you for weeks till you back down and agree to go on a date. He tells you that you are the most amazing woman he's ever met and he's fallen for you which is strange because he tells you he's easily bored but you are different. You spend every minute of your time with him watching movies. going camping, canoeing and the rest going partying or in bed. You are infatuated. You can think of nothing else but him. He makes you feel special. He makes you feel like you're the only girl in the world. He makes you fall hook line and sinker in love.

After several months and as the relationship progresses you find out he drinks heavily. Well, you think to yourself, if I could just stop him drinking. He stops drinking and turns to drugs and online poker. Well if I could just make him see there's another way to fight his demons. You see his anger and blame all of the above.

You watch him flirt and cheat, you blame all of the above.

In hindsight years later the realisation dawns on you.

No it isn't the drugs or the alcohol that makes him who he is. That is actually him and  the girl in the story was 22 yr old 3rd year Nursing student me.

Spot the red flags waving clearly in my face!

I've read the psychology and cut the psycho babble for those who have just come across this and are reeling in shock from the horror of it all.

Once We Begin To Study Personality Disorders We Come Across The Red Flags

Recognise any of these? I've been unlucky in love. My ex was crazy. They cheated on me. They used to hit me when they were drunk. Oh I loved them but I had to leave them.
This is the bait from a narc trying to reel you in with their poor me and bad luck stories. All their stories will have the underlying thread of them being painted as the victim and nothing is EVER their fault. Dig a bit deeper and this is a massive red flag to run!

The Nex used to say to me "Everything I've ever loved leaves me," very early on in the relationship. What an amazing 'poor me' hook that is for a nurturing empath who set out to love him and prove to be different than the rest of his 'batshit crazy exes!'

What Is A Narcissist

Narcissistic personality disorder (NPD) is a long-term pattern of abnormal behaviour characterized by exaggerated feelings of self importance, an excessive need for admiration, and a lack of understanding of others' feelings. People affected by it often spend a lot of time thinking about achieving power or success, or about their appearance. They often take advantage of the people around them.
The behaviour typically begins by early adulthood.

Narcs are manipulative and they lack empathy and compassion so are capable of causing intentional harm to others without considering the consequences of their behaviour. All their relationships follow the same pattern without exception. They love bomb the victim in the idealisation phase then they use the victim up and devalue them until they eventually discard them.

A narcs real true self is a wounded child whose emotional development was stunted due to neglect from a primary caretaker and emotional and often physical abuse.

Why?
If you repeat a lie often enough, it becomes the truth.'

Behind the mask: The "False Self" of the Narcissist
Narcissists develop what's called a 'false self.' The severity and intensity of NPD comes from the desperate pursuit of a sense of self. They live in a false reality and believe their own lies about who they are.

What is the Authentic Self?
The core of whom you really are, not what people tell you that you should be or the 'you' defined by people who do not really know you: the doubters, critics, and others who only see the part of you that you choose to show. An authentic person is aware of their behaviour and the consequences of it and it's impact on others.
They strive to take the right actions that are both beneficial and non-destructive to others.

Secondly what is the False Self?
Narcissists despise their authentic self and can't risk showing their vulnerability to others, especially themselves.
They need to believe and continuously reinforce the false self to themselves and others.
They make up a fictitious false self who is everything the narcissist is not. This being an entitled, superior, inflated, and grandiose self fed by the narcissist's fantasies and what they can squeeze out of various sources of narcissistic supply.

What is the purpose of the false self?
This mask, which the narcissist thinks is real, hides the insecure and damaged part of them and chases away their feelings of depression, abandonment, and shame.
It protects them from painful feelings and Narcissistic injury.
If they're not forthcoming, they demand them in one way or another in the ways that make the relationship a wild ride on a rollercoaster.
The Narcs success in maintaining this illusion makes you continually doubt yourself since you rarely receive validation of what you are going through in the relationship.
They are very good actors capable of duping even the most experienced professional.

The problem with the false self
It takes a lot of energy to keep the fragile, superficial mask in good enough

shape to protect against what Narcs see as 'attacks' from the outside world, e.g., complaints about their self-absorbed and abusive ways.

This destroys the illusion and might force them to take a closer look at themselves. That's why they protect the mask so aggressively in ways that make you continually doubt yourself. It's extremely painful to have your feelings rebuffed by someone whom you feel so much love for.

You can't rip the mask off the Narcs face without hurting yourself in the process. They will hold on to the mask and attack back which we see when trying to distance ourselves and leave them. This is when the mask comes of for good and we see their real self in the form of Narcissistic rage.

Ok I know what they are now,
They are telling me how sorry they are,
They are telling me they will do anything to make another go of it!
They have even agreed to go for anger management therapy!
I miss them so much.

Does A Narc Know He's A Narc?

To any one of you thinking you can educate your Narc as to what they are and how they behave. There's literally no point sending them any of this material. In fact it may educate them to be a better Narcissist.

You will teach them how to pretend to behave. Also you are showing them if you are still communicating that your boundaries are weak and they can come back at anytime and hoover you back in if they fake the good behaviour you are teaching them.

Things can't change and improve for you unless you 'let go' and initiate 'no contact' for real.

Why Do I Want to Contact Someone Who Hurts Me?

I'm doing no contact like a pro now for several months then I suddenly want to contact them! Why?

Because you love them or loved them deeply.

You have a good heart and if they hadn't turned into the person that did all those evil things you would still be together and life would be great right? Wrong! Yes you love or loved them only they couldn't love you back. Their love was toxic and was all about controlling you.

Now you are a few months out you are remembering the love you had and thinking of the shattered future you had planned. It's ok to grieve for the person you fell in love with and the fictitious mask they had. Just remember that that wasn't really them and why you left. You left because you deserve real true love and you don't deserve abuse. These feelings will pass but for now never forget what they did to you and never forget what it taught you.

Can I stay married and make it work if my partner has NPD?

I write this with tears in my eyes nearly twenty years later as the wife that stayed and tried to make it work. My husband was all the things I desired in a man handsome charming and generous spirited. However he had a dark side, and as our marriage progressed that dark controlling mean side took over and I saw less of that man I fell in love with.

It wasn't until he put his hands round my neck and I called the police nearly 16 yrs later that I ended it with him ( still deeply trauma bonded I might add) and had to get a years injunction so he could no longer abuse me.

It was only then, as the brain fog cleared I began to find out what the man I lived with was truly like and during my research stumbled on cluster B personality disorders particularly Narcissism.

I understand and I know how hard it is to leave but if your partner has NPD I'm here to sadly tell you they get worse, you can't fix them by loving them and they will bleed you emotionally and physically dry until you don't recognise you anymore.

Please learn from my experiences and get out now while you're young. I won't judge you if you don't leave immediately. I didn't straight away either. It's tough to walk away from someone you love.

Educate yourself and you will learn why you need to grow strong and make that break.

# The Narcissists Playground

## Social Media

You will probably find that the narcissist will not immediately un friend you from social media because it would deny them the pleasure of cyber-abusing you by parading their new love by splashing sensational pictures on their page and mutual friends pages, gloating about how happy they are and lying about you as the crazy ex in vague or outright statements to dupe their friends and family.

This is just another attention seeking manipulation tactic to deceive you and especially everyone else into thinking that you were at fault for the relationship's demise and they finally found a person who is worthy of their greatness.

It helps to remember that the new victim is being love bombed at this stage.

If you are still 'friends' you need to protect yourself. Go to your Nex's page and delete every comment you made on every post then delete your Nex's comments on your own page. Delete all the pictures of your Nex or save them to a file on your computer to delete at a later time if you haven't the heart to do it yet. Now you're ready to delete and block them from social media.

Now delete and block all the Nex's family members and any mutual friends that you suspect may be turned into a flying monkey.

If you are co parenting change your Nex-name in your phone to Psycho or something that will make you think twice about answering. If you receive a phone call, let it go to voicemail. If you receive a text, don't respond. Keep all the messages in case you need them in court to get an injunction.

If you are not co parenting change your number.

Set up an email account for co parenting purposes to correspond only about the children.

Otherwise block their email address.

"Once we initiate no contact we can begin to heal.
A huge part of the healing process is educating ourselves on how these insidious people tick."

"YOU are all much stronger than you think you are! This is all about taking back the power and saying this is my life and you're not welcome anymore.
You have NO place in my beautiful life!"

Ending The Relationship

Projection You Are The Crazy One

If you don't feel like you are a 'batshit crazy' ex then you are reading the wrong book! Seriously this is how they want you to feel and they've projected all their crazy onto you so it's no surprise you feel this way right now.
Breathe read and learn and you will see that this was never about you.

The Latter Stages of a Relationship With a Narcissist

You know your light bulb moment? The bit where you realised they're a bully. You're onto them and want out but you are still trapped. The bit where after years of abuse you realise and tell them they're not right in the head. That's when they begin to point their finger and project it all onto you.
The Nex spat at me, "It's not me bitch it's you. you're the one who needs help. You're the one who needs pills for depression. you're a cheat and a slag. you've never been faithful to me! I was right about you!"

Why? Once a Narcissist is cornered this way they will throw it right back at you.
After years of abuse they want to break you down as they know you are going to discard them soon. They know you have worked out their deep down pathology is the 'true' them. You are waking up! You can't be duped anymore and you are going to reveal their hidden pathology to everyone.
So now they have to point the finger at you for all their dastardly deeds. They need to make you literally look insane, so they can walk away from the mess they caused into another 'normal' relationship (they've been grooming) unscathed as the victim pointing a finger back at you saying "Look at him or her they're mental! See what I've had to put up with and why I left?"

"This is the stage where you realise that you are not dealing with a person but you are in fact fighting a psychopathy that is so hidden and insidious that unless you have experienced it you struggle to believe it exists."

"I've come to the conclusion that narc shit is like bullshit except deeper and harder to shovel!"

The Smear Campaign and How To Survive
Turning Friends Family and Children Against You

So they have bad mouthed you all over town. to anyone who'll listen! How dare they after everything they have put you through?

This involves some all of the following:
Befriending your friends and family and initiating contact with mutual friends to ask them to join their campaign against you.
Continuing to escalate the attack by widely posting insults and snide remarks in public online forums in an attempt to engage you.

The Flying Monkeys That Enable The Narcissist.

What is a flying monkey?

Flying monkeys are the people they get to do their dirty work for them, so their hands remain clean.

The term flying monkey comes from the Wizard of Oz where the wicked witch used flying monkeys to carry out her attacks. Today in psychology a flying monkey remains just that, someone who does the narcissists evil bidding to inflict more suffering on the victim.
Most collude with the narcissist in a vicious smear campaign without even realising they are being used. Sadly flying monkeys can be well meaning friends and loved ones who have also been manipulated and duped by the narcissist in their hate campaign. The only course of action for the victim to take when a previous ally has been manipulated in this way is to block all contact with them and hope they work out the truth one day.

Why Do They Create an Evil Smear Campaign?

Narcissists love drama, they feed off its energy and anyone they can create drama around. They love nothing more than lighting the touch paper and running away ( because they are actually cowards as well as bullies) then when it all blows up pointing and saying "Well would you look at them!" Then muttering "Well I'm not getting involved it's nothing to do with me. I just want a quiet life!"
Their very lifeblood is chaos and mayhem that they themselves have caused unknowingly to other unsuspecting victims.

"Sooo they can't have you! So now they are going to smear your name all over town! Hold your head up high do not respond and do not get into a 'word salad' defending yourself! This is a pathetic Narc tactic when they realise you are no longer willing supply! Be strong!"

I remember sitting with my therapist crying and saying "I just wanted him to say well done! Just you're great at this or that! I know I'm a good Mum so why does he not see it? Why is he doing this? Why is he belittling my name and smearing me all over town like I'm sleeping with all his friends? When he was cheating on me for years!"

I know now of course. You see you're trying to get your head round something so twisted and evil! You left them so you caused a huge Narcissistic injury so now they must destroy you! You hurt them! How dare you leave!

They function on three main emotions envy jealousy and greed.

This is when you see you weren't in a relationship. You were in competition with them. As soon as you started doing better than them, be it a better parent, better cook, better at balancing the books, better looking, more popular than them you became the enemy.
Now they must set out to 'show' everyone that you are terrible at all those things you excelled at in the relationship.
Inside of that huge inflated ego of self importance that is their mask to the world they know they are a broken dysfunctional person.
Now you know and you have information about who they really are and must be trashed and destroyed before the truth leaks out!

## Do 'No Contact' Like A Pro

The minute you are no longer willing to be narc supply and begin to tell others what they are really like they will protect themselves from being revealed.
They lie, they cheat and then turn the finger to pointing at you.
The only way to deal with this is not to respond and to maintain no contact.

## Perfect Projection

The Narc flips it around.
They pretend now they are everything you were: good, virtuous, faithful and a super parent, kind, and law abiding and everything they were: a liar, a child abuser, a cheater and evil is what you are. This is what they do to project their sickness onto the victim so it remains hidden from others and now the fingers point at you. This is how they deflect people from looking for the real perpetrator.

## So What Do I Do?

Give up defending and explaining yourself. It's not easy and I'm not going to pretend it is but continue to be you.
The you that is a good kind person,. the you that is a super parent.
Eventually the real you will shine through and that finger pointed at you? Swings back at the real perpetrator. Their black soul can't hide in the shadows forever.
When we are going through a smear campaign of manufactured lies designed to discredit us as a person and a mother or father we automatically want to shout "This isn't me! You don't know me!" We feel violated angry and upset at the thought that someone who said they loved us so deeply now has set out to hurt us. Some of our mutual friends now avoid us, there is whispering in corners and we begin to feel paranoid.
So what do you do? Do you defend yourself and tell people they are lies? That depends whether the Nex got to them first and turned them into a flying monkey that swallowed their lies and is joining them In the assassination of your character.

The Nex did this to me, he visited all my friends telling them they didn't know me I was in fact mentally ill and I had spent all our money and I was lazy and I had cheated and when he found out he had moved out.

The truth was of course he had cheated and I had found out and thrown him out!

The only method that works is to stop explaining 'your side' to people.

So step away from their lies, walk with your head held high and build a new virtuous life for yourself.

As time goes on people quickly see the truth and who you really are. Oh and those that don't? The ones that become a part of his enabling entourage? Well them and their opinions don't matter.

Leave them in the past where they belong.

How do I react to gossip amongst my friends from the narcs smear campaign?

You can use humour. If someone says "Your Nex said you cheated on him with three of his friends" you can say "Yes have you been to my brothel too?" Then laugh and say "tell a story Jackanory" ( a children's programme where they tell stories to children) or you could say "Don't believe everything you read on the back of a cornflakes packet" then skip on by with a smile on your face!

If they see you react in an unbothered amused way and you don't defend yourself you are clearly innocent. If you say "What a lying pos he cheated on me, he lies he is this he is that" it sounds like you are deflecting the blame.

Always react to smears on your character in an unbothered way.

It's difficult after being targeted by a Narc smear campaign to trust anyone.

Trust your gut and if in doubt don't discuss it. Make all social media private so they have no ammunition to use. It almost goes without saying never ever retaliate and ignore the Narc like they are invisible!

"A fire needs oxygen to burn like a Narc needs attention! Take away that oxygen supply and it will stop burning! Total silent treatment literally starves the Narc of attention and eventually extinguishes it! Not immediately, you got to hang in there a while, but it works each and every time."

"Dig deep and find the superhero within you."

A fellow Thriver Jayne shared with me the tale of Edith Eva Egar and she said she thought of my friends surviving and recovering from their own personal Narc-induced Auschwitz'.
Those of you that are struggling today saying they can't go on think of what those poor people went through need to dig deep like they did.

"You can take away everything from me but you can never ever murder my spirit."
Edith Eva Egar

To the Narcs.
"We will live laugh and love while you fester in hate till the end of time."

Maya Angelou
You may shoot me with your words,
You may cut me with your eyes,
You may kill me with your hatefulness,
But still, like air, I'll rise.

"When we initiate 'no contact' the Nex will try to regain control This has nothing to do with love as they always were incapable of that. They will do this by whatever means they have available. It becomes a twisted game of chess they're playing with your life. Children, pets, your family and friends, new partners, houses cars anything you have together become pawns to be used to either regain control or if this is impossible to hurt you."

I know it's hard not to respond to the Nex smearing your reputation all over town, but keep this at the forefront of your mind.

"Let go of what and who you can't control. The only thing we can control are our reactions to the lies. No reaction is the right response to take back your power.
Ignore them and their enablers and flying monkey's.
Don't defend yourself with words defend yourself by virtuous living and slowly people will see that you stepped away from the drama and they are still in the thick of it. Trust me on this one."

Why do they want to destroy me and take my children despite being with a shiny new toy?

"They want to destroy you because you will no longer tolerate their abuse and be willing narc supply. You took all their fun away now and you are a loose canon full of secrets of their psychopathy so they have to make you look like the crazy one. They take the compliant kids as pawns in the game of your life purely to hurt you and to win. The new shiny toy is supplying their needs right now but as soon as he or she is onto their pathology or quits they will go through the same process.
1.Love bomb and idealization,
2.Devalue while they bleed the victim dry emotionally and financially while they groom the next victim,
3.A painful discard.
Stop explaining your story or the truth to people that just don't get it!
Channel that energy into healing you and living!
In time the ones that matter will see through new eyes."

Dividing Your Family

It is common practice for a Narc to triangulate and try and divide and conquer the whole of your family so they still have control over your children and their useful financial support. Following our divorce the Nex tried to turn my incredibly close family against me, trying to seek out would be flying monkeys. In many long rants to my Dad saying "I'm sorry you don't know your own daughter!" He also chased my Mum through the shopping centre! He told both my sisters I had kicked and punched my daughter. He tried to break us all but none of us would or will engage with his poison! During alienation he ranted to my Mum and Dad that he still wanted them to take my children out and buy them things, but they want nothing to do with their mother. He was that blatant.

Narcissists then turn to their own children by lying about the victim and alienating them against him or her.
They try to rally up supporters to help to achieve total alienation of the victims children.
Dr Childress states 'An ex spouse becomes an ex parent' In child custody battles.

The Narcissist In the Courtroom

Narcs are self entitled creatures who think the world and you owes them a living.

Narcs believe they are superior beings and everyone else is inferior to them.

They are devoid of empathy so have no conscience to pay back any money they borrow from anyone.

They would sell their own Granny down the river if they thought they would financially gain from it.

Just for a moment imagine having no conscience and no empathy and never considering consequences of how your actions affect others.

Now you're getting it!

Narcs are above the law and believe that laws and rules do not apply to them.

They despise authority figures and will do anything to get one over on others who are above or superior to them in job status or class.

Belittling them or cheating them is just another game.

Narcs are simple playground bullies at heart and are only deterred by bigger bullies.

Those being the police, or the judge and prison and the bullies there.

They will tell outrageous lies and drop you in it to save themselves from any consequences of their unlawful behaviour in the courtroom.

Unfortunately due to their superficial charm they manage to convince authority figures they are in fact telling the truth.

They will try also to love bomb and charm the victim in domestic violence cases and custody battles.

This is often successful as the victim still has loving feelings towards their abuser and very often makes decisions from the heart and gives the abuser benefit of the doubt or drops the case altogether thinking they can work it out between them in a civilized manner.

Narcs are not civilised or reasonable,

They fight dirty, and it's a battle of good-v-evil,

I say this from my heart do not give them an inch and make all your decisions based on the wellbeing of you and your children.

Do Not Get Dragged into Legal Tit for Tat

The pathogenic parent will show your children legal papers to sway the child's opinion of you. Your child or children may say "You stole our

house" or "It's all your fault" and then express a wish to break contact with you, which is the alienators mission.
What Not To Do.
Put your side across and say well those are lies!
What do I do?
Write and say I understand you are upset and I'm sorry you have been involved in adult issues that you shouldn't have to be worrying about, then carry on the letter as usual telling them you love them and keep it light and humorous.

Your Fight is Not Over

The worst alienation occurs on the lead up and during a custody battle. Most of us then feel defeated after losing to the Nex in court! I'm here to remind you all that getting court out the way ( a source of constant drama and conflict) does not mean your fight for your kids is over it has just begun, because once you step away from the drama you cannot be instigated in it, you cannot be blamed and your children have a chance to see the cause of all the chaos for themselves. Please pour some of that energy you have used in the battle into building yourself back up and continue to reach out to them and drip love however you can.. Their fight to see you has just begun.

Brain Fog A Few Weeks to a Month of No Contact

While embroiled in a relationship with an NPD individual you cannot think straight due to their insidious tactics but In the first few months after bravely leaving the Narc and after the brain fog clears you begin to see clearly and you finally stumble on the letters NPD on the internet through insomnia and tears.
Finally I'm not alone. There's reasons for all their shitty behaviour. It's a bolt out the blue that it's all about them. The devalue and discard would inevitably happen no matter what you do. Then you begin to look around you with your new knowledge and see traits of narcissism in other people you know. It's like on Sixth Sense when the little boy says "I see dead people". Suddenly all around you are emotional blood suckers. Was my Geography teacher one? Is my boss one?
It's quite chilling especially if you see traits in a high conflict family member. You become highly attuned to spotting Narcs, but you've got

to keep it in perspective and remember that there are beautiful people out there. Remember that Narcs are attracted to childhood wounds of insecurity and low self esteem and fear of abandonment.

"As you work on your inner wounds you get a healthy human shield of good positive people in your life surrounding you.
And the Narcs? Well as you heal they fade away."

Cognitive Dissonance Kicks in

A Month To Three Months Of No Contact

In Psychology cognitive dissonance means simply

"The state of having inconsistent thoughts, beliefs, or attitudes, especially as relating to behavioural decisions and attitude change."

As we go forwards with no contact it's normal to feel tearful and fearful and unsure.
The full extent of your cognitive dissonance is kicking in right now as you have been away from the toxic person sometime. This is making you reflect back with your new knowledge on that person you used to 'love. ' You are seeing the dysfunction in them now from the past, when you were with them and now thinking of things they said and did differently. It's ok right now to feel utterly violated. Its ok not to trust a single soul as your trustometer has been blasted to bits.

It will take time to heal from this. You need to cry it out, rest and recuperate and spend time alone. Work through this devastation and grief for the lovely person that never existed.
Feel violated at the monster you now know them to be. You need to get strong emotionally to 'deal' with this person especially if you have children with them.

Counselling is also a useful tool to get you through this tough time to help you understand why you are feeling this way and enables you to work on your 'inner wounds.'

As you move away from the toxic person you will experiences flashes of understanding as your brain tries to make rational sense of it all.

You ask yourself "Is it me? Maybe I am crazy after all?"

You fight the illusion of the charming good person you fell in love with ( their social persona) You struggle to believe that the person who promised you so much who told you it was you and him against the world and held your hand with tears in his eyes as you gave birth to his child is inherently evil. This causes confusion and pain as the realisation dawns on you that you were tricked by a master manipulator that tried to suck out your soul!

Hang On I Think I'm The Narcissist

Do You Have fleas?

No I'm not talking about the pesky creatures that prey on our furry friends. For those of you that don't know, Fleas are the bad behaviour patterns and habits picked up from living with a person (generally a parent, sibling or partner) who had total and unhealthy control over us. Fleas are the crazy making, and unhealthy ways of coping, the pain and guilt patterns we had to take on as children or partners in order to just survive in that toxic environment.

The good news is they're completely un-learnable. One of the worst fears that newbie's worry about is the overwhelming fear that they themselves have NPD.

All human beings do Narcissistic things and in recovery when we are learning to love and take care of ourselves these self-serving things make us question, "Am I a Narcissist?" It's a perfectly understandable fear to feel guilty about possibly having hurt someone's feelings or being self-centred.

It can really be upsetting, even terrifying because that's what we have been taught to do when serving the Narcs in our life. So let me put your mind at rest and show you the difference. In order for someone to recognize, acknowledge and feel guilty about their own Narcissistic behaviours, they first have to have a level of empathy and sense of emotional responsibility and accountability that Narcissists do not feel as they don't have the insight to do that.

If you're that worried about the impact of your behaviour on others you don't have NPD you just have fleas.

Grieve For The Person You Thought They Were

I find it easier to remember two separate men in my marriage.

The one I fell in love with who was charming funny and generous who would do anything for anyone.
Then the other man who was callous cruel degrading unloving scheming manipulative and abusive.

I grieved for the first man and it's much easier now to say to myself the second man is a stranger. I never married him and I would never have married him.
He never did and doesn't deserve a place in my beautiful happy life. He doesn't and never did deserve to even breathe the same air as me.
That's all, there's nothing more to say and I'm not wasting another second of my time or thoughts on that stranger.

Do you see now you have been no contact long enough to start to question their behaviour ,lies, and manipulation?
You will ask yourself "So it doesn't matter what I did, he would still behave like that?"
Yes there is not an ounce of decency in them.
It takes a lot of sleepless nights and fighting yourself, fighting our inner belief of the love bombing partner we originally met at the start of the relationship with these questions before you finally admit this wasn't about you it was caused by a person with a mental disorder. Once you hit that wall you must find a way to climb and clear it. Only when you are safely on the other side can you begin to heal and you are going to start finding the missing pieces of you.

How do I clear that wall?
Maintain no contact and that wall will disappear like a mirage in the desert so you can safely cross it with the Nex on the other side.
You are out of the situation. the brain fog is clearing. rational thoughts are starting to kick in now so we can ask how and why do they do what they do?

How and Why Do They Do That?

146

You will have read bits about gas lighting and triangulation and words like 'Stockholm Syndrome' will trip off your tongue as you research at 3am and piece together this person you thought you knew so well.

So here I'm going to put it all together and show you exactly who this person really is and why they behave the way they do.

Why Do They Do That?

Narcs Are driven by envy and greed overlying deep shame and loathing of their true self.

I don't usually quote Sam Vaknin But who better than a narcissist to explain how they envy others?

"Envy is at the core of my being: seething, foaming-at-the-mouth, destructive, morbid, and potent. I envy other people's happiness, possessions, accomplishments, status, spot in the limelight, contacts, you name it. I disguise my envy. I rationalize and intellectualize it. I do my utmost to ruin the source of my frustration while pretending to be his or her friend. I lie sleepless at night, rebelling Impotently against the injustice of it all, that any one should surpass me, perfect as I am. My pathological spite drives me to extremes of behaviour: I plot and provoke and collude and spread malicious gossip and strive to damage my opponent and reduce him. I Imagine his downfall in great detail and revel in his forthcoming misery and humiliation. I spend inordinate amounts of time, resources, and mental energy on nurturing my envy and mollifying it."
Sam Vaknin


Why A Narc Targets You

When a narc targets us they do so because we have something they want and admire that they don't have. We are bright and bubbly, with an active social life and a wide circle of friends.
As the idealise phase continues they monopolise your time so you don't have time for your friends. Their aim is to groom you to meet their needs while love bombing you so you become hooked. It's all exclusive and you believe that this wonderful person that texts you hundreds of times a

day and spends all their time with you is hopelessly in love with you. As infatuated as you are with them in fact. However it is not in their interests for you to have friends. This is when they begin to test and trample down your boundaries.

Their way is to divide and conquer you by sabotaging your friendships and triangulating all your close relationships this way including your family. It's much easier to abuse you if you have no allies.

So how do they achieve this?

If you make plans with anyone other than them they insult that person behind their back and tell you lies about them that are supposedly in your best interest because they care so much about your wellbeing. They might say "she's got a real reputation" if you were planning on a night out with a girlfriend. While being utterly charming to this persons face. They lie different individualised lies to each person concerned to deliberately pit people against each other.

You can't have friends of the opposite sex because you will be accused of fancying them. You won't find out while in the relationship but they threaten anyone who speaks to you so you become isolated.

However they have double standards and they will explain, as my Nex did about the long list of girls on their friends list that they go way back and are just friends even though you know that some are past girlfriends. They will use this information to taunt you, saying "We broke up I know she still fancies me."

So now they have you exactly where they want you insecure and dependant on them with no boundaries and fully in their control and ready for the devalue stage where they can abuse you freely.

The Trophy Wife or Husband

To the narcissist you are nothing but a new leather handbag, or a shiny new car.

They kept you as a trophy to show off and make others envy them and make themselves feel better about their empty existence and fed their ego.

Narcs don't see their partner as someone in their own right with feelings.

148

The Games Narcs Play

Once they have you hooked with love bombing techniques and drips of love to keep you just where they need you then follows the silent treatment and their game of cat and mouse of "Will they call won't they call?" Leaving you for hours at a time or overnight pondering "Are they cheating on me?"

Triangulation with other partners coupled with these other tactics are all immature pathetic treatment from a man or a woman who is still emotionally potty training.

Why do we put up with this 'love'?
Do we deserve this?
If the answer to this is 'Yes' then we need to work on our inner wounds. Our insecurity and feelings of worthlessness.

The Mask They Wear

They Learn To Mimic Emotions

Narcs study other people.

The Nex used to say to me "I know people. You don't know people like me, there's only a few types of people" That now sends chills down my spine because now I look back and see that what he meant was those who could be duped and manipulated and those that could not.

Narcs merely mimic human emotions by learning from watching us empaths.
They can cry or rage or mimic fear or love. They can also lie with no conscience about having an illness or say they are dying when we try to leave. They often pretend they are sick to get us to respond or behave the way they want us to. Especially once they feel you are slipping away from their control.
They are very convincing until you walk away and look back and see the faked emotions. Think of a toddler bawling for a biscuit if you say "no" they try different emotions till one works. Remember everything they do is to secure Narc supply. If you threaten to remove yourself and take their

control away then they will go through the whole spectrum of emotions like an Oscar winning actor using every tried and tested tactic from super nice to rage to find one that works to reel you back into their web of lies and chaos.

If the tactics fail to work because we are strong and walk away this is when we see the mask slip and Narcissistic rage is released.

Love Bombing

We miss the mask! The non authentic person. That sweet guy or girl from way back at the beginning. who wined and dined and kissed and courted us. What happened to them? Their real self came out to play once they had hooked you.

Normal people don't love bomb when they meet someone they like. They do not flatter and make promises of eternal love on a first date. They don't say they have fallen in love with you without getting to know you first. This is a huge red flag and common behaviour of a predator looking for a victim to use.

Narcs use love bombing techniques to initially secure you and to create an unnaturally strong bond to them.

When victims are still in the idealise stage of the relationship it's very hard to believe that this wonderful charming person who appears to have fallen in love with them and claims to want to take care of them intends to use, devalue and ultimately try to destroy them.

Taking On the Identity Of The Target

They take on the identity and interests of the one they are love bombing and maintaining supply from. When me and the Nex met those many years ago he morphed into this countryside loving outdoorsy person. Perfect for me as I loved all that. Enter my perfect soul mate cooking me eggs and bacon on the campfire. Going for long walks and sleeping under the stars.

Once my marriage ended he love bombed the OW this way too.

Now a few years on and after my son broke free he said to me "We don't do any of that family stuff anymore Mum ,when I first moved in we went camping and canoeing or walked the dog."

He love bombed me this way when he needed to draw me back in after an aggressive outburst or after a suspicious cheating episode. Now he's doing same to the OW. Taking her camping to their caravan if things are rough after a fight and then everything is ok again for a while or if she accuses him of cheating, according to my son.

Once out of the relationship you can see that these interests wane and that the fun outdoor guy was part of the false self created to reel me or the new victim in and thus keep a plentiful narc supply.

Word Salad

Word salad is a 'confused or unintelligible mixture of seemingly random words and phrases', most often used to describe a symptom of a neurological or mental disorder. The words may or may not be grammatically correct, but are semantically confused to the point that the listener cannot extract any meaning from them.

If you cast your mind back to a typical conversation with the Nex you will remember the way they ranted at you. One long rant where they shouted at you without making any sense. An unintelligible mixture of repeated sentences when you called them out on their behaviour. This is 'word salad' and it's designed to confuse and put the victim of the rant off balance.

You try to reply and to reason but you can't get a word in edge ways. You end up apologising for something that wasn't your fault and they end up getting away with what you called them out on. Your head is mashed and you just want the conversation to end.

When you address their bad behaviour they will point their finger at you and remind you that you were late for your second date. You let them down five years ago. They say something like "I should've left you then" so you go into defensive mode pleading your innocence. Before you know it the original wrong doing you called them out on is forgotten. 'Projection' and 'Word salad' at its best in the world of Narcdom.

Gas Lighting and Lies

A major part of the word salad comprises of gas lighting. That is distorting the truth and lying to create a new reality that fits their false mask where everyone else is to blame and they aren't accountable for their behaviour. This over time leaves you questioning your reality and perception.

Gas-lighting is the psychological manipulation by an abuser.

It is one of the most extreme, dangerous and effective forms of emotional and psychological abuse and is mostly carried out intentionally. Gas-lighting is a game of mind control and intimidation that is often used by narcissists and sociopaths as a way of confusing and controlling their victim.

It was named after the 1944 thriller 'Gas-light' starring Ingrid Bergman. The husband used forms of manipulation in an attempt to drive his wife crazy, so he deliberately dims the gaslights in the house but told his wife that she was imagining it. and he moves a watch and pretends he hasn't to make her think she's losing her mind. With the use of these and other various tricks he tried to convince his wife that she was going insane and also that she was losing her memory.

Gas-lighting gradually makes the victim doubt their own sanity and decreases their self-esteem and self-confidence so they are unable to function independently which is the abusers aim.
They eventually become so insecure that they will fail to trust their own judgment, intuition and find themselves unable to make even simple everyday decisions.
Over time it will actually damage your trust in yourself and your experience of reality.
The abuser always plays the role of the victim. Whenever the true victim bring up a problem, they find themselves apologizing by the end of the conversation to the abuser.
They begin over time to consider their point of view as normal.
They start to lose their ability to make their own judgements.
This leads to complete dependence on their abuser.
By the time they are in deep the victim is not confidant in their judgement and perception of reality anymore.
They find themselves questioning different scenarios
Did it happen or did it not happen?
You reason with yourself "I'm sure he came back at 3pm but if he says it was 2pm then why would he lie?"

"I'm pretty sure I put my purse in my bag but if he says it was on the fireplace then ok it was."

The victim begins to blame themselves saying, "Maybe I'm getting old, maybe my memory is going."

Gas Lighting Stages

The first stage is disbelief when the first sign of gas lighting occurs.

The next stage is defence where you are defending yourself and argue against the abusers manipulation." No I didn't" you say indignantly. "Yes you did you stupid bitch, you have such a bad memory, seriously you're just a crazy lady" is the Narcs reply.

"I'm not crazy I know where I put the keys! I didn't move them!" I would reply indignantly.

The Nex then would square up to me and shout aggressively gritting his teeth! "Are you calling me a liar?" I would shrink and lower my voice and back down so as not to release the crazy "No ok I'm sorry." I would say.

During this stage, you are driven into confusion by the word salad conversation. going over and over, like a broken record in your mind. You can't stand that they see you as a liar so next time you go along with it and back right down. Gradually over time your perception of reality becomes skewed.

Sometimes however the Nex did not respond in anger but instead would look me in the eye, put his hand on my shoulder in feigned compassion and say in a caring way "Look I know you better than you know yourself! You're not right in the head, you're just a crazy lady!"

The final stage is depression and you begin to lose touch with reality until you hardly recognize yourself anymore.

Some of your behaviour feels off.

You feel isolated and withdrawn from friends.

You start to avoid discussing your relationship as you know your friends don't like him and have noticed a change in you.

You can't put your finger on it but blame yourself.

I became panicky because I couldn't find the 'right' kind of sausages. I knew he would accuse me of not caring about him saying "You're too busy and you can't do any simple thing I ask! Why is everything too much trouble for you? What kind of wife are you! Why would you want to wind me up?"

Incidents like this were happening more and more frequently and he had flung the sausages at me the last time and I didn't dare tell him they don't stock those ones anymore. I began to believe he was right. After all, what was more important than keeping my husband happy? Why wasn't I a better wife?

I began to blame myself for everything. If I was a better wife I could get the right sausages, the house would always be spotless, dinner would always be on the table no matter what time he came in.

Gradually over time I began to lose touch with reality and failed at that point to see anything else wrong with the relationship, besides that I was a terrible wife. It took a long time, and many counselling sessions for me to shift my thinking back to reality.

So how do you know if you are being gas lighted?

You are constantly doubting yourself and find decision making increasingly difficult, as you feel that whatever you choose will be the wrong choice. Everything you do or say is wrong, so you feel that you are no longer capable of making rational decisions about anything, so you will leave even simple decisions up to your abuser giving them all the power and control.

You ask yourself, "Am I too sensitive?" several times a day.

You often feel in a state of bewilderment and confusion finding it increasingly difficult to trust your own mind, and constantly doubting your thought process.

If you have a moment of clarity you are very quickly told that it is wrong reinforcing the belief.

You're always apologizing to everyone for doing things wrong, even if you have done nothing wrong.

Feeling sorry for everything means that the accountability and responsibility for everything that is wrong lies with the victim. This ensures the perpetrator remains innocent.

You can't put your finger on it but you are constantly unhappy.

You find yourself apologising and making excuses and rationalising your partners behaviour saying "If only you knew them like me, you just have to get to know them."

You find yourself censoring information from friends and family so you don't have to constantly explain or make excuses for their behaviour.

You become withdrawn and often reclusive as you feel so low and beaten down that you have little confidence left to socialise with anyone.

You will feel safer spending time alone than with other people, as when those around them question what is wrong, or what is happening within their relationship, you will not have the answers to justify what is going on.

The abuser at this stage has won the battle for control, as without anyone to confide in you will find it very difficult to work out that it is the abuser that is causing the damage.

The abuser will not want anyone to figure out their game plan so, they will work hard to make sure that you become isolated from anyone who could offer support and the real truth.

You become indecisive and find yourself looking for approval for the simplest things like what you should eat or where you should go for the evening.

You have the sense that you used to be a very different person, much more confident, more relaxed and more fun.

You feel hopeless and joyless and worthless.

You continuously wonder if you are a 'good enough' person and this affects you at work as well as at home.

You begin to doubt your ability and struggle with simple tasks like answering the phone or dealing with colleagues.

The main reasons we may not recognise this insidious mind game is that we live in denial not wanting to believe those we trust and love are capable of manipulating us and that they have our best interests at heart.

Triangulation

Triangulation is another manipulative string in the narcs bow. They create a situation where one family member won't communicate with another so uses a third party to convey information. This indirect communication serves the narc well as they can fabricate and twist the truth to suit themselves. This is used alongside gas- lighting to change the victims reality.

Dramas are created with the narc at the centre controlling the conversation lighting the touch paper then standing back to watch the inferno loudly exclaiming that they hate drama.

The narc controls the information between the parties and tries to prevent them directly comparing stories so they can add ,fabricate and twist the information to use to their advantage.

Narcs enjoy pitting people against each other and love the power trip it gives them as they emotionally feed from it.

Why Does Your Narc Want To Pit People Against One Another?

For anyone who doesn't fully understand 'Triangulation' and why your Narc wants to set everyone apart to hate each other It's a case of divide and conquer. It's easier to gain control of someone if they lose all their allies.

As you look back on your relationship and talk to people who didn't dare tell you the truth while you were in it, you will see this clearly. You may have disliked people who you now realise are good people. You may have liked people who you now know were just like them. Once your Narc radar is up and running you will see things clearly.

It is not normal or healthy for a person to enjoy chaos and destroy relationships.

The Nex made me believe he was Gods gift and every woman he knew wanted a piece of him. He still saw all his exes socially and I believed they still fancied him. It was only after I left him these women spoke to me or it came up in conversation that they really felt uncomfortable around him.

Some of my good friends came back and told me this too. It's shocking how they do this and you see it so differently once you are away from them.

The Nex did this to the new OW telling her I'm still obsessed with him when I had gone 'no contact' for years but he was actively stalking me. It's truly crazy making!

Triangulating Other Supply

The abuser will triangulate other women and deliberately create distrust in the relationship to make the victim feel they either cheating, or considering cheating. They may mention another woman like my Nex constantly did in passing, "I saw my ex today wow she looked amazing." They do this to make the victim feel off balance thinking "Will they cheat?" throughout the relationship. They do this to make their victim feel insecure and jealous then they will say the victim is paranoid and has trust issues. When they are continuously gas lighted like this it changes their self perception and they begin to feel they really do have trust issues and are paranoid.

The victim will be accused of over reacting and being too sensitive the abuser will laugh at or sneer at the victim, but when called out on it will say "I didn't mean it like that, really you are paranoid! Why can't you just trust me?"

Sex As A Weapon

Narcs do not enjoy intimacy in a relationship. The partner is merely exploited to fulfil the narcissist's selfish needs. They lure you in with lots of sex and intimacy because they want to hook you, so it's all love bombing dates, fancy gifts and future faking where they paint a rosy picture of your future together. After a while and during the 'devalue' stage things change.

Sex is used as a weapon and just another way to control the target. Withdrawing sex and affection and giving the 'silent' treatment are common tactics as is triangulating other partners keeping you feeling 'off balance' and never secure so we keep on supplying them and jumping through new hoops.

Narcs and Intimacy

Intimacy confuses the hell out of anyone in a relationship with a Narc.
Sex for a narc isn't about intimacy it is about feeding their ego and control. You will most probably find that those moments of great sex looking back were ego boosts and they may well have actually told you that too bragging. "See how good I am? See how lucky you are to have me?"
They also use sex as a weapon as either a feast to reel you in or a famine to control you.
They like you to beg for cuddles since they do not need or enjoy this normal physical intimate contact.

Kisses start slow and sweet then over time you have to beg for those too. Sex is just an act to them and a way to get their primal needs met.

Once you leave the relationship you look back and realise it never was the intimate eye contact vulnerable moment you perceived it to be that is a two way street in a normal mentally healthy relationship.
With a narc it's just another power struggle and another manipulative string in their bow.

Think back to a day when you went out with your Nex and they upset you or became aggressive tainting the day with their nasty outburst.
Is upsetting and scaring you and ruining the day going to make you feel like you want to be physically close to them?
No, when we feel abused and bullied we feel anything but sexy and would want to avoid intimacy at all costs.
So why is it after a short period of time has elapsed after they have verbally or physically abused you do they suggest "Lets go to bed."
Is it because they feel guilty about the way they treated you and want to make amends?
No, they don't feel any remorse for the way they just treated you. They do however need some reassurance that you accept the previous abusive behaviour and they still have access to you and your body.
They also get a sadistic high out of the abuse they just inflicted on you making them feel sexy.

So what if you refuse?

No doubt if you flinch as they touch you they will say,
"You're not still carrying that on are you?" or project onto you so you have to defend yourself saying,
"You're cheating on me aren't you?" as that must be the only reason in their mind that would prevent you wanting to be intimate with them.
Then they will repeat past conversations using 'word salad' and gas lighting to confuse you blaming you for previous events and then silent treatment if you don't give in to their sexual needs.
To avoid this you go willingly upstairs to avoid further abuse or violent behaviour.
This tells your abuser their previous abusive behaviour was acceptable.

158

Sex then becomes just another way to exert power and control and just another form of abuse.

Stonewalling When The Victim Is Non-Compliant

The silent treatment is another emotionally abusive way a Narc controls you. The narc simply does not respond to you when he or she is not compliant with your wishes.
This puts the abuser in a place of control and punishes you for not complying or behaving how the narc wants them to.
The narc now has you jumping through hoops to please them just to stop the deafening silence.

The victim will continuously reach out to the abuser via email, phone, or text to resolve the misunderstandings and conflict.
Any attempt is typically met with continued contempt, and silence to ensure the victim understands the extreme disapproval from them so they learn that they must not behave like that in the future.
Survivors of abuse frequently complain of the lack of validation they feel when being stone walled in this way and that they began to feel non existent in the eyes of the narc partner.

The Nex shut me down verbally so I no longer had a voice. He would shout and scream and swear and call me vile names but if I so much as raised my voice back even saying "Stop shouting, Calm down!" his posture would change. His eyes would glaze and he would grit his teeth and take on a fighters stance. "Who do you think you're talking to!" he would spit at me through gritted teeth. Then he would become extremely aggressive and push or shove me into a corner.
After a violent episode he would say "How dare you shout at me? Why would you wind me up?" To which I would mutter "You were screaming at me!" His response? "Yes but you're better than that! Do as I say, not as I do!"

This kind of aggressive behaviour shut me down over a period of years to the point where I would stand there frozen and just let him rant at me shouting "Look at me you f**king bitch when I'm talking to you." If I tried to walk away he would physically stop me as I said "I don't want to do this, I don't want to fall out with you!" He would grit his teeth and clench his fists and threaten me "If you walk away from me I will throw you through the f**king window!" I would apologise just to feel safe, and often I would dissolve into tears saying, "Look I'm sorry can we just forget it!"

He would smirk at me and say "Look at you you're f**king pathetic!"

As a result of this since I left him it's taken a long time to find my voice, accept anger as a useful emotion and raise my voice. It's only through counselling I have learned that anger is healthy and normal in a mentally healthy relationship. It's okay to say "Hey I'm unhappy about this!" It's ok to protect your boundaries by raising your voice as in a normal relationship it does not lead to an aggressive fearful situation.

Future Faking To Reel us Back in

One very powerful way how the Narc keeps us hooked when we try to break free is 'Future Faking' During the early intimate love bombing stage when we bared our soul and swapped intimate stories with the one we thought was our soul mate, had our back and would never hurt us because they loved us, we revealed the future triggers they are now using to keep you exactly where they want us.

They know exactly what you've yearned to hear the entire relationship. "Give me another chance, I will buy you a ring!" they plead.

"We will go on holiday just you and me" the Nex would promise. It's hard to be strong and see through this bullshit as it's music to our ears. We think "They really do love me!" and fall straight back into their trap! So when we're tired of 'giving it another go' and going back to more of the same escalating abuse we have to let go of the future we think we could have had with them.

This was another illusion created only to secure Narc supply and ensure it was plentiful until they find another victim.

Keeping You in A Box

Narcs destroy our social networks and isolate us so post narc it is important to re connect with like minded people we can talk to and laugh with.

"Post narc recovery and getting out that box the Nex put you in is difficult. Who am I? You ask yourself as you step outside into the sunlight. It's time to find your voice and stop editing who you are. Stop apologising and be wonderful you!"

## How Do They Create A Cage?

"So you got me where you wanted me. After all the accusations that I cheated and was cheating I stopped accepting invitations from friends. It was easier that way than to deal with your wrath or you physically grabbing me and pinning me up against the wall asking who had I been with.

Well meaning friends asked if everything was ok and persuaded me to go out just for coffee but I always had excuses. I was always too busy or too tired. I had to pick the children up or had to work or I simply couldn't afford it. Meanwhile you lived the life of a single man, going out when you pleased and coming in when you pleased.

I remember the last time when I dared to ask where you had been till 3am and you threw me in the corner of the bedroom and spat in my face. "Don't you ever ask where I've been, you're not my mother! I go where I want."

The following day you took me out for lunch as if the whole night was a figment of my imagination but I never asked you again.

I became reclusive and stopped going to the gym. The girls at work asked me if I wanted to go camping and I told them I couldn't. They asked me to birthdays and leaving do's but I never went.

Bubbly me disappeared and I even became scared of answering the phone and began to doubt all my abilities at home and work because of your constant criticism. You began to ask me if I wanted to go out like you were trying to persuade me, like you were my friend. Yet you knew I would say "No I'm tired."

Friends from the past tell me now they invited us out and you told them I was quiet and liked to stay in the house. Male friends from the past told me you threatened them if they spoke to me.

You created a cage for me so I was just available for you."

## Putting Our Needs On Hold To Provide Narc Supply

In the confines of an abusive relationship we are conditioned to put our life on hold and our needs last. They don't care if we are tired hungry cold or poorly. You will have noticed their lack of compassion or empathy and the fact that they can't see things from your point of view. All they care about is you meeting their needs and fulfilling their narcissistic supply. They may be quite charming when they want something and you mistake this for 'love.' This is a toxic one sided love. As we leave this relationship it's hard to fathom not only who we are anymore but what we need to feel better. So I want you to think about right now what do you need to feel better?

Nothing You Do Will Be Good Enough

"Narcs diminish our achievements to build themselves up. They only compliment our achievements if they can somehow bask in our glory and turn the compliment on themselves."

Nothing you do for them will be good enough. This is the nature of abusers. This is not because you are lazy or worthless this is because they want to keep you in a permanent state of gratefulness so you keep serving them. This is not a loving relationship where they care for you but one where they want to tear you down and destroy your confidence and self esteem.
This pathology will get easier to grasp as we go along. Just remember this isn't about you. The narcissist is all those labels they are projecting onto you. So if they call you lazy and worthless they are looking at a mirror of themselves as inwardly they despise themselves. In a loving relationship a partner who truly loves you will support you and empower you to grow as a person.

"For anyone unlucky enough to be dealing with a narc right now let go of what and who you can't control. The only thing we can control are our reactions to the bullshit and no reaction is the right response. Take back your power and ignore them. Don't defend yourself with words defend yourself by virtuous living and slowly people will see that you stepped away from the drama and they are still in the thick of it."

Are They Capable Of Change?

For those of you who think your Nex sailed off into the sunset with their new love. Narcs don't change. They simply hide their true selves a while and love bomb their new victim to draw them in and secure Narc supply.

Under the mask they're still the same flashing red ten Narc they were with you.

Trust me on this one they will find out soon. Be glad you left their abuse.

So according to social media they have moved on and appear to have sailed off into the sunset with their new beloved serenaded by a string quartet of harps.

How do you feel? Have they changed? Have they miraculously with his or her love changed into a loving caring new partner? Excuse me while I stifle a giggle, no they have not changed. No he or she isn't lucky or happy and enjoying the rewards of all your hard work teaching them to manage their anger and teaching them how to be sociable and accountable for their mistakes.

She or he is simply being 'Love bombed' to secure Narc supply and fed the same tired lies they fed you at the start including that they had a bad childhood and a string of crazy exes and you are the worst.

Wait, hold the harps, and keep watching. Soon you will hear the karma truck is rolling in the distance as anytime now that mask will slip and she or he will see what you saw. The anger the chaos the lies and their knight in shining armour is about to reveal themselves as a 'true tyrant in tinfoil.'

See how you dodged a bullet now?

How Can They Get Married So Fast After We Broke Up?

Narcs groom their prey before discarding the last. This is to ensure an uninterrupted narc supply. The new victim is being love bombed and lied to right now and they're marrying fast before their true psychopathy comes out to play.

I know it hurts right now but remember your own wedding and the love bombing turning to devalue? It's ok to feel alone and broken that's why we are here. You need lots of time and learning to love yourself before you even consider letting anyone close again. It's ok to be afraid you were violated and duped in the worst possible way.

You escaped and now must heal your heart body and soul.

In moments of weakness when we forget what the Narc did to us and we begin to look at their next relationship through rose tinted specs believing the fake happy family pictures that are being paraded on social networking sites.

Feeling things like he never bought me flowers, or he never took me away on holiday.

I want you to take a pen and a piece of paper and write the words 'behind closed doors they...' and then scribble every single vile thing you can remember they did to you while the world was not watching.

Once you've done that look through all these posts and remind yourself they're incapable of change.

They are still the same flashing red ten toxic Narc you remember. Just because we can't see this now don't ever forget that!

Narcs are so obsessed with image they endeavour to 'edit' or 'delete' reality to fit in with the image they want people to see, their false persona. On social networking sites they show a new house or car depicting a life of luxury when really they're deep in debt, or they show a picture of themselves and their latest conquest when things are very rocky or they're cheating, or they put up pictures of their children when they fall out with them.

Scratch beneath the surface and all is not what it seems.

How Narcs Condition You To Meet Their Needs

Think about the way the Narc conditioned you to meet their needs and ignore your own and constantly remind you that you were not important. Was their time always more important than yours? Did they constantly let you down? Did they call you fat lazy and useless despite the fact you worked really hard?

Every time I sat down the Nex called me lazy. If there were a few plates left by the sink he would storm in and scream "Look at this shit hole." If we heard his car me and the children would jump up. Chloe would start arranging cushions in the front room and Matty would run to his bedroom and I would run in the kitchen and be busy even though the place was tidy and dinner was on.

As a result post Narc it was really hard to sit down to let Joe cook me a meal without asking him "What do you want me to do?" He would steer me back to the sofa and say "Nothing I want you to sit down!" bringing me a glass of wine.

Three years on I take positive delight in leaving a few plates by the sink in a spotless kitchen. It's my snub to the Nex. I take delight in walking around in my pyjamas and not getting dressed without being called lazy and I don't miss the sound of his diesel engine and the feeling of panic and my heart in my mouth as he stepped through the door.

Jumping Through Hoops To Provide Narc Supply

I have countless stories of the Nex birthday, Christmas and Easter where I jumped through hoops cooking favourite foods and buying well thought out gifts. Planning things months in advance and paying for special treats. He was never grateful and they were never right even if he had asked for them. He wasn't ever happy or grateful for anything. I remember saying to my therapist "I just wanted him to say thanks! I just wanted some approval." I have since learned you cannot, I repeat cannot ever get a thanks or approval from a Narc.

Why?.

They will keep moving the goalposts so you keep jumping through more hoops and therefore providing their ever demanding narc supply.
The Ways Narcs Sabotage Your Life

Did you feel that your Nex time was always more important than your time? Were they always late for every appointment? Did they lie about how long they would be? Did they lie to others on the phone about where they were when they were with you? Did their lies just trip off their tongue when they spoke to your family and friends? Did they say "I won't be long I'm just round the corner," when they were miles away?
Did they frequently sabotage your plans because you had to stop and do something important for them? Deliberately stopping you from working or going out?
The Nex used to wait till I was just going out the door to deliver important parcels for my business and run downstairs and demand that I must write an invoice out for him right now! If I refused he would say "I ask you to do one thing! You are my wife!"

He would wait as I loaded the washer after the children came home from school and demand I take it all out and wash his work clothes first.

He would be late for every important event in mine and the children's life to the point where I would lie about the time just to get him there on time! So a three o clock parents evening became two o clock.

Despite the fact I paid for and ran two vehicles I stopped asking for lifts relying on my legs or taxis as he could never get me anywhere on time. He claimed always that he was busy but I see now that he actually didn't care.

If it wasn't important to him he didn't care about anyone else's life or commitments. Not even his own children. We didn't matter to him and it took me a long time after I left him to realise that I did matter and my time was as important and sometimes more important than everyone else's time.

Addiction and Compulsive Behaviour

Narcissists cannot face the shame of their true self and low self worth so they develop their false entitled self persona ( the mask) with addictive and compulsive behaviour. Sex, alcohol, food, porn, drugs ,gambling and especially money.

Narcissists are often compulsive shoppers (with their targets cash). Unlike a mentally healthy person with bills and a mortgage to pay they have no 'off switch' and do not care about consequences of their impulsive behaviour. They will empty your bank account the day before the mortgage is due and they do not think or care about the consequences.

They will specifically befriend the wealthy to get their needs met. The Nex told me very early on, he had many wealthy friends and would brag about them to me and his get rich quick schemes that failed would then be blamed on me.

Their entitled self has to have the very best of everything from small items such as socks to larger status symbol items such as a car.

The 21 year old Nex changed his car every few months because he got bored and wanted an upgrade and he would spend huge amounts on speakers and radios even if we were struggling as a family financially.

Narcs are inherently envious of others with more than them so if you have a better phone or car they will despise you for that.

Of course this deep emptiness cannot ever be filled with material things

166

as they cannot feel like you or me and cannot derive pleasure from a simple sunset. The Nex would appreciate things like that better high or drunk.

So they continue throughout their empty lives to pursue anything that will give them a 'kick' or a 'high to make them feel something.

They have no impulse control and will con or steal anything that they feel they are entitled to without remorse or fear of the law. They feel they are above the law and because of this are huge risk takers driving too fast and stealing from others. Anything that they acquire through life ( usually from someone else's hard work or money) instantly becomes theirs and they will lock things away and hoard things like rats. Hell they even lock up their own children!

But nothing can ever fill that empty black soul so they continue to pursue these material things till the day they die.

## We Can Go Banging on About Narcs Till the Cows Come Home!

Once we have learned who they are and why they do what they do and that they can't be fixed by us or therapy and the only course of action is to escape from the Narcs in our life then we have to concentrate on 'us' and healing. Posts about evil Narcs then becomes detrimental to healing and keeps us 'stuck' in victim mode feeling helpless. Thriving post Narc is about learning to thrive and embrace our new life.

## Studying Narc Behaviour Then Becomes Empowering

"Knowledge is power. Installing new software in our brains as to how these creatures tick and how to deal with them is empowering and stops us feeling defenceless.

So read and research and Google away!"

The more you study their behaviour the more empowered you're going to feel and the more empowered you feel you're going to reach the stage where 'jerks' have no place in your life because you won't accept them. That's the point where everything changes. We can't stop self absorbed jerks or Narcs being themselves but we can change everything for ourselves.

We can change our reaction to their daily drama and chaos and cut off the Narc supply we once provided by going 'No Contact' Then we can go back out into this world with our renewed self confidence and faith in ourselves and fulfil our dreams. We can show everyone a true version of ourselves. The one the Narc wanted to keep in a box. Then together we can put the good the beautiful the kindness the joy and the peace back into our world.

If you feel alone right now feeling unsure and bewildered by everything. I want you to know that thousands of people have been where you are, some of us are just a little further down the healing road than you.
There's a beautiful peaceful happy place waiting for you when you take your life back.
Come take our hand and join us!

So Let's See How an Emotionally Toxic Environment Effects The Brain

Here's the science bit made simple.

Through Magnetic Resonance Imaging we can see that Post Traumatic Stress Disorder following recovery from an abusive situation results in atrophy of the hippocampus.
The hippocampus is involved with memory.
It is responsible for our verbal memory but also plays a very important role in the memory of context that is the time and place of events.
Memories associated with strong emotions such as fear and pain are highlighted and then cause triggers once out of the abusive situation.

This is what happens in Post Traumatic Stress Disorder (PTSD)

Those who've been in abusive relationships, like soldiers in combat often end up having brains that are hyper-vigilant as the brain constantly scans our environment for danger.
This is a natural survival instinct that over develops as the brain becomes responsive to things that it perceives are a threat that are not dangerous such as a totally dark room or a slamming door.
These non threatening situations then bypass the rational part of the brain triggering a fight or flight response where adrenaline is released.

Also the trauma of the verbal abuse and the other forms of abuse you were subjected to may also result in cognitive impairment or memory problems causing what many survivors look back on and refer to as 'brain fog.'

So trauma from abuse and PTSD damages the Hippocampus in the brain and slows down Neurogenesis ( just reading some of these words will get your brain cells dancing!)

PTSD After Narc Abuse

When you have been trapped in a situation over which you had little or no control at the beginning, middle or end, you can carry an intense sense of dread even after that situation is removed. This is because you know how bad things can possibly be and you know that it could possibly happen again and you know that if it ever does happen again, it might be worse than before.
People who suffer from PTSD may feel shaky, as if they are likely to have an embarrassing emotional breakdown or burst into tears at any moment. They may feel unloved or that nothing they can accomplish is ever going to be 'good enough' for others.

So What Can We Do To Reverse The Damage To The Hippocampus?

Okay so we've heard the gloom and doom bit about how being in an abusive situation damages the brain.
So how are we going to reverse the atrophy of the hippocampus and the decreased capacity for production of new neurons?

To reverse the damage to the brain, the atrophy of the hippocampus and the decreased capacity for production of new neurons, that's been caused by an abusive environment we need to keep learning new things, challenging ourselves, taking physical exercise and try as tough as it may be to look on the bright side of life!

After Narc abuse it's possible to  rebuild positive brain pathways to rewire the brain that was 'addicted' to the painful pain peptides. How do we do this? Little by little and by being kind to ourselves day by day. Scheduling something in to make us 'Soul Happy.'
Think about what makes your soul happy?

So We Can Think Ourselves Happy

Being focused on negative thoughts slows the brain down and stops it functioning effectively and at it's full capacity.
We cannot fire on all four cylinders.

Previously we touched on the feeling of 'brain fog' that survivors of abuse experience.
Survivors of abuse including myself report a feeling of losing their mind, their ability to remember simple things and feelings of depression caused by the 'brain fog' they are experiencing.
"When I left my toxic relationship I could not string a sentence together either on paper or verbally as effectively as I can now after three years out of that toxic brain fog."

From a survivor:

"I didn't realize at the time that I was living in an environment that was resulting in the death of neurons and, of course, ensuring that new ones weren't developed through the process of neurogenesis, either. Fortunately I did maintain enough cognitive functioning to realize that this was indeed a toxic environment in which to live and furthermore, things were probably going to continue to grow worse rather than better. I felt the environment was destroying my spirit and strangling my soul. I didn't know to be concerned about the well-being of my brain."

Suffice to say trying to think more positively and creating happy, hopeful, optimistic, and joyful thoughts counteract the negative state of the brain. This in turn decreases the stress hormone cortisol and produces the happy hormone serotonin, which creates a sense of well-being and a natural euphoria or high.
This over time helps your brain function at peak capacity.
Happy thoughts and positive thinking therefore speed up neurogenesis. Neurogenesis supports brain growth as well as the generation and reinforcement of new synapses especially in your prefrontal cortex (PFC), which serves as the integration centre of all of your brain-mind functions thus repairing the damage that being in an abusive environment has done.

So we must try to build a happy brain!

Laughter not only provides a workout for your muscles, it releases a rush of stress-busting endorphins. Your body can't distinguish between real and fake laughter either so any giggle will do. The elation you feel when you laugh is a great way of combating the physical effects of stress. When we laugh, our body relaxes and endorphins (natural painkillers) are released into the blood stream.

Therapy is recommended to dig deep and find and heal the cause of our inner wounds.

Do I need therapy and can I afford it?

I asked myself this question while I was in financial ruin after the Nex tried to destroy me, took my children, my dog and bullied me out my house.
While dealing with solicitors and police due to his stalking me and when I retaliated with the police he used this to further alienate the children.
He told my children "That bitch is crazy kids!"

I said to myself I will just go for the first 8 free sessions.
I spent the first one trying to convince the therapist I was wasting her time and surely she should be helping others who have really been battered and bruised. I spent the next four crying and developing a really close relationship with my therapist who was now my friend. The next three realising that it wasn't me and finally beginning to learn to think of 'Me' in this mess instead of saying "Yes but he had a really rotten childhood!"
I began to feel lifted and happier in session 8.
I knew I had to continue the sessions and began to consider therapy the way I bought a new dress to 'cheer myself up' So I stopped buying things to cheer myself up and bought myself a new therapy dress every week. It worked much better than shopping!
So I tell you this therapy is like buying a new dress. One that you pull over your head that instantly gives you confidence, makes you feel loved and you cannot buy that in the shops! How can you not afford to change your life?
Therapy is life changing as I wear my new dress all the time!
Being in therapy is a very brave step and it will uncover a lot of pent up emotion you've had bottled up! It sounds an old cliché but with time and working through these feelings it will get better! But expect to be on an

exhausting roller coaster for a while. A roller coaster of anger guilt and pain.

Please remember you aren't crazy and have been conditioned to think it's all you.

## Counsellors Are Not One Size Fits All

If you find you and your counsellor do not hit it off or cannot build a relationship or isn't empathetic to your situation, Or God forbid doesn't even understand the abuse process then it is your right to say "I'm sorry I would like to see someone else." Shop around till you find one that fits. You need to find that person who you can develop a therapeutic relationship with. A friend to have coffee with.

Otherwise how are you going to bare your soul? Keep searching till you find the one that 'fits' for you.

I struck gold when I met mine and she changed my life. Please find the one that changes yours.

## This is An important Message For Healers

So you're starting to understand and feel better and are chatting with others who are just starting out and you want so badly to help them through this.

When we've been through abuse if we listen to and help others when we aren't fully healed we 'trigger' ourselves and relive our own abuse. I'm sufficiently out now not to re abuse myself and if I get upset or overwhelmed I take a break. so to all of you who are a few steps behind me and not fully healed step away from other people's pain when you find it too much.

You are re abusing and triggering your abuse. You are damaging your own healing as I did. You cannot help people when you feel stressed and struggling.

Go do something that makes your soul happy to fill yourself back up. When you feel your reserves are topped up then you will feel less hopeless and can help others again. It is one of the hardest things to learn in life that we cannot fix people including family members who live in denial, we can only be there to support love and guide them as they get their own 'light bulb moment' remember YOU are Important and cannot heal others from a broken place.

Your Doctor or therapist may recommend:

CBT therapy

"Cognitive behavioural therapy (CBT) is a talking therapy that can help you manage your problems by changing the way you think and behave. This therapy identifies the self-talk that causes our false beliefs about who is responsible for the abuse. The first step in this process is to think of specific abusive incidents and the comments made by the abusing partner and then to think of some of the negative things you may have said to blame yourself for the abuse.
The next step is to reflect on how your feelings and emotions that made you think that way.

EMDR

Eye Movement Desentitizisation and Reprocessing Therapy is an increasingly popular choice for abuse victims.

This is an account of an abuse survivor, Jennifer, talking through EMDR therapy after her first few sessions.

"It works. What you will do is talk about something that is upsetting. You will then give it a number from 0-10. 10 being you want to kill yourself. Then you will shut your eyes and do your breathing exercise as the small electrodes simultaneously stimulate your hands or you watch the fingers of your therapist go from side to side.
What happens here is your brain is reprocessing this traumatic event and desensitizing you at the same time. You will naturally let the traumatic event play out until another image, usually calming, enters your vision. You then give another number. It can be high or low. You work it out until you are calmer. But first, you have to create a safe place to go a few times a day. That's so if you are having a really bad time in therapy you can train your brain to quickly go there and calm you down. You will also do your breathing exercises here as well."

Chrysalis To Butterfly Healing Blogs

As I began healing I thought of myself as a caterpillar gathering knowledge and working towards a transition of huge changes towards a fully fledged butterfly.

I want you to think about how far you've come?
Are you a caterpillar just starting out gathering knowledge but still in a state of shock? Doubting yourself! Are you a chrysalis? You're in the process of change? You're absorbing all the information and working through the cognitive dissonance where you are beginning to see that this wasn't your fault. Are you stuck in that chrysalis waiting to emerge from your comfy cocoon? What can you do to ease your way out? Do you feel ready to emerge? Are you dying to just get out in the sunshine and dry your wings and fly? Where are you today?

Feeling Broken

Do you feel too broken and that you will never get through this or recover from this? The very fact you wound up here shows you have a huge strength and determination to understand what has happened to you and to help you move forwards with your life. Recovery is especially challenging if you have both parents with NPD or a sibling and then gone on to marry an NPD partner or partners.
If you have tried a therapist and it's going nowhere but you see your bank balance going down change your therapist.

You can also learn so much about how to cope and heal by reading and talking to survivors. You may benefit from less therapy once you have dug into the past to find out why you are a 'Narc magnet'. Then you can work on that in your daily life.
A huge part of recovery is rebuilding your self confidence by pushing yourself and stepping out of your comfort zone a little everyday.
I tell everyone to 'Fake it till you make it.'
Work on being less critical of yourself  and gradually over time change your internal dialogue of the way you look at yourself and the over critical way you have been conditioned to judge yourself.
It takes time and patience and it takes giving yourself a break and beating yourself with a smaller stick.

You will get there and you've got the rest of your life to get it right.

For Anyone Doubting You Can Heal

With the right help and support you can and you will.
It's a process and it takes time. In time you will beat yourself with a smaller stick, in time beautiful people who care about you will come into your life.
Once the darkness and evil has left it amazing people and opportunities will be attracted to you and you will begin to live the life you were supposed to live.
One of love and abundance.
So wherever you are on your healing journey today I promise with my hand on my heart it will get better.

I Just Want Closure

Don't expect to get any closure from a Narc.
Someone who never takes responsibility for their own actions and always blames others for their problems. This is never going to happen.
If you want any kind of closure you will find it through your own healing, through education, through loving yourself, and through your own personal growth.
This is what enables us to move on and say "I deserve better."

Why Do I accept Abuse?

Many of us believe that it was bad luck to become involved with a narcissist. This is simply not true and it was in fact a big wake up call that one day in the not so distant future you will understand. Narcissists feed off our inner wounds. If we grew up with conditional love based on our performance from critical parents and we never felt we measured up or we went through school being bullied and ridiculed as a child by friends or siblings for being too fat or too skinny or just different, then we will carry these wounds.

When we become involved with a narcissist we are carrying those inner core beliefs that we are worthless or not enough so we feel extremely significant and valued in the idealisation period. The love bombing phase makes us feel loved like never before so once the Narc begins to devalue us we cling to that love and acceptance. We accept the drips of love they give us as all we are worth, as we carry the deep childhood wounds of not being important and fear abandonment.

Many of us were also brought up by a mother who stayed at home and was looked after financially by a man so we grow up with the belief that a man should provide. This reinforces our feeling that we need a man to feel whole and to survive. Once we dig deep into ourselves and consciously recognise these wounds we can move forwards and work on our low self esteem, lack of confidence and our deep fear of abandonment and become whole on our own.

How We Measure Our Self Worth in an Abusive Relationship

We feel so special when they are pleasant showing that our levels of self worth are in our boots. This shows that our view of ourselves is directly related to how the Narc feels and treats us at the time. ( they have negatively conditioned us to believe that we are to blame for everything) So when the Narc is nice ( the mask) we feel so good, we feel loved and get a euphoric high. ( due to our addiction to them) and we try constantly to up our game to gain approval from them to feel this high.
We want a simple "thanks" or a "well done." "We want to be appreciated for the hoops we are jumping through because we love them but when the narc is nasty or cruel ( their true self) we feel wretched and unworthy as it triggers all our childhood feelings of abandonment and feeling unloved. It is only by changing the way we feel internally and our inner self worth and confidence that when the narc is nasty that we do not internalise their criticism and blame but instead realistically see that they own their own behaviour and it is not created by us or anything we did or did not do. This is the breakthrough we need to change and escape the abuse.

How Did I Become Narc Food?

You are a kind loving person and selfless in a relationship? In fact perfect Narc food. They love us empaths to feed on. You haven't done anything wrong, there is nothing wrong with you. You just attracted a mentally unhealthy partner that manipulated and used you because they could.

You deserve love and a healthy relationship but you have to believe that yourself inside.

So you are broken and need fixing.

How do you do that? You learn to love yourself and work on your self esteem issues and lack of confidence and fear of abandonment. The very childhood wounds that the Narcs feed on. When you feel whole and worthy you will not entertain toxic people.

Co Dependency

It is highly likely that you are Co-dependant. This is excessive emotional or psychological reliance on a partner, typically one with an illness or addiction who requires support.

Co-dependency is a learned behaviour that can be passed down from one generation to another. It is an emotional and behavioural condition that affects an individual's ability to have a healthy, mutually satisfying relationship. It is also known as 'relationship addiction' because people with co dependency often form or maintain relationships that are one sided, emotionally destructive and abusive.

The disorder was first identified about ten years ago as the result of years of studying interpersonal relationships in families of alcoholics.

Co-dependent behaviour is learned by watching and imitating other family members who display this type of behaviour.

"Until we are at peace and heal our childhood wounds of not being enough and fear of abandonment the patterns that kept hurting us will repeat themselves in all our relationships."

Your heart is torn in two.

Why Did we let someone so evil so close?

Someone who professed to love us so much.

Why did we not see it coming?

What do we mean when we say, you just need to work on your inner wounds? Narcissists feed off our wounds. A bit like having a psychological scab from childhood and after the love bombing phase is over they take this scab and pick pick pick away at it. Your insecurities your lack of confidence and any defects you shared with them in the process of sharing your inner thoughts with them during the love bombing phase. You may have revealed that you hate your teeth, or you were a fat child and were bullied. Whatever it is they will find out and use it against you in the devalue stage.

Years of being conditioned in our childhood that we are not good enough, not smart enough or not pretty enough led us into the arms of a narcissist who then picked at the inadequacies we already felt we had.

Narcs sniff out insecurities like a vampire seeks human blood. Conditioning us to believe these things like they were set in stone, so hearing positives about yourself without cringing, being uncomfortable or feeling vain is to be expected.

It takes time to destroy someone's worth and credibility so they stop believing in themselves.

.

Constantly reminding you of your flaws or insecurities never allows that psychological scab to heal.

Dealing with your insecurities and lack of confidence and any perceived flaws you have means you are water tight against another disordered soul. If you are happy inside about yourself and you show yourself love then there is nothing for another Narc to pick at.

Counselling addresses these issues and you will reach the stage where you feel whole and good enough. You will not entertain abuse and bad treatment because you not only accept yourself,
Sisters and brothers, you actually like the person you have become!

Please be kind to yourself if you are embarking on this journey it takes time to heal recover and get the lifestyle and career you want post narc. Do the inner work on yourselves, eat well, catch up on sleep, learn relaxation techniques and please be gentle with yourself.

I developed these exercises within my abuse recovery group to help survivors.

The Narc Accountability F**k It Bucket Exercise!

Once we begin to start thinking positively about ourselves again it's time to begin purging ourselves of the Narcs poisonous lies and this is when the 'Narc Accountability F**k it Bucket' is a useful exercise.

You can either do this virtually on the pc as we use in my group and have a virtual rubbish truck empty it at the end of the day. Or far more effectively you can get a real bucket write the words 'Narc Accountability F**k it Bucket' on the side and scribble the lies on paper and toss them into the bucket!

You're going to purge yourself of those nasty lies all the Narcs have told us repeatedly about ourselves. You know the ones you deeply believed or still believe about yourself?

You are going to chuck their poisonous words in the bucket and say aloud the name of the abusive person that said them which will make your Narcs accountable and give you some closure.

Who Am I?

Confidence Builder Exercises

So running alongside the Narc F**k it Bucket exercise we are now going to get the truth out there. If a Narc says you are awful at something you can bet your bottom dollar that you are pretty amazing at that particular thing! When we have a go at thinking positively about ourselves and thinking about the qualities we know we have we begin to realise that they're the ones the Narc was envious of in fact. It will take time and work to change your 'inner critic.'

Practice saying . I'm a good person, I'm beautiful,. I'm clever without cringing.

So now you can find a beautiful box and decorate it how you like and write down your qualities on little coloured notes fold them and put them in your box so you can keep them and refer back to them when you are feeling bad about yourself. This exercise is a toughie if you're just starting out but have a go. Here is your chance to shine and remind yourself who you really are.

Reversing Negativity Exercise

We are used to hearing negative derogatory comments about ourselves. Such as "You are fat, lazy, useless, ugly or old ,No one will want you! You are lucky I put up with you!".
So we are going to redress the balance here. By listing five or more things you are learning or have learned to love about yourself since leaving the narcissist.
Come back to this exercise as you heal.

Pour Love Into Yourself.

We have been negatively conditioned to put ourselves last.
We have to try to pour all that love into ourselves to heal.
You will feel very uneasy and undeserving at first, but as you practice doing nice things for yourself you will cringe less and smile more.
Tell yourself you are worth it.
Other people will treat you how you treat yourself.
So teach them well that you are a prize!

To reverse the negativity after living under King or Queen Narc in Narcdom when everything we did was wrong! We all think negatively sometimes. Especially when we are in that 'pit of shit' post Narc.
Okay this one's about simply changing our mindset. so every time you think a negative thought push it away and say a positive one out loud. So "I'm so fat" becomes "I'm so curvy and womanly!"
"I feel stupid I'll never get that job" becomes "if I study and try hard I'm going to get that job! Watch me!"

Are You Grateful?

Can you pinpoint the exact moment in your life you became grateful?
Grateful for scraps while everyone else had a full plate.
Dig deep into your past.
Why as an adult did you give yourself leftovers, the chipped cup and the burnt pork chop?
Why did you put yourself last?
Who made you feel 'less than'?
Who made you feel unworthy?

We must identify and heal these inner wounds to become whole.
Do You Say You Shouldn't Have?

When a friend does you a favour or helps you out or buys you something do you cringe with embarrassment and flounder around looking for something nice to do back in return?

Let us look at why decent genuine people do nice things for us in return for the things we have done for them in the past.

These are the people our toxic Nex repelled. The friends who know our worth and appreciate the things we have done for them. They see we need a favour or help and step in as we would.

When we leave a toxic relationship we are negatively conditioned not to know our worth and to think we are less than everyone else.

Practice accepting compliments and favours with gratitude without putting yourself down.

Learn your worth as others learn your worth by watching how you treat yourself.

The further away from the Nex you get the more beautiful people who see your worth can reach you now.

They 'see' who you truly are before you will see yourself.

Are You Grateful For a Sandwich?

I wrote this while reflecting back on my toxic relationship.

So how do you become grateful that he brings you a sandwich? I mean a lot of thought went into it. He had ordered exactly the filling I wanted and hand delivered it to me so he must love me right?

After many years of being let down.

Home late for dinner and never called.

Stayed out all night and never called.

Said I'll take you out but something came up.

Never turned up for his daughters birthday.

Forgot mine and spent all day hunting for my perfect present to come home with a cheap handbag.

Refused to get up on Christmas Day because he hates it so letting the in-laws down.

Had to be begged to get the Christmas tree out of the attic when I had a bad back.

Promised to help pay some bills and then wriggled out of it or worse, paid some money then took it back because he said "you taking my money ruins my business."

Refusing to help his son learn how to ride a bike. Instead throwing it at him and saying "if you don't learn this then I will take your X-box away. "

Saying he will cook tonight if I peel some spuds and nip to the shop. Then as it's cooking asking me to watch it as he has a phone call to make.

Shouting at me "well sort it you're a bloody nurse" and accusing me of seeking attention when I found a lump in my breast and was scared.

Calling me "lazy" when I had sciatica and couldn't hoover but refusing to do it himself.

There are so many more reasons but that's how I became grateful for a sandwich.

Isn't This What I Deserve?

I can understand how you feel when you accept your life as it is following years of abuse. I used to go round muttering the same. "This is it! this is my lot I'm meant to be unhappy and alone!" No! We all deserve happiness but if we subconsciously believe that we deserve a life of pain and misery then we will attract that ( as I did) and continue to live that. The day we take control of our own life and say "no I deserve more, I do not deserve abuse" is the day things change. Now you might need help and support getting there with a counsellor but you must work on the inside changing your unworthy perception of yourself. Work on your inner wounds to become whole then you will attract beautiful loving people into your life! Hand on heart, It's a game changer I promise you.

Are You A People Pleaser?

If you are an empath and grew up in a people pleaser role it is easier to give others advice, take care of others needs, empathise with them when they're down and bereft. This is what we are used to and it's one hell of a skill to develop caring about yourself the same way. When you are feeling low you are so hard on yourself. You are your worst critic. The moment you start being gentle and loving yourself the way you care about others is the moment true healing can begin. Ask yourself "if this was my friend what would I do for them right now to make them feel better?" Then do that for yourself.

Feels wrong? Feels indulgent? Of course it does the Narcs in your life conditioned you to feel that way so you provide the best Narc supply by putting your needs on hold. Keep loving yourself this way and it gets easier.

What Do We Know About Boundaries?

Were you a people pleaser in your relationship with King or Queen Narc? Of course you were. They tore down and trampled all of your boundaries. You were there to please them under the guise they cared about you. They didn't care if you were tired or poorly or upset.

You may have tried at first to reinforce and lay down your boundaries but this was met by Narc rage or the silent treatment or emotional blackmail and tactics to get you to change your behaviour.

The Nex would scream at me. "You never do anything for me! I ask you to do one little thing! You are my wife!" I always knew that I was being slowly trampled down and I should have had stronger boundaries but when the crunch came to the crunch I would never implement them because of his predicted bullying behaviour.

Once you've had a brush with a Narc and looked at those boundaries it has a knock on effect of making you look at all your relationships and their boundaries. "No" becomes easier to say without guilt. You learn that you can be assertive and say actually "I'm sorry I can't I'm busy!" Without giving excuses and without guilt! It is a huge leap in healing and becoming an assertive person.

This is learning to love yourself and put yourself first sometimes and is another step towards FREEDOM!

The biggest lesson is people treat us as we treat ourselves, so if you put yourself last others will too. In fact not only that they will use abuse and wipe their feet on you.

Loving yourself is about caring enough for yourself to show others your boundaries and how we expect to be treated.

Once those boundaries are in place for good you will walk away from disrespect and people that hurt you.

Re-Defining Our Boundaries

We are redefining our worth and creating new boundaries
We are saying "No it's not okay."
We are walking away from toxic partners because we deserve better.
For those of you who have recently left King or Queen Narc do not risk
being hoovered back in because of rose tinted specs of good times.
Pick up a pen and write down every little thing he or she did to you.
Do not minimise the emotional abuse.
Top of the page It is not okay that they ignored me for several hours.
It is not okay that they swore at me.
It is not okay that they pushed me.
It is not okay that they hit me.
When you are done keep it for weak moments and re read it.
Stay NO CONTACT from this toxic person.

Am I Crossing Over To the Narc Side?

# Understanding Your Dance With the Devil

When you're recovering from your dance with the devil you may wonder if you yourself are going over to the 'Narc' side.

Narcs do not have the ability to self reflect and have no insight into their shortcomings or past behaviour.

Quoted by a fellow Thriver Julia "I worry that because I am building myself up, staying positive on a personal level and in personal relationships, that in the midst of it all, perhaps I have narc tendencies as well! I fear becoming the very thing I loathe. I can see myself doing that, since I have a mean streak where douche is concerned."

This is simply you developing boundaries and becoming assertive.
Being a little more selfish with your time and being more selective on who you spend it with,
This is you deciding how you want to spend your day and not playing second fiddle to others all the time.
This is you fine tuning your narcometer so it flashes a warning every time you come across a toxic person who has the potential to harm you.

This is you becoming in touch with your 'strong independent' woman

This is you HEALING Julia...rock on!

Learning To love Yourself

Help Yourself As You Would A Friend

We've all been down there in that 'pit of shit' it takes time to climb out of it and everyday we climb a little higher away from it. Sometimes we have dark days when everything seems pointless and the pains too much. On those days reach out to others but also think about how you would help a friend who felt like this today. reach out to yourself like you would a friend.

"Most women are starving to receive something from a man that they need to give to themselves."
Sherry Argov, Why Men Love Bitches: From Doormat to Dream girl A Woman's Guide to Holding Her Own in a Relationship.
"Love Yourself" my therapist said to me in those early sessions! I thought she meant some new age hippy mantra and after years of being a nurse with two children and under King Narcs rule clearly misunderstood. "You remember when you were nursing taking care of others and your family? What did you do for them?" she said. "Well I made sure they were comfortable, they slept well and they weren't in pain and they were eating properly and drinking enough." "Do you do these things for yourself?" she asked. I paused and said "Well no there's not enough time" I replied. "So you are worth less than King Narc your children and your patients?" she said. "Why should others love you if you treat yourself so appallingly?"
Ask yourself this question. Others measure your worth by watching the way you treat yourself.

"There is only one person who can make things happen for you the way you want and give you the life you have always deserved and that's the person looking back at you from the mirror."

Time To Step Out Of Your Comfort Zone!

"You will be more disappointed by the things that you didn't do than by the ones you did do, so throw off the bowlines, sail away from safe harbour, catch the trade winds in your sails. Explore, Dream, Discover."
Mark Twain

You are awesome as you are. yet you've been negatively conditioned to hate yourself through years of criticism. Your fat thighs. your big nose, the bits that make you, the unique bits. So fall back in love with every inch of you the good the bad and the ugly.
Go shopping learn how to flatter your body and learn what colours suit you,.
Go for a makeover and learn how to do your makeup and hair so you feel amazing. Learn something new,
Learn a craft.
Read new books.

186

Watch different programmes than you usually watch.
Take up a sport.
Talk to new people.
Cook different foods from around the world.
Travel and open yourself up to new exciting opportunities!
Yes you will feel scared stepping out your comfort zone. That's ok.
Baby steps firing those brain cells everyday with something new! No one controls you now.
Throw yourself back into life!

The Gift Of Empathy

Since I was a little girl I used to enjoy the challenge of getting a grumpy sad looking person to smile!
While under Narc rule I stopped communicating and smiling and lost my voice. Hearing the Narcs devil on my shoulder.
"You sound stupid!"
"Why are you talking to him?"
"Do you realise they don't really want to talk to you!"

After Narc rule I found my confidence return and now I pass the time of day and share a smile with many people. A smile is enough to change someone's day, so if you see someone old and shuffling say "Hello "If you see someone young and upset ask "What's wrong?" This is how we should naturally be without Narc influence.
Enjoy having our greatest gift of empathy and compassion for others.

Finding Your Voice

Ok what happened to you? When I say you I mean the you that you were before you met that insidious person who proclaimed to love you. The bubbly you, the happy confident you, the you that loved getting up in the morning, the you that got things done?
While you were with that dysfunctional abusive person do you remember that little voice inside you that fought for you? "You won't tell me what to do, I will wear what I want, I will be friends with who I want, I will hang out with who I want and I will go where I want." You need to re-ignite that feistiness,. that drive, that rebel in you that is there inside you still.

The narcissist squashed the real you till you turned into a former shadow of yourself. It may only be a quiet voice right now, testing the water, tentatively deciding to wear those shorts they hated, but not having the confidence to wear them outside the house or to leave a few plates by the sink in an otherwise pristine kitchen,. or to go out with a friend they told you had a reputation, just for a coffee so you can make your own mind up but that is YOUR voice and as you work on yourself and on your inner wounds of insecurity and lack of confidence and begin to turn around the inner beliefs of 'hating yourself' and negative beliefs they drummed into you it will get stronger and louder.

You are becoming the 'YOU' you were meant to be. The you they kept in a box for themselves. Only you fought your way out and are FREE!

Missing Pieces

While we are healing we are finding the missing pieces of ourselves. The Narc has conditioned you to put your needs last and only satisfy his own.

Take it day by day to find the missing pieces of you. It's a process and it takes time.
Like a jigsaw puzzle of "Who am I?"
You can be that person again.

My counsellor said to me in the very early days "Who is Tammy?" I couldn't answer for crying but as the weeks progressed I thought about who I was other than a wife and a mother and a nurse. I really didn't like me much because the Narc had conditioned me to think negatively about myself. Then in one of the sessions when she asked me I blurted out "I'm actually ok, In fact I quite like myself." That was a breakthrough and progressed over the weeks to "I'm fun, I'm bubbly, I'm clever, I'm me!"

Think about those attributes that the Narc tried to steal for themselves.
Think about the parts of your personality they tried to put in that box.
What are they?
Who are you now?
How have they changed who you are?

Forgiving Yourself For Staying

You were sold a lie, a fiction and a dream by a manipulative actor which turned into a nightmare.

Healing can only take place when you begin to forgive yourself and find a smaller stick to beat yourself with.

I too beat myself up for staying and It took a good chunk of therapy to see that I couldn't have left then as I wasn't strong enough to stand up to him. You also need to forgive yourself.

I know it's going to be the hardest thing you've ever done but celebrate every breath of fresh air you take from this moment on away from their toxic poisonous trail.

You get to write your own story now of peace happiness and love.

Working Towards Forgiveness

This is a working progress and one of the toughest parts of the process but it is vital to our healing.

Forgive them for your own peace.

Work towards pitying their black evil soul.

Anger bitterness fear and distrust are negative emotions that will consume you if you let them.

Hating them is another way they cling on to your life and keeps you embroiled in their chaos.

They have no place in your beautiful life so let those emotions go.

Feeling Numb?

Give yourself Permission To Feel

It's Okay Not to be Okay Sometimes.

It's ok to feel after years of negative conditioning and minimising your feelings. It's okay not to be okay.

It's okay to be angry and upset and it's okay to cry,

It's okay to have really bad days where we get nothing done without guilt,

It's okay to be a recluse sometimes,

Its okay to have lazy days,

It's okay to sit watching sad films and eating ice cream in our pyjamas.

These bad days are allowed and help us recharge from the grief and pain in recovery. Embrace these days then give yourself a big kick up the bum and push yourself out the house and out of your comfort zone!

I Need Closure

We can't have closure from someone who is incapable of seeing their faults but we can have closure by educating ourselves on NPD and seeing it wasn't us and that they have a mental disorder.

Grieve For the Person You Thought They Were

Express and own your grief anger and hopelessness and work through it. If you internalise these feelings they will eat up your soul.

"We must revisit painful memories to completely rinse them out of our body and mind for good. It is only by acknowledging our pain, processing it, discussing it, writing it down, and understanding its origin that we can finally let go of it so it can no longer hurt and cause us pain and let us move on from that in a healthy way.
Do not block pain. Work through it till it no longer hurts.
Remember pain is a teacher."

Processing Grief

After a Narc attack we need time to process the grief and let go of the person we thought they were and the future they had faked us into believing was real. This takes as long as it takes and is a huge part of the healing process.

So We're Empaths

Human beings with real feelings of love and compassion.
We don't lack empathy, in fact it spills out painfully too fast. We're hurting after the discard, or if we woke up first and discarded them.
Why does it still hurt when we know they are rotten to the core?
Where does this burning rage come from?
The uncontrollable anger that at first makes us question ourselves.
How dare they lie about me to my children and friends?

How dare they smear my reputation all over town?
How dare they try and destroy me! I'm so angry!

We Ask Am I The Narc?

This is I quote "A normal reaction to an abnormal amount of bullshit."
It is normal to have angry feelings and indeed we must release them to feel better.
So we need an outlet for our anger.
This could be any physical activity that helps you to vent.
Personally Kickboxing got me through the last few years of anger and yoga helped to chill me out if the Nex or the children upset me. If you can't process your anger yourself it's imperative you ask a therapist to help you.

After the fear and crying has subsided we are left with many negative emotions after leaving an abuser! It's really important right now for you to get all that anger and frustration out! Anger is a horrible negative emotion that feels wrong and can make us physically sick. Get it out so it can't hurt you anymore!
Hitting something, any type of physical activity and shouting or singing loudly are all ways that get rid of anger and other negative emotions safely.

Coping With Anger

Feeling angry for a long period of time can have really negative consequences on both your emotional and physical wellbeing.
It can leave us feeling sick and unable to eat and completely unable to focus on anything,
It can cause us to lash out at those around us which can seriously affect our relationships with friends and supporters.
It also leaves us feeling so stuck and so overwhelmed that we end up using self-injury to try and deal with it.
Or we end up crying or going to sleep to make it go away. It can be different for everyone. It can even cause things like high blood pressure, or auto immune disease so addressing our anger is of extreme importance so as to keep our physical and emotional health topped up through this tough time.

You escaped their control right?
If you still let them control your thoughts and emotions,
If you still let them anger you,
If you still let them upset you,
THEY still control you!

Take back your power and steer those thoughts away from them and their never ending chaos.

How do I do this?
Grieve and allow yourself to feel for a set part of your day but do not wallow in it for long.
Do something uplifting and positive for you everyday.
Are you not worth it?
Do they deserve another minute of your precious time after everything they did to you?
Do they deserve your tears?
Maintain NO CONTACT
Ask yourself what YOU need today to get you through this?
We were not allowed to feel in Narcdom while under Narc rule. We learn to suppress our emotions to keep them on a level of pleasant. We walked on emotional egg shells so as not to feel hear or see their rage and protect our children from it, so when we've escaped and we finally feel anger and express it we feel like we are going over to the 'Narc side'!
Anger is healthy if it is channelled in the right ways so when the Nex pushes your buttons find a healthy outlet for that angry emotion.
Vigorous physical activity of any type helps.
Cleaning or destroying something in the garden in a controlled way are good ways to get rid of that knot of emotion inside.
One Thriver told me she threw ice at the wall outside and watching and listening to it shatter helped her release her anger.
If you can't deal with your anger ask a therapist to help you. Do not sit and seethe. Yoga meditation and breathing techniques are really good ways to calm yourself down after an angry episode.

"People say I am strong and I'm going to tell you how I got there.
For years I kept all my feelings hidden.
Now I shout, I cry, I write.

If we internalise our feelings of grief, loss and anger they will eventually destroy us."

Pretending to be ok and walking on emotional egg shells is what we do in an abusive dysfunctional relationship to keep the Narc on a level of pleasant. We might not see while we are involved with them that we are checking and altering our behaviour and emotions but their nasty comments when we raised our voice in reaction to their lies and their gas lighting when we tried to extract the truth led to a stage of learned helplessness and giving up who we are and what we stand for.

Post Narc then it's important to be strong but not silent. It's Important to learn to express the feelings that the Narc suppressed in us.

The whole range of emotions through from love for others that we weren't allowed to show ( I used to watch my loving daughter hugging her friends and feel uncomfortable and sad that I couldn't openly show love to people like her).and on the other end of the spectrum anger and rage at him and his smear campaign. are all normal human emotions and if expressed around healthy people do not create a problem.

So if something isn't right say so! If you are unhappy cry.

"When we have one of those days where we are 'stuck' we have to learn to throw it in the 'F**k it' Bucket and move forwards. Look forward to a brighter tomorrow."

Stop being hard on yourself!

Stop suppressing your emotions!

Go somewhere safe and quiet and let them all tumble out!

Healing after narc abuse is a rollercoaster of ups and downs, and feelings ranging from "Yay I'm all better" to today "I can't go on." Accept these peaks and troughs as part of a long process. The ups will soon outweigh the downs!

Cry and vent a lot, and don't push yourself through the process too hard. Be kind to yourself and nurture your inner child.

As hard as it is let go of what the Nex is doing right now. You are caught up in anger and frustration as you can see them for who they really are and you're watching other victims being duped by them. Annoying and frustrating right?

Just remember they aren't capable of a real relationship. They will simply be using any relationships they have for their self serving needs. Going through the only relationship they know:
Love bomb,
Devalue,
Discard.
Now if you let the past go you can go out into our beautiful world and live an amazing life. While you are checking on them you are 'stuck' and you cannot move forwards unless you close that chapter and pick up the pen to write a new one.
You can do this!

Focus on The Future

When we are healing we can still feel 'stuck'. These feelings are normal as you are still healing from your Narc experience. Give yourself time. Focus on the future and on happy things. Work through your feelings with a counsellor if you can and only devote a small amount of time to that.
Try and wean yourself off watching Narc related material, limit the reading and refocus your time.
Please read the blog about our addiction to pain peptides as in effect what you are doing is reinforcing painful brain pathways by going over the same material over and over again.
Breathe enjoy and try and fall back in love with yourself and with your life.
I promise you positive things and people will start coming when you do this and you can gradually build the life you want.

How Do I Deal With This Burning Rage?

It is normal to live and breathe the hatred of your Nex for months. It is normal to want to talk about them all the time. It is normal to feel 'in love' and hate them at the same time .You have a beating heart that feels. that's what got you into this mess in the first place with a monster!
You feel incredibly raw as you are processing all this and feeling all this. It is very cathartic and a huge part of the healing process to cry and talk

about what they did. You are angry upset and you want validation that you never got in the relationship.

Now you can say 'they did this, they said this' and you have friends that will say "OMG That's awful" and that's what we need to hear many times before we see it wasn't anything we did.

Only then can we move on emotionally.

So cry, rant, and explain things over and over again until what happened to you becomes so wrong so wicked and abnormal you would never be treated like that again by any living thing.

How Dare They?

Let me explain why but let me give you all hope that you will move past this sadness and the emotional pain.

When you have worked through this very draining but healing process you will reach the stage where you will be left with a healthy level of "How dare they do that to me?" anger!

That shows great healing because now you know you would never accept that from anyone else for the rest of your life!

Rebuilding a happy life post narc starts with replacing every sad, scared, upset and toxic memory with a happier one and gradually day by day collecting new happy memories.

Fleeting at first and barely undetectable in the confusion and pain of what the Nex is doing to you to sabotage and destroy you when you dare to go no contact. Until one day you will look back and say I am happy now. You won't predict that moment it will just happen.

Attracting Good People

Narcs Destroy Our Social Network

Narcs destroy our social networks so we have to rebuild new ones. Recovery isn't just about learning the 'why's' and 'how's' it's about rebuilding a new better life so 'meeting' people on the Internet who have been through the same experiences and sharing their stories is healing and therapeutic for all of us.

Let go of anything toxic in your life.
Partners, friends and family members, and dead end jobs.
Anything that no longer serves you.
You will see huge positive changes in life.

As you move away from your Nex and their entourage's toxic cloud of chaos and destruction you allow space for good happy positive people to come into your life. People the Nex repelled. Remember those?
This is why it is imperative you escape, go NO CONTACT with NO exceptions so you can close that chapter of your life shut and seal it. Then fully in control you can pick up your pen and begin to write your new life how YOU want it.
Once you surround yourself with a human shield of good people and positivity the evil will bounce right off.

Existing Behind Closed Doors

"You gain strength, courage, and confidence by every experience in which you really stop to look fear in the face. "
— Eleanor Roosevelt

So he turned you into a former shadow of yourself? a recluse that exists behind closed curtains?

Getting Yourself Out There Baby Steps

Start by smiling and saying hello to people you don't know and starting a conversation when you're out shopping.
Accept invitations from well meaning friends you trust.
Visit places you're interested in.
Join a group or volunteer for something you are genuinely interested in.

Your enthusiasm will draw people in.
Push yourself out that comfort zone everyday at least once. It takes time to get out the box the Narc put you in. Be kind to yourself and set yourself small goals.
If you can't cope with PTSD find a therapist to help you with techniques.
I learned to breathe through panic attacks triggered by the Nex stalking me. Try and 'bring yourself back' this way by concentrating on a clock

or an object in the room or outside that is distracting. Lessen anxiety by making sure you never leave the house without a charged phone and telling someone where you are going. It's these little things that make us feel 'safe' and allow us to work through panic attacks with breathing techniques. Concentrate on the fresh clean air and feeling 'free.'

What are you doing to push yourself out your comfort zone?
To climb out that cage the Narc had you in?

## Coming Out Your Comfy Cocoon

To come out of your comfy cocoon you have to actively want change enough to become a butterfly! What are you going to do today to make one of these changes?

## Making New Memories

Avoiding visiting places where we used to go together as a couple kept me stuck a very long time as he was stalking me. It was only by mustering the courage, ignoring my fast beating heart and breathing through an impending panic attack and actually facing my fears head on telling myself "I can do this" that revisiting places and actually doing things that we used to do as a couple became therapy.
It allows you to finally lay old ghosts, build new happy memories and move on in your head. Do NOT give him or her the power to take your favourite coffee shop, that beautiful part of the beach, that river you had a picnic by, your favourite music, the food you ate or cooked for them away.
Take it back and reclaim it NOW!

## Is There A Fill Up Station

Oh there is a fill up station guys. When you are empty and drained and can't carry on don't. Learn to listen to yourself. If you hear "I am exhausted with no reserves and nothing left to give" Ask yourself "What do I need? What do I need to feel better right now?"
When I'm rock bottom I pick myself up and I hear my counsellors voice asking me?

Sometimes I know a bath would help, sometimes sitting watching a comedy or in the middle of the day a ten minute breather and a cup of coffee. Oh to breathe! Sometimes I need to let it out and just cry all that pent up emotion out. Sometimes I type furiously to a friend or my sister or I kickbox or calm myself with yoga.

Sometimes I can't figure out what I need at that moment but the important thing is to ask yourself.

Does it feel self indulgent? Of course it does as the narc conditioned you to put your needs on hold to satisfy their own.

# The Importance Of Alone Time
## In Abuse Recovery

In recovery 'alone time' is crucial to process sadness and grief so we can recharge and face the world again with renewed energy.

"Embrace your time alone like an old friend. You are getting to know YOU and what makes you tick. It's ok if that's where you are right now. Don't rush healing. When you're ready to socialise you can take daily baby steps to push yourself out of your comfort zone."

So important post Narc to appreciate our time alone either doing nothing but calming the mind or just sitting and thinking or listening to music, or being outside in our beautiful world connecting with nature.
When we are in an abusive relationship we are in 'survival' mode struggling just to get through the day. Enjoy your peace and appreciate the simple beautiful things around us.

Regaining Our Trust in People

When we are healing we need firstly to spend time alone as our trust has gone in people and we no longer feel safe even though we may have well meaning friends there. All abuse is tough to recover from but it is the psychological abuse that stays and affects us for so long. Accept that this is where you are right now, allow only people you trust implicitly into your personal space and explain to them how you feel. Socialising is a new skill and one that can be built on slowly over time. So even having few friends over can be exhausting so when they are gone be kind to yourself and know these feelings are normal after being violated and abused. It will get easier, give it time and give yourself love.

Mood Shifting

"I like to start my day with a few minutes of mood shifting. When I just wake up I might feel tired or groggy, so I'll lie in bed for a few minutes and change my vibration from I don't want to get up to, I love being alive. Im happy and I love everything. It really changes my whole outlook on my day." – Angela, Yoga Instructor

Post Narc we sometimes forget the little things about caring for ourselves, so here's a gentle reminder.
These are better than any product bought in the pharmacy.

The Power Of Exercise

Exercise helps with balancing the endocrine and nervous systems which can be affected by stress.

The physical benefits of exercise on our heart and circulatory system are well known. Exercise also gives us a natural mental boost by increasing happy hormones called endorphins in our brains. These little fellas give us a natural high! These highs increase our metabolic rate and make for a more productive day kick starting us into action! This has a knock on effect on all our days activity! Great for if you are feeling fed up and miserable! Especially on days when you feel low drag yourself out
Think about what exercise you might enjoy.
What are your fitness goals?

I have always been a fitness freak or fanatic or whatever you want to call it! In my twenties I used to run on the treadmill and do weight training for 40 minutes on my way to the hospital and I would bounce round for the whole 8 hour shift. it gave me huge amounts of energy! The Nex stopped me going over the years once I had the children then I became weak and damaged my back suffering excruciating sciatica. Not helped by the fact he actually kicked me because I could no longer nurse ( our bread and butter) I had set up a retail business to help make ends meet and that was making more money than nursing! Yes really! That's how badly nurses are paid! Anyway I digress!
Once I asked him to leave for the first time him for being abusive to my daughter I finally sought help.
The consultant told me after extensive physio the next stop was steroid injections into my spine.
I crawled out the Doctors office left nursing and began to try and heal myself.
I had dabbled in yoga so began the stretches eight times a day through excruciating pain. If I was round at someone's house I would have to get on the floor! I was on very strong painkillers.

Over the months I joined a gym and sat in the Jacuzzi in agony as pain shot from my ankle up my leg and up to my original lower spine injury. I began to work through the burning pain and managed a full length. Over the next six months I came off the painkillers upped the yoga and was smashing 25 lengths at the pool! I began to get pretty fit again despite what the surgeon had said!

8 years later I swim when I can but I do yoga everyday and have added kick boxing to my repertoire and very rarely take painkillers! If I feel a twinge then I'm down on the floor!

My point is Narcs destroy us physically and getting away from them is a massive step to being well and healthy. I know post narc you don't feel like doing anything.

I was there I had to push myself, but if you do something everyday be it a gentle walk or a run or a few lengths in the pool it not only strengthens your body and clocks up a lower blood pressure and gives your heart a fantastic boost but it also strengthens you on the inside too!

It's a great stress buster and there is no better way to get rid of pent up anger than smashing a kick boxers bag shouting "Take that you lying cheating B****d!" Also it means you can have that extra slice of cake!

Never Underestimate The Restorative Powers Of Sleep

You have been taught through years of negative conditioning from the Ncx that you are not worthy or important and sleep is something lazy people do.

At the end of this toxic marriage I could have slept for six months and still been tired!

The Restorative Powers of Sleep

Never underestimate the restorative powers of sleep. When our bodies and minds are going through extreme stress as is the case after leaving a Narc (unless we have to run from immediate danger and Adrenalin kicks in) our bodies shut down. We become uncoordinated and clumsy and suffer memory loss. There are different stages of sleep from very light stages 1 and 2 up to stage 5 when our brains go into REM sleep. This is Rapid Eye Movement or dream sleep ( just watch your pets eyes rolling round to see this!) Studies have shown that if we miss out on deep REM sleep, when we constantly get woken through it leads to symptoms of psychosis over a period of weeks. So bearing this in mind try really hard to get enough sleep and learn to catnap ( a skill I learned after I left the Nex) when we catnap and are sleep deprived our body bypasses the light stages and goes straight into REM. This is restorative and an instant pick me up.

Avoid long naps other than power naps shorter than 30 minutes though during the day as this will affect your night time sleep routine.

If you attend counselling it is also very draining and exhausting triggering yourself in the session. Try to book your counsellor on a day when you're not busy or at the end of the day so you can take a nap. Our bodies are amazing tune in and listen to yours.

There Are Too Many Tabs Open In My Brain

Sometimes it's hard to sleep because our brains are too active like a computer with too many tabs open.

All survivors frequently complain about over thinking.

Shut all those tabs and relax before you try to sleep. Try yoga meditation warm baths and a good relaxing book. If you wake in the night tossing and turning and over thinking and are just staring at the ceiling fighting sleep get up. Once it's a battle and you shut your eyes then look at the clock to see another hour gone by it becomes a war zone so get up out of bed and do something that makes you naturally tired like housework or a hobby then make a milky drink put on some music get something light-hearted to read ( not about Narcs) get comfy and read till you are nodding off.

If you did your housework in the night then it's like the cleaning fairy came which is an added bonus if you're still tired in the morning!

Don't feel guilty about working a catnap into your day if you're at home either. When our bodies are under huge psychological stress this is how we restore them and heal.

So how do I develop good habits to help me sleep through this emotionally stressful time? Try to ensure the lead up to sleep becomes a regular routine encouraging your natural biological clock by going to bed and getting up at the same time every day, including weekends.

Limit caffeine, alcohol, and nicotine. Stop drinking caffeinated drinks at least eight hours before bed time. Alcohol can relax you and make you feel sleepy, but it interferes with the quality of your sleep so is best avoided and nicotine is a stimulant. Try to avoid eating late and at the very least avoid heavy, rich foods within two hours of going to bed. Fatty foods are difficult to digest and spicy or acidic foods can cause heartburn. Getting regular exercise is helpful and can improve insomnia by naturally tiring the body. Aim for 30 minutes or more of aerobic exercise daily but not too close to bedtime.

Ensure your bedroom is quiet, dark and not too hot as excessive noise light, and heat can interfere with sleep. Try using earplugs to muffle outside noise, and sleep close to an open window or use a fan to keep the room at a cool temperature. blackout curtains or a sleep mask can be used to block out light.

Avoid stimulating stressful situations before bedtime. This includes, vigorous exercise, and if possible big discussions or arguments, or catching up on stressful work. Instead, switch your focus onto quiet and soothing activities, such as having a warm bath, light reading, or listening to soft music, while keeping lights down low. Turn off screens one hour before bedtime. The light emitted from TV, tablets, smart phones, and computers suppresses your body's production of melatonin the sleep hormone which can severely disrupt your sleep. Stop emailing, texting, watching TV, or playing video games an hour before bed.

Food As Medicine

Prolonged high cortisol levels from stress can wreak havoc on the body in a variety of ways. Maintain good adrenal health. Pay attention to your hormones.

Research foods and herbs that help you with hormonal balance.

"Let food be thy medicine and medicine be thy food." Hippocrates

Post Narc we can't eat!
We just can't. there it is!
The 'Post Narc Diet' is probably one of the best out there for rapid weight loss after a Viral tummy upset!

We feel nauseous with all these negative emotions going round in our heads, we feel sick at every interaction with the Nex, their involvement of our children, breaking the trauma bond, having no sleep. It really is a downward spiral.

So we grab and eat rubbish on the run! We snack on high carb quick snacks and we feel more rubbish!

We ask ourselves "Why do I feel bad?"

We chastise ourselves and say "I should feel better now I left that relationship!"

"Why am I still in that brain fog?"

Diet plays an important role in brain health and neurogenesis. Excess refined sugar has a detrimental effect on the brain, and refined and processed foods should be avoided when possible. The brain is 60% fat, and the right fats are essential to healthy brain function. These may constitute a certain proportion of plant and animal fats. Omega 3 fatty acids, seems of particular importance with regard to neurogenesis, with rich sources including oily fish and some plant oils, hemp in particular. This fatty acid is a major structural component of the brain and many other parts of the body.

At times of stress our digestive system shuts down for a reason.

Our bodies are in adrenaline mode. This is 'fight or flight' preparing our bodies for attack! Adrenaline either prepares us to fight our attacker or flee! It is not helpful to have a full belly in case we need to run fast or physically fight someone so our brain damps the digestive system down! It's normal. Go with it! Eat little and often! Eat little nutritious portions for fuel. Your body is a finely tuned machine! Eat only what it needs. Slow burning carbs for energy like porridge is good. Easily digestible fruit or shakes or puddings and soups are the easiest options.

Your appetite will return when your adrenalin levels return to normal when your body no longer feels under threat.

Sabotaging Meals

As I was cooking the dinner tonight I thought about how I felt when I was at my lowest. I was used to cooking large meals for my family under enormous stress and on a tight family budget. That all changed when he took them and I grieved cooking for my children. I worried so much about what he was feeding them, whether they brushed their teeth and whether they did their homework.

As well as the big worries on the lead up to going to court to court, attending police interviews to report the Nex behaviour and almost weekly solicitors appointments and the constant stress of his smear campaign.

This ruined my appetite and I stopped eating and became thin and unhealthy. I would stand in the supermarket and be clueless as to what I wanted to eat. I was in some kind of fog. I tried to eat but a few mouthfuls would make me sick until the court ruled one years injunction and he was no longer allowed to come near me in my house or on my street!

Several months passed and I began to treat food as medicine to make me well. I began to once again enjoy food as I always had. I wrote 'A Thousand Joys' at that time. Food became a pleasure again. Choosing and cooking food I liked was important.

I had a good few quick easy recipes that required little effort and time that I began to make again. If you are in that 'pit of shit' the last thing you feel like doing is cooking an elaborate meal.

So think about some easy recipes you like to cook through this stressful time? Inspire yourself to go into the kitchen and practice some self love. Every meal no matter how simple should be a celebration.

Getting Away From The Poison

When I was under Narc rule and after years of being downtrodden and abused my sparkle was gone, my complexion was tired, my hair refused to grow and would break off through stress. I was too skinny as I couldn't eat. I suffered headaches and unexplained stomach pains. The Narc free diet is the best plan yet for putting a sparkle back in your eyes! It's only when you look at old photos and compare them to now that you truly 'see' the damage they do! It's like being injected daily with a toxin that saps the life right out of you. Then a few months out you suddenly feel better. It's much like getting over a long term illness.

Women like us are bombarded by the beauty industry daily with anti ageing serums, Botox, pills to lose weight, pills to accelerate the growth of our hair and nails. We spend millions globally on lotions and potions that support a multi million dollar industry. Companies claim their miracle products will iron out wrinkles and halt the march of old Father Time.

However it is never more apparent after escaping from a toxic relationship how stress is the true cause of ageing on our face and bodies. No amount of lotions, pills or makeup can cover the tired dull grey dragged down appearance of an abused woman or man.

The stress of living with the daily poison has to come out somewhere.

Likewise women including me suffered horrible gastric and digestive problems and lost a tonne of weight or gained it during the abuse. It is also common to suffer long term auto immune diseases after a prolonged period of stress.

As you get away from the Nex rest and recuperate and take gentle exercise. This combined with a healthy diet and relaxation techniques will support your recovery.

During the toxic relationship we honestly don't think it's all due to stress and living on eggshells at the time but once you get away and relax you will see it was. Just flick through before and after photographs of any abused woman or man and you will see the physical toll that living in that 'fight or flight' environment does to us.

Every woman and man has the potential to blossom and radiate health once they escape those conditions.

What Are Toxic Energy Suckers?

Do some people just drain the life out of you? You know, toxic energy suckers? Surround yourself with a human shield of positive people who care about you that toxic people can't infiltrate. You can change who is drawn to you and how people interact with you by changing the way you think and feel about yourself.

Believe in yourself and others will too.

Respect yourself and others will too.

Help I'm A Narc Magnet

So you left the Narc in your life? You're doing no contact like a pro! So where now are all these toxic people coming from? "It's me I'm just a Narc magnet" I hear you cry. No! These Narcs have always been there only now you are getting wiser.

You are finely tuning your Narcometer and now you can spot them before they do you harm. These toxic people are coming as lessons that you are winning.

Celebrate the fact that you now 'see' them! It's overwhelming isn't it? It's also quite ok for you to want to hide too and block them from your beautiful life because that's you developing boundaries to protect yourself and becoming a warrior against the Narcs! Yay you!

As we get further away from the toxic Nex we begin to re-evaluate our family and friends and distance ourselves from other toxic people that we have attracted in our life! Removing toxic people gives us the peace we deserve.

Being Re-Targeted

I was prompted to write this after being re -targeted myself many times and also after talking to a fellow survivor who met a particularly vicious jealous Narc in the disguise of a loving friend while recently recovering from a romantic Narc relationship.

As you step away from the toxic relationship you will begin to feel quite determined. You vow to yourself that you will never let any toxic person hurt you again and you mean it. Sadly Narcs are attracted to your kind heart and your considerate nature like bees are to honey so be aware in your vulnerable state you are a sitting duck ready to be targeted again.

Until your Narc radar is faultlessly up and running don't beat yourself up if you mistakenly fall for another Narc or let another in your life. These are lessons.

He or she may come in the form of a concerned empathetic co- worker or someone who seems to really care, who you pour your heart out to thinking they are an empath like you.

Not so fast! Be careful who you trust "Oh no tell me everything" they exclaim while handing you a tissue feigning compassion and then you begin to spot the red flags! Guard your soul and don't let people into your circle until you can be sure you can trust them.

# Narcissistic Parents and Siblings

Are you beginning to 'see' your parents or parent differently? When we are growing up we have nothing to measure or compare the 'love' we feel from our parents to.

That is our 'normal.' Looking back were they loving parents or what you perceived at the time as loving parents? Were they overly critical? Did you jump through hoops to please them only to be told you weren't good enough? clever enough? or pretty enough?

Were you compared unfavourably to your other siblings? Did your other siblings get away with things you were chastised for? I think when we've been attacked by a narc it makes us analyse everyone but that's not a bad thing.

However It's upsetting at the time to see narc traits in people we love but realising where your 'inner wounds' originated from is liberating and healing and why we became people pleasing narc fodder in the first place. It's painful at first accepting that our parents or indeed siblings made us feel 'less than' but remember their narc traits were likely passed down from their parents. Understanding your family dynamics is the key to set you free. It may not necessarily mean you can't love your parents as you always have. It just means you can create boundaries for yourself to ensure your mental health.

Narc parents cannot love their children normally.
They love them as possessions and a boost to their own ego.
They do not see them as individual but rather an extension of themselves.
They use their children for narc supply by looking like a great parent.
They feed off their children loving and needing them.

Narc Father

He has an overly inflated view of his own importance.
He has a tendency to exaggerate his accomplishments.
He has an excessive need for admiration.
He excessively envies others.
He has a constant belief that others envy him.
He has a condescending manner towards others.
He has a noticeable lack of empathy.He has a sense of entitlement that he brings to his relationships.

You used to think that by the time you were in your twenties and definitely by your thirties you'd have your act together – you'd be establishing a successful career have your own place , be in a committed and stable relationship, visit the gym enough to have the body you always wanted and your social life would be vibrant.

But, you're nowhere near where you thought you'd be, and the tiny boxes next to the list of achievements that you'd hoped to accomplish are still unchecked.

As your confidence deflates, you look back on your own upbringing, and think about your father – Mr Self-Assured. He seemed to have it all – charm, success, popularity and he never seemed to be plagued by self-doubt, unlike you. He was the hit of the party, knew everyone and made things happen. You couldn't get enough of him.

How Kids Experience Narcissistic Traits:

Come to think of it, did his confidence border on arrogance? Is it possible that you were raised by someone with Narcissistic Traits? And if so, why is it Important?

We take our families for granted – it's natural that we do. Each family is a miniature sociological experiment, with its own set of unwritten rules, secrets, and nuanced behavioural patterns. We take our Mom and Dad for granted; like this must be what it's like for everyone. Your dad may have been narcissistic, but you just assumed that all fathers were like him.

Here are some signs that your dad had narcissistic tendencies or was an out-right narcissist.

Dad was self-centered and pretty vain. He had an inflated sense of self-importance that led him to believe he was superior and entitled to only the best.

Dad used people for his own good. He would take advantage of others, to the point of exploiting them when it suited him. Everybody seemed to cater to him, or at least he expected them to.

Dad was charismatic. Everyone wanted to be around him and he relished admiration from others. He loved being in the spotlight and the positive reinforcement that came from being the centre of attention.

No one had an imagination like Dad. Grandiosity is alluring, and so were his fantasies of success, prestige, and brilliance. He would often exaggerate his achievements, and his ambitions and goals bordered on unrealistic.

Dad didn't take criticism well. Nothing stung him like criticism he often cut those people out of his life, or tried to hurt them.

Dad's rage was truly scary. Some people get mad and yell a lot. Dad could hurt you with his anger. It cut to the bone.

Dad could be aloof and unsympathetic. Narcissists often have a hard time experiencing empathy; they often disregard and invalidate how others feel. Of course, he was exquisitely sensitive to what he felt, but others were of no mind.

Dad wasn't around a lot. He got a lot of gratification outside the family. Other fathers hung out with their families a lot more. Plus, he craved excitement and seemed to be more concerned by what others thought of him, rather then how his own kids felt about him.

Dad did what he wanted when dealing with you. Narcissists don't step into someone else's shoes very often. He did things with you that he enjoyed; maybe you did as well.

Dad wanted you to look great to his friends and colleagues. You were most important to him when he could brag about you; sad but true.

You couldn't really get what you needed from him. Even if Dad provided on a material level, you felt deprived on a more subtle level. For example, you wanted his attention and affection, but would only get it sporadically, and only when it worked for him.

When you go through these traits, some may hit home; while others may not be relevant. Some may ring as very true; while others as less so.

Another characteristic typical of narcissists is a disregard of personal boundaries. Narcissists don't always acknowledge the need for boundaries which is coupled with their failure to realize that others do not exist merely to meet their needs. A narcissist will often treat others, especially those that are close to him, as if they are there to fulfil his needs and expectations.

Now that you have a firm grasp on what a narcissistic father may be like, let's take a look at how he might affect his kids.

How a Narcissistic Father Can Hurt his Son or Daughter:

Narcissistic parents damage their children. For example, they may disregard boundaries, manipulate their children by withholding affection (until they perform), and neglect to meet their children's needs because their needs come first. Because Image is so Important to narcissists, they may demand perfection from their children. The child of a narcissist father can, in turn, feel a pressure ramp up their talents, looks, smarts or charisma. It can cost them if they fulfil their Dad's wishes - and it can cost them if they fail. No winning here.

In general, here's how a narcissistic father can affect a daughter or son.

• Daughters of narcissistic fathers often describe feeling "unsatiated" when it to comes to getting what they needed from their fathers. They never got enough and would have to compete with siblings for time with Dad. As a young child, Dad would comment on how beautiful you were. But as you grew older, he would rarely miss out on commenting on weight and attitude. You probably carry these concerns into adulthood, even if you found success. With a Dad like this, it's never enough. With men (or women), you often feel vulnerable and worried you'll be dumped for someone else. Anxiously avoiding commitment or taking on the narcissistic role are both natural ways to keep relationships safe; it's understandable and self protective.(But, you lose.)

A daughter needs her dad's adoration; it validates her and helps her internalize her specialness. Healthy fathers give their girls that gift. You are special and deserve love, for being you.

• As the son of a narcissistic father you never feel that you can measure up. Dad was so competitive, that he even competed with you. (Or, didn't pay attention to you one way or the other.) You may have accepted defeat - you'd never outdo your dad. Or, you may have worked hard to beat Dad at his own game just to get his attention and some semblance of fatherly pride. You somehow never feel good enough even when you do succeed, you still feel empty and second rate.

Just like girls need to be adored by their fathers to feel validated, boys also need their dad to believe in them. You may even become a narcissist yourself. This way you get Dad's attention (after all Imitation is the highest form of flattery); and you learn from your old man how to manipulate and use people.

So how do you survive a narcissist father?

Every narcissist is a hero and a legend in his own mind. And, so was Daddy.

Get into a good therapy. You want to come to terms with Dad for who he is, and how he hurt you. He' is your father after all, and you will need to differentiate from him in order to enjoy his presence without being undermined. It's no small task.

His arrogance and constant need for ego stroking can be annoying. Accept

Dad for who he is. If you put him into place in your mind, he may simply end up being a lovable, but annoying father. Take the best, as long as he doesn't still have the power to hurt you.

Do not let Dad hurt you. If he has a rage attack, you may decide to get in the car and leave. Limits are often a good thing. "Dad, this is not constructive."

Cut ties if it is too toxic or dangerous. Some narcissistic parents have violent or abusive tendencies. It goes along with their self righteousness. You are now and adult. Take care and take caution.

Has your Dad affected your dating habits and choices? Some identify with their father by becoming arrogant themselves. Others are anxious in their attachments because they could never trust Dad's undivided attention. Do you date narcissistic people yourself?

Keep your expectations realistic and low. Don't expect a relationship with a narcissistic person to be based on mutuality or reciprocity. Narcissists are selfish and can't put your needs on par with their own. As an adult, you can keep these conflicts with your father at a distance; but if you date or marry a narcissist, it probably will wear you out.

21 Signs of a Narc Mother.

http://psychcentral.com/lib/2010/narcissistic-mothers/

http://www.wisegeek.com/what-are-the-signs-of-a-narcissistic-mother.htm

http://parrishmiller.com/narcissists.html

Be concerned if she has many of them.

She has to be the centre of attention all the time. This is a defining feature of narcissism. She will steal the spotlight or spoil any occasion if someone else is the centre of attention.

She demeans, criticizes and makes derogatory remarks to you. She always lets you know that she thinks less of you than your siblings or other people.

She violates your boundaries. You feel like an extension of her.

There is no privacy in your bathroom or bedroom; she regularly goes through your things to find information she then uses against you.

She 'favoritizes'. Narcissistic mothers often have one child who is "the golden child" and another who is the scapegoat.

She undermines She will pick a fight with you or be especially critical and unpleasant just before you have to make a major effort.

Everything she does is 'deniable'. Cruelties are couched in loving terms;

aggressive acts are paraded as thoughtfulness.

She makes YOU look crazy. When you confront her with something she's done, she'll tell you that you have "a very vivid Imagination" (common phrase that abusers use to invalidate your experience of their abuse) or that she has "no idea what you are talking about".

She's jealous. If you get something nice, she'll take it from you, spoil it for you or get something the same or better for herself.

She's a continuous liar. To you, she lies blatantly. To outsiders, she lies thoughtfully and in ways that can always be covered up.

She manipulates your emotions in order to "feed on your pain".

This behaviour is so common among narcissistic mothers that they are often referred to as "emotional vampires".

She is selfish and wilful. She makes sure she has the best of everything and always has to have her way.

She is self-absorbed. Her feelings, needs and wants are Very Important and yours are irrelevant or insignificant.

She is almost absurdly defensive and extremely sensitive to criticism.

She terrorized you. Narcissists teach you to beware of their wrath. If you give her everything she wants, you might be spared; but if you don't-the punishments will come.

She's childish and petty; "getting even" with you is Important to her.

She is aggressive and shameless. She doesn't ask, she demands. She won't take no for an answer-she will push, arm-twist, or otherwise manipulate or abuse you until you give in.

She "parentifies". She sheds her parental responsibilities to the child as soon as she is able.

She is exploitive. She will go to any length to get things from others for nothing (work, money, objects)- including taking money out of her children's account or even stealing their identities.

She projects. She will put her own poor behaviour or character onto you so she can punish you. For example, you refuse an especially outlandish request of hers, she becomes enraged and furious at your refusal, then screams at you, "we'll talk about it after you've calmed down and aren't hysterical".

She is never wrong about anything. She will never, ever genuinely apologize for anything she has done or said.

She is not aware that other people have feelings. She will occasionally slip up in public, and because of her lack of sympathy, will say something so callous it causes disbelief in people. The absence of empathy is another defining trait of narcissism and underlies most of the other signs that are on this list.

My Mission

My mission now is to work through the psycho babble and put it in an understandable format so target parents recovering from abuse by proxy at the hands of their Nex and suffering resulting brain fog can understand what is happening to their children.

Once you understand you can educate your friends family and children by sharing my blogs and articles and help this very sick pathology stop hiding behind closed doors. Let's blow it up out of the water!

Only then others will see Parental Alienation in all its ugliness and bring about change for our children and our grandchildren and break this circle of abuse.

When we begin to understand our family dynamics we can go back and heal the inner wounds they caused us.

Children of Narcissists are triangulated and pitted in competition against one another and taught to compete for the Narcs conditional love.

They are taught to hate their siblings and it's often many years later that they begin to see that this was not theirs or their siblings doing.

If we become bitter and twisted as we do not understand psychotherapy will help us to heal.

## Hiding the Crazy

In a family ruled by a Narcissist, we live in denial of their underlying pathology. We all know something is seriously out of whack but we can't understand quite what. The message at all times is pretend to be normal. The skeletons in the closet are hidden, by appearing perfect at all times when on public display. It's important to dress impeccably in the best clothes we can afford and to behave like the perfect family at all times. We take our cue from the Narc himself who tells us to straighten up and asks us "What will the neighbours say" and we become Oscar winning actors at hiding their crazy! We minimise their abuse, and we make excuses for him or her that he or she was tired or hungry, because we want to cling onto that wonderful person who we fell in love with at the beginning of the relationship, when we were being love bombed.

We don't want to believe that that person is not real and simply a lovely fictitious mask and that this crazy irrational aggressive person is truly who they are.

Their abusive behaviour becomes accepted within the family as normal and as my daughter used to say and smile "You know what Dads like! That's just Dad."

Did the Narc Love Me?
Do They Love Their Children?
That would be a resounding 'no'
Narcs lack compassion and empathy and therefore don't have the capacity to love anyone in a mentally healthy way.

They simply use the term 'love' to gain all the financial and status benefits of a relationship or a normal marriage and then a family without lifting a finger!

Why?

This set up serves their narcissistic needs and provides the best unlimited supply as they hide behind a veil of normal. The relationship and marriage smoke screens their lying cheating true behaviour to the world. They know deep inside how weak spineless and insecure they are and they fear exposure. When anyone tries to rip the nice mask off their face and show the world true them they fight back and rage and go into attack mode for fear of discovery and the shame that people now really know who they are.

Narcs are simply predators looking for long lasting supply for their self serving needs.

So who do they target?

They target the best looking, the most intelligent, the most loving, the most generous kind, the most compassionate, and sparkly people on the planet! That is the people who have all the empathetic and beautiful qualities the narc lacks and they are inherently envious of.

So where do we find these people?

As you recover you will meet these empaths on narcissistic recovery forums all over the world.

So they target you because they need what you can provide for them and they will remain in a 'relationship' with you until you are so depleted financially and emotionally from taking care of them that you are completely sucked dry of the resources they need or until you put an end to it by discovering who they truly are and calling them out on it, or until they find a better supply.

So they target empaths, who have the childhood wounds of abandonment and feeling not good enough because we believe that love will heal them. We have endless patience so can supply them with what they need for the longest time.

Narcs pick us off the way a lion hunts a wounded antelope. Our inability to see evil in people is attractive to them and our empathetic qualities and childhood wounds make us easy prey.

They look for us hunt us down and target us as a predator finds his prey.

So let's come back now to why they have children, what better ready made source of narc supply than your own child!

Stop Creating An Illusion For Your Children.

While unknowingly in a relationship with a Narc we minimise and downplay their abuse to ourselves.

We teach our children to handle their volatile parent.

They learn by watching us making excuses, that the NPD parent is in a bad mood because they're tired, or hungry, or because they lost their job. They learn that they are allowed to behave this way, because they had a bad childhood and they learn coping mechanisms from us to keep their parent on a level of normal, because no one wants to see them rage, right? They watch, as we chastise our self as they rage anyway, then blaming ourselves for not correctly guessing how to stop it.

We say "Well if I had just made them a sandwich, cleaned the kitchen, guessed they were tired."

The whole household learns how to spot the first signs.

We get really good at it and we all work together to prevent the next rage episode looking relieved that we stopped it.

We become masters at second guessing that moment when the NPD parent is on the lead up to a meltdown.

We notice the footsteps as they enter the house and the pacing and the clenched fists and gritted teeth.

It is therefore not surprising that once we leave the abuser, that our children empathise with the Nex and take their side.

Poor Dad or Mum they had a bad childhood and they rage but that's 'normal' for them. and I love them.

After the relationship breaks down we continue to run around doing all the arranging and keeping things normal because it's important that our children have a normal relationship with both parents, right?

Creating the illusion that the NPD parent loves them normally because we don't want them to suffer like we did, when we realised they just doesn't care.

We must stop this and let the parent with no empathy show their child they don't care.

Let them screw things up!

This will hurt our children short term as it hurt us, but it will help to prevent a situation where they continue to believe that their Mum or

Dad is normal, thus letting a normal relationship without any boundaries develop with them, where they as the pathogenic parent then have the opportunity to psychologically damage them without exception and destroy or try to destroy loving bonds with the real safe loving parent in their life.

# The Ticking Time Bomb

"As I studied NPD, a psychological cancer that spreads through generations. I began to realise that parental alienation is just a ticking time bomb. Activated the day you say no more to the abuse."
Do you recognise Alienation before it's too entrenched?

Badmouthing the target parent in front of the child,
Limiting contact between the child and the target parent and the family,
Erasing the parent from the life and mind of the child,
Creating the idea or impression that the target parent is dangerous or mentally unstable,
Forcing the child to choose a parent.

Diagnosis Of Parental Alienation
Dr Craig Childress

"The complete suppression of the child's attachment bonding motivations toward a normal-range and affectionately available parent, in which the child seeks to entirely sever the attachment bond with this parent.
The child displays a characteristic set of five specific narcissistic/ (borderline) personality traits in the child's symptom display, toward the targeted rejected parent:
Grandiosity: The child sits in a grandiose position of judgment of the targeted parent as both a parent and as a person.
Absence of Empathy: The child displays a complete absence of empathy and compassion for the targeted parent.
Entitlement: The child expresses an entitled belief that the child's every desire should be met by the targeted-rejected parent to the child's satisfaction, and if these entitled expectations are not met to the child's satisfaction, then the child feels entitled to exact a retaliatory revenge on the targeted parent
Haughty and Arrogant Attitude: The child displays an arrogant attitude of haughty contempt and disdain for the targeted parent.
Splitting: The child's symptoms evidence the pathology of splitting, in which the child displays a polarized perception of his or her parents, with the supposedly favoured parent, characterized as the ideal all-wonderful parent, whereas the targeted parent is characterized as the entirely bad and worthless parent."

Here I have summarised Dr Childress Attachment Theory of Parental Alienation as I understand it,

"Alienated children internalise the sad angry feelings they have been taught towards the once bonded parent, when really they are feeling grief like that parent died. They think these feelings are their own and don't realise that re bonding the relationship would remove those sad angry feelings and make the child feel better again."

How Does my Child Become Aligned with the Alienator?

"AB-PA and Complex Trauma The origin of the attachment-based pathology of "parental alienation" (AB-PA) is to be found in the childhood attachment trauma of the narcissistic/(borderline) parent, who is then transferring this childhood trauma into the current family relationships, a process mediated by the personality disorder pathology of this parent that is itself a product of this parent's childhood attachment trauma. "
Dr Childress

So how can my once loving child or children now treat me with such disrespect and cruelty?
This change in behaviour is very hard to accept and understand.
The target parent goes from being a much loved parent to a subject of hate.
The alienator encourages and rewards any disrespectful behaviour towards the target parent, by bad mouthing the target and repeating lies about them which distorts the child's reality.
The child enjoys his new found elevated status and attention from the once critical parent.
The Alienator continues to abuse the target parent that they can no longer get physically close to, by using the child.
This is called abuse by proxy.
So because the alienator is angry at the target parent, the angry behaviour is reflected from the confused and brainwashed child, onto the target parent.
This can be verbal or physical and many target parents see their once lovely child become out of control.
My son ripped down Christmas decorations and threw a stool at me during this pre-alienation period.

As the anger escalates the loving feelings and happy memories of the target parent are overcome by it.

Once feelings reach this stage, it's very difficult to emotionally reach a child and bring them back from alienation but it can be done if you understand the process of Alienation.

The child buries all the positive feelings for the target parent because they are fearful of losing the alienator, who is the one constant in the child's life.

He is being told by the alienator that the target parent doesn't care and doesn't love him, so he clings onto the alienator.

In this way he becomes aligned with the alienator.

The child sees the alienator become extremely angry if he dares to show any loving or positive feelings towards the target parent.

He becomes frightened that the love of the alienating parent will be taken away, if the alienator sees him care about the target parent.

Over time he denies his loving feelings for the target parent, so they become buried so deep inside him that he becomes brainwashed into the new reality the alienator is teaching him and begins to outwardly 'hate' the target parent.

"When we are dealing with someone who severely lacks empathy, there is no level that they will not stoop to to make the target parent look like an unfit parent, even if this involves harming or upsetting the child or children they profess to love."

A Twisted Game of Chess

"When we initiate 'no contact' the Nex will try to regain control of you. This has nothing to do with love as they always were incapable of that. They will do this by whatever means they have available.

It becomes a twisted game of chess he or she is playing with your life. Your children, pets, your family and friends, new partners, houses cars anything you have together become pawns to be used to either regain control or if this is impossible to hurt you."

"The only way to deal with a Narcissist who is playing a twisted game of chess with your life, using your children as pawns, is to step away from their drama using the grey rock method and refuse to play."

"It is only when we shake off the 'victim mentality' that we are powerless and the Narc controls everything, walk away from their smear campaign as if we were untouchable, that we can be in a strong enough place to help our children."

How Parental Alienation Stays Under The Radar

How the pathogens of narcissism and parental alienation survives by staying under the radar.
The way they stay hidden is simple.
They deflect the blame from them onto the one that exposed who they are.
They turn the fingers of the law and social services and child protection that is pointing at them onto the one they are abusing by proxy.
The only way to survive is stepping away from their twisted game, even if that means stepping away from your own children caught up in the Narc web of lies and deceit.
You cannot rescue them, you have to wait for them to work out the truth and free themselves of the evil pathogen.

Preventing Parental Alienation Before It Becomes Entrenched

While you still have contact with your child.

For parents who are seeing signs of their children being alienated by the Nex.
Act now,
Read Divorce Poison by Richard Warshak,
Familiarise yourself with Dr Childress Attachment theory of Parental Alienation,
Look up Ryan Thomas who is a reunited alienated child and has done lots of helpful videos and books and online courses for target parents, to help you reconnect with your child.
Keep teaching unconditional love and boundaries to your child.

Preventing Parental Alienation is much easier than reversing its effects once it has taken hold.

## Validate

The most important word when communicating with an alienated child is 'Validate'. They have internalised the alienators script and they believe their thoughts are their own, so validate them using age appropriate language. Say to them "I understand you think I've done some horrible things, can you tell me what those are then maybe I could fix them?"
Validate their feelings "I'm sorry I make you feel uncomfortable or unsafe. Why do you feel like that? What can I do to make you feel better?"
Say to them "I'm sorry you are hurting, I understand you are in a difficult spot right now."

## Validate Your Alienated Child's Thoughts

When your child is being alienated and comes home to you repeating lies and you say that's rubbish.
"He or she is a liar do you not see!"
"Do you not see he or she is alienating you!"
This is the damage you are doing.
You are saying to your child,
"You are rubbish and your thoughts are rubbish!"
You are not giving him any validation for his own thoughts.
Hang on I hear you cry "but those are lies!"
Once the lies that the alienator has taught your child become entrenched and internalised, they become his own thoughts.
Your child needs very careful handling to prevent total alienation from you.

## The Alienator's Script

So how do I handle this?
You say "Ok Why do you think that about me?"
They have been taught the alienators script and you want them to once again think for themselves beyond what they are parroting.
You must calmly validate how they feel and what they are saying and you can then ask them why they feel that way. This gives you a great insight into the alienators script and strategy.
Over time they will see by your behaviour not your words, that you are not the person the alienator is painting you to be.

222

Knowledge and Love are the Strings in Your Bow

Right you're going through the court system fighting for custody. Social Services and the family courts have let you down and no one is listening. They are believing the alienators lies and false allegations against you.

What do you do before Parental Alienation becomes entrenched?
You are not unarmed and you are not defenceless.
The only person who can help your child is you.
So keep calm and educate yourself on Parental Alienation.

Empower Yourself with Knowledge

You need to empower yourself as much as you can, then teach your child before she or he is alienated that you love them and always will.
You can clearly say to them "even if someone may tell you I don't care about you in the future don't be fooled by them, don't listen to them."
Teach them to remember always to think back to this conversation and give them something to remind them of it. Something to keep and to look at everyday, like a locket for older children, or for younger children a teddy bear.
Tell them everyday when we are apart, you can look at this and remember "I love you always, no matter what anyone else says."
Tell them never to keep secrets from you.
Tell them "I want you to know you can tell me anything!"
"I will never be shocked or upset by anything you say, so if there's ever a time there's something you can't handle, or someone upsets you, I will help you."

Teach them other safe adults they can go to, like a school teacher or friend, if at anytime they can't reach you.
Teach strong boundaries.
Teach your child they have choices of what to eat, what to wear, what places to visit and ask them often to make these decisions and support them by saying "That's a great choice."
Teach them they do not have to choose who to love and they can love who they like.
Teach them that their body is their own and they do not have to hug or kiss anyone they don't want to.

Do not bad mouth the alienator or respond to the alienator and get caught up in drama they can use against you.

Wait for a time when your child is relaxed,

Reinforce these messages every time your child comes to visit.

'The NPD Parent Will Damp Down Your Child's Emotions.

They don't care if their child is upset, tired, or angry as it serves no purpose to them. The NPD parent will ridicule and call the child names for crying or being emotional. As a target parent of a child that is being alienated the most important thing you can do for them is to validate their feelings and tell them "it's ok to 'feel' as that's what makes us human." Let them cry and cuddle them, let them be sad and say "it's ok to feel negative emotions." Even anger is a useful emotion when channelled correctly and expressed in a healthy way.

The alienator will tease the child and call him names to drive a wedge between the target parent and the child such as "You're a pathetic Mummy's boy grow up!"

This will shame the child into not showing love and positive emotions for the target parent and is a classic alienating tactic.

"It is only when we begin to understand how the Narc views their children and doesn't have the capacity to love them or anyone else that we can get our head round Parental Alienation.

How could a parent that loves their child cause them pain just to hurt the other parent?"

Reversing the Alienators Programming

I know from my child's behaviour that he or she is being slowly alienated from me.

How do I deal with their abusive behaviour?

How do I try and reverse the alienators programming?

The following behaviour is extremely common with a child that is fighting alienation programming.

The child arrives from the alienators like a tightly coiled spring, withdrawn and hostile. It's important not to say anything regarding this behaviour but to be as warm and loving as you can and let them unwind for a resettling in period in their own room. Resist the urge to be too physically close immediately or ask lots of questions and wait for their cues that they are relaxing. As the visit goes on you will see your authentic child return and totally relax and be their usual loving self. Once you feel the barriers come down a bit spend time with your child and try to be the opposite of what the alienator is saying about you. Be loving, be fun and spend time reconnecting happier memories of happier times.

Towards the end of the visit you will find the child may withdraw and become agitated hostile and verbally or physically abusive as they are returning to the alienator. They will be feeling uneasy and may lash out verbally or physically.

Do not allow yourself to be abused and tell them calmly and firmly that you do not accept their behaviour. Say "I brought you up to be respectful and I don't accept the way you are speaking to me."

Tell your child calmly that you understand their anxiety and empathise how hard it is living between two worlds. Tell them you love them no matter what even if they are told otherwise.

Your child is in a really tough place.

Show your son or daughter the unconditional love that is sadly lacking in the alienators house.

Hate is Taught.

Children do not naturally ever hate a parent they once had a strong loving bond with. The alienator teaches them to disrespect and behave like they hate the target parent. Over the years as we drip love to counteract the poison and as the children grow and think for themselves, the very same 'hate' they have been taught boomerangs back into the alienators face. The real perpetrator is revealed, as the child escapes to the loving parents arms.

I've personally experienced this and I've seen this text book behaviour many times in action.

Please hang in there, we have to play the long game.

I want you to change your thinking.

I want you never to say my child hates me.

I want you to say my child loves me but isn't allowed to show it, or he is subjected to the wrath of the alienator.

Where a loving connection with a parent turns to what appears to be hatred, remember that true rejection is being indifferent to that parent. Hate is Taught.

If a child is showing hate through actions or words, then this can be rekindled into love.

A Glimpse Into the Narcs Alienating Playbook

Love bombing

"Narcs only give conditionally, if they want something in return and to manipulate and control their victim. This is why they dangle presents, treats and days out that never materialise and their children jump through new hoops as the goal posts are moved to secure the love they have never felt from the emotionally unavailable parent."

Don't Fall Into The Alienators Trap!

Why Love bombing works so well as a tactic to alienate your child I hear this all the time and I have been on the receiving end of this.

"The Nex love bombed him or her back with stuff."

Okay put yourself in your child's shoes.

Stuff is important to them so new clothes new toys games and holidays are all used as a bribe by the Narc, provided they do as they are told and come and live with them. Your child is being shown conditional love. However your child who has a weak attachment and has previously felt unloved by the pathogenic parent suddenly begins to believe he's important. He or she will do whatever it takes to get this 'love' from their over critical parent. So right now he mistakes that for love, which will be reinforced by the alienator who will say things about the target parent, who is likely being bled dry through the family court system and being narcissized. The alienator will say of the target parent, she or he doesn't care as they bought you nothing. This form of manipulation works and children who previously learned unconditional love from the target parent, will learn that being bought stuff is love. The difficulty is they crave the love from their emotionally unavailable parent.

What do I do?

Do not compete as your attempts will be bastardised and the alienator will say you are trying to buy them.

With a narc we are damned if we do and damned if we don't!

Do not let your child rule the roost on visits and feel obligated to buy things you cannot afford, or you are fulfilling the role that the narc parent is teaching your child, that you are to be disrespected and are only there to be used and to provide stuff for them.

Show your children your boundaries are strong.

Buy little meaningful things instead, as these are the things that will help the light bulb go on and teach your child the right things about love.

Keep showing unconditional love to your child and dripping love alongside the poison, however you can.

Tools from the Alienator's Handbook.

Emotional Blackmail

Anytime the Nex made me or the children cry when he was abusing us, he would say through gritted teeth "Look at you you're pathetic!" and we would quickly stop through fear.

Throughout our marriage the children never saw him cry.

The very last time the Nex assaulted me and he was arrested he told me through gritted teeth I had betrayed him and he told me I had ruined his life, so now he was going to ruin mine.

He cried like a baby in my daughters arms and told her I had stabbed him with a garden fork and he pulled up his trouser leg and showed her a wound he had previously.

This was to be the first time he used this waterworks tactic.

I then witnessed the Nex cry, when I was telling him I wanted a divorce and he got on his knees grabbed my sleeve and sobbed!

Before he was alienated from me, my son told me "Dad cries when we come to you as he cannot cope and misses us so much."

My son also told me his alienated sister phones and guilt trips him when he is with me to come back saying she misses him too.

It's common for Narcs male or female to use this emotional blackmail tactic and the children become parentified, that is, to feel responsible for the pathogenic parents emotional state.

They then feel they have to stay with the unstable parent for fear they will harm themselves.

Stripping You Of Your Mum or Dad Status

One of the ways a pathological parent alienates you from your child is by stripping you of your 'Mum' or 'Dad' status.

They begin by encouraging the child to call the new step parent Mum or Dad, thus removing the need for you in their life. Their mission is to erase your important status and encourage your child to disrespect you. Then your child will begin to call you by your first name. My son during alienation messaged me back after I tried to reach him saying "You are a liar Tammy!" Once his eyes were opened several years, later hearing "Hi Mum" for the first time had me in tears!

My brainwashed daughter still calls me "that woman" or worse when talking to my son. If your children or teens are at this advanced stage of alienation, you cannot push them or defend the lies. This makes it more entrenched.

You have to step out of the Narcs game, throw yourself back into life and wait for the children to see through adult eyes! Children are smart they will get there to the other side.

Your Child is Totally Alienated

You don't deserve to be here! Yes! You heard that right YOU don't deserve to have had your children ripped out your life! This is the work of a pathogenic parent who has alienated and brainwashed your children. You had your faults as a parent we all do and life was especially tough while trying to co-parent with a person who you now know, has a personality disorder.

You are an awesome Mum or Dad, You loved your children then and still do, and just for the record they love you too! Only they're not allowed to show you love right now, or they face the wrath of the alienator. They are rewarded for hating you! Sick right? Yes sick! Did I mention this isn't your fault?

Take my Hand

I may as well be dead! My life is over now, he's taken my children. What's the point in anything? I have nothing to get up for.
I hear you! I said all those things and meant them, as I lived from bed to chair after he ripped the children out my life. There are no cries of "Mum where's my maths book? Mum he's eaten all the chocolate cereal!" No arguments no nothing, just a deafening silence! No morning cuddles or giggles! No school rush no letters to sign, no lunches to pack, no texts during lunch break no last minute "Mum can I bring a friend home for tea!" or "wait till I tell you what happened today" texts.

There is only an echoing silence, as you stand at the entrance to their eerily tidy bedroom which used to be a hub of noise and activity after school. I remember her school bag and coat was flung down on the bed and there was cries of "Mum can I talk to you?" "Two seconds I'm just coming" I would shout, and run upstairs to hear about my children's day, as they jostled for attention saying "Hey I asked her first! "and "Mum can I just have a hug? I've had a bad day you know that boy I told you about, well I think he likes someone else. I just want him to notice me Mum."

Standing in the supermarket in a brain fog, crying over the chocolate cereal, not being able to move like your feet are stuck in glue, looking around at all the people with a purpose, rushing around buying food for dinner. Asking myself "What do I even like for dinner?" Grabbing a ready meal and a tiny milk carton and scurrying home with your head down before someone you know bumps into you and wants to know "What happened?" or asks "Where are the children?" Running in the house bolting the door just in case the Nex is stalking you!

This is where the alienator wants you! Scared and alone and deep in that 'pit of shit' so you can't climb out and fight back! So what are you going to do?
You need to hold on with your fingertips and pull yourself up and out of that deep hole! Your children are depending on you finding the YOU that is lost again!
Take my hand I'm going to show you how.
To crawl out that that 'pit of shit' we need to empower ourselves with knowledge.

Psychological Splitting

Dr Childress psychological splitting attachment theory.
The child develops insecure attachment with the target parent where they
have to align with the abusive parent in order to survive.
The abuser creates delusional beliefs in the children, causing them to go
into the victimised role.

In order to understand how your alienated child thinks we need to grasp
the concept of 'splitting,' which is a polarized perception of events and
people into extremes of all-good, ideal, and wonderful or all-bad, entirely
devalued, and demonized. In splitting, thinking and perception are black-
or-white.

At the moment those are the thoughts planted by the alienator that he or
she now has internalised as their own thoughts.
My son told me he would never see me again and he told me he did not
have a Mum, before we reunited.
This is the script of the alienator. Your son or daughter has gone back to
the infantile coping mechanism and 'psychologically split' to deal with it.
However his or her authentic self still has the same loving feelings for
you and like my son when he came out the fog, he or she will be loving
again.

When our children are brainwashed, that means they are psychologically
split into believing that the target parent is black and all evil and the
alienator is all white and good and nothing they do or cause is wrong. If
your alienated child or children are thinking like this, then anything they
see on your personal page, any rants at your Nex anything about court
or custody will be used against you. The Nex will run with the word
narcissism and in the twist that is so unfair in these situations, you will
be painted black and evil and this will be discussed with your children,
which will push them further away.

Take a Step Back

Unfortunately if the alienation of your child is severe and becomes
entrenched and they are psychologically split and aligned only with the
alienator like my eldest daughter you have to take a step back just to keep

230

your sanity. Particularly if you have been accused of harassment or could get into trouble for breaking the law. It's heartbreaking and you have to become like an Armadillo soft on the inside and hard on the outside to cope.

## The NPD Parent is Still a Flashing Red Ten Narc

Remember that the Nex is still the same flashing red ten narc, though and he or she will be trying to control every aspect of your child's life and be triangulating and manipulating all their relationships, in the same way they did with you. Our children get wise to this and one day they will get strong enough to leave, as my son did.

Until then live your life and get yourself mentally healthy so you are ready when they make that first tentative move.

## The Dysfunctional Family Structure

### One Parent Narcissistic and the Other Orbiting.

The family dynamics that appear normal to the outside world are not visible to anyone outside the family, yet are extremely destructive behind closed doors.

Narcissists have a charming demeanour and come across as loving caring family orientated individuals to anyone on the outside looking in.

The Nex in my case always had to have a family picture to display on social media, if we went out for the day.

These were invariably what I would now call 'grin and shoot' photos. The time before the photo, bullying the family to smarten up and come here and smile and if anyone said they didn't want to have a photo taken, he became angry and aggressive towards them.

The first most important message in this family, is we don't discuss family business with the outside world and anyone doing so is reprimanded for disclosing secrets.

The second message due to the Narcissists false self, was they are a cut above everyone else and anyone outside the family is inferior.

If one parent is narcissistic, the other parent must revolve around the narcissist to keep the narc on a level of pleasant and to meet the narcs needs. The narc is the king or queen of the house and everyone in the house is simply used to serve their every whim.

Everyone in the Narcs life serves a purpose and is used to provide narc supply.

Children are only seen as merely an extension of themselves and to stroke the grandiose ego of the narcissist.

Unfortunately the orbiting parent is so busy jumping through hoops to meet the Narcs ever changing needs (as the goalposts constantly move) that often the children's needs are unmet.

If I was busy doing something with the children and I was summoned and I didn't drop everything this was met with "You are my wife I asked you to do one thing!" Or emotional blackmail "If you want to do it alone carry on winding me up!"

The Children's Roles In A Narcissistic Family

To help you understand and get in your alienated child's head I'm going to explain their family dynamics from what I've learned from my own situation and my research.

In a normal family structure, sibling rivalry occurs naturally as part of growing up and with good parental guidance turns into respect for each other as children mature. Siblings are encouraged to be close and love each other and to take care of each other.

In the narcissistic family system there is typically a golden child and a scapegoat child or children.

The narcissistic parent picks the Golden Child to be an extension of himself. The narcissistic parent's other half, and they are lavished with attention and praise. Successes are celebrated and failures are diminished. The Golden Child can do no wrong. He gets love bombed and given the best of everything. The Scapegoat on the other hand becomes a target of criticism, the one whom all the problems of the family are projected. They can do no right. The scapegoat is taught to carry the anger of the family and becomes the target of rage and ridicule.

They are frequently blamed and shamed. They are systematically ridiculed and belittled carrying responsibility for the narcissist's own self hatred ,and whatever bad that happens through the day. Their major achievements are dismissed. Any money spent on them is the bare minimum and is spent unwillingly. If the scapegoat succeeds at something the reaction of the parent on the surface is one of praise and they will say the right things but their body language and facial expressions will convey displeasure and disapproval and subtly suggest that they're angry at this achievement.

The Scapegoat grows up understandably feeling very jealous of the Golden Child. Over time this leads to resentment leading to increasing conflict. This is the sole aim of the Narcissistic parent.

The Narc parent knows that if he divides the children this way there is more opportunity for triangulation. The Golden Child will be encouraged by the Narcissist to bully the Scapegoat, which adds to the increased conflict and drama.

In a narcissistic family dynamic, the siblings are triangulated by the narc parent and are taught to compete for love and affection, so despite being close when growing up might not be as close to each other as they otherwise would be as the disordered parent pits them cruelly against each other.

The result of these tactics like emotional abuse, lies, and neglect, ensures his or her children are always on their toes, working to earn their conditional love and provide them with an unending source of narcissistic supply.

The scapegoat is truly in a no win situation. The abuse is usually so insidious that it's not picked up by child protection services, so there is no option but to endure this situation, until the child becomes older and mentally strong enough to leave.

The Scapegoat is actually the most likely to escape these unhealthy family dynamics.

The damage done to the golden child is less obvious, but they are just another pawn in the Narcs twisted game as they are parentified and their role becomes that of the emotional caretaker of the disordered parent.

They grow up as merely an extension of the narc parent losing their own sense of self and all their boundaries are trampled by the narc as they learn that they are only valued for doing whatever makes the narcissistic parent feel better about themselves and if life choices are made that the narc disapproves of, the child risks total rejection.

The Golden Child's sense of self can end up being swallowed up by the Narcissist and she can end up being so enmeshed in them that she loses her identity.

She may well grow without proper boundaries and proper self identity. She is likely to remain, for a long time, as a puppet of the Narc, and if she does manage to break free, that process will be infinitely more painful for her than it is for the Scapegoat child.

The Scapegoat on the other hand, is the independent one. He's the one that begins to question and who's driven to seek answers leading to a light bulb moment, about Narcissistic Personality Disorder. He's the one who can break free from the toxic dynamics of the family and go on to create a healthy life and recover from the lies he was told about himself, since the day he was born.

How do siblings cope in a narcissistic family?

Some children cope by complying with the narcissistic parent and ignoring their own needs, Some rebel against the narc parent and some cope by identifying with and imitating the narcissistic parent, so that they end up becoming narcissists as well.

If one sibling copes by rebelling and another by complying, even if they were once close this drives a huge wedge between them. The compliant child sees the rebellious child as selfish.

If one sibling copes by complying and the other by identifying with the narcissist, the compliant child can end up being totally focused on the needs of his narcissistic sibling and parent, never thinking about his own needs. This pattern can continue into the child's adult relationships.

The Golden Child's Role

The golden child is another pawn in the narcs twisted game. She is one of the chief sources of narc supply and will be encouraged to form a strong alliance with the narcs new partner and both will be used to enable the narcs continuing abuse of the target parent and non compliant siblings. The golden child has undergone a process of parentification so she feels responsible for the narcs emotional well being and often financial state too. She will work hard to keep the parent happy and on a level of normal. She will be emotionally bullied and lied to by the narc if the target parent files any charges for assault or harassment against the narc. She will be roped in to get the target parent to drop child maintenance payments and she will join the bullying team to get the target parent to hand over their house or other assets to the narc. She will also be used to help to alienate her non compliant siblings from the target parent and she will be rewarded and encouraged to 'hate' the target parent.

If the golden child doesn't comply with the narcs wishes at any point she will be psychologically abused, using tactics such as the silent treatment. The golden child will therefore learn to comply and be rewarded for this with the love she has never felt from the emotionally unavailable toxic parent.

Slowly Slowly Catchy Monkey!

Once you have established which role your alienated child or children play, either the golden child or scapegoat in the new family structure, we can work out the best strategy to reach them. This usually involves making a considerable effort to reach out to the scapegoat child who is less enmeshed and less aligned with the alienator. Yes I know you want to reach out to both or all of your children but you need to treat them as separate and work out a different strategy for each one, based on what you know.

The golden child is the one that provides the narc with supply and is the one that is therefore being love bombed mistakenly believing they are loved in a normal way.

These children are the hardest to reach, as they will do anything to finally secure the 'love' of the over critical parent as they have searched all their childhood to feel that love.

You will have to take a step back from this child's anger and abusive behaviour.

Concentrate your efforts on the scapegoat child as this is usually the one that is treated badly and the narc will discard first because they do not comply and provide little narc supply.

They usually end up rebelling against the alienator.

Its usually quite clear cut as to which of your children are in each role ( please refer to my previous blog on the narc children's roles and do your own research)

When we have identified the scapegoat child we can come up with a long term strategy to reach them and steer them towards their light bulb moment by showing or sending however we can drips of love alongside the poison they are being taught.

After we rescue the scapegoat child, as I have we then encourage the scapegoat child to reach out to the golden child.

The narc will lock down the golden child and want to divide and conquer the siblings to hang onto the remaining child for narc supply.

The golden child as per narc protocol will be encouraged to be verbally abusive and block the scapegoat child, but gradually over time as the enlightened target parent we can encourage our child to maintain a relationship with the golden child.

As the scapegoat understands and moves away from the toxic parent he or she is in a much healthier place to continue to reach out and drip love alongside the poison to help the golden child reach their own light bulb moment and escape the narc parents daily abuse.

The Bubble of Denial

The comfort of denial is a tough place to leave for a brainwashed alienated child.

Who wants to believe that their parent has a mental disorder? A parent they've worshipped and adored since they were tiny.

Once the bubble of denial pops for good there's no going back to that comfy place.

They have to face the same grief process that we did upon discovering our partner never loved us and never cared.

Put yourself in your daughter or sons head.

Would you want to go through that pain?

Realising the love you have been yearning for, the approval you have searched for your entire life from this parent, is never going to come? Learning that your parent is incapable of love?

Then once they have got their head around that, they have to face the harrowing guilt of the horrible way they have treated you, the loving target parent.

They don't understand the hate they have been taught, they want to love you.

This is where our young adults are as they try to break free from a toxic parent.

Be gentle with them, love them however you can and be there to catch them when they fall.

"Turning 18 is not a magical age of understanding. Your child may wake up at 17 or 18 or could still be brainwashed and controlled into their twenties. However following this advice and dripping love helps to create a series of light bulb moments over time to reach your authentic child. Have patience and understand if they are not ready to listen just yet."

The Obsessive Alienator

The obsessive alienator doesn't have anything better to do. They live empty lives so are hell bent on causing revenge drama and pain as they see us quite simply as having wronged them. How dare we see through their public facade and threaten to expose who they really are? Threaten their very existence? Remember they will protect their public mask at all costs.

How dare we try to leave? This triggers their deep childhood wounds of abandonment for which we must be punished and so they can't let us move on. Thus follows the smear campaign where they project their faults onto us so the finger of the authorities swings from the perpetrator to the victim. This is how they hide their pathology by deflecting the blame onto the victim.

We are Fighting a Pathogen not a Person

Thanks to all of you who share your harrowing stories with me. I'm so sorry for all you have endured at the pathogenic exes hands. I'm going to send out some tough love to you all.

For those with anger deal with it! Step away from the manufactured drama that the Nex created or is still creating. Try and put the lies your Nex created into a box now where they can't hurt you. Stop wasting time explaining your side to people who don't care and don't understand. You need that energy and drive for yourself to heal. You need to channel it constructively.

The very first step to helping your children is to heal yourself from the Nex abuse and work through the stages of grief at missing them and build yourself a virtuous and beautiful life.

Let go of the guilt you have for moving forwards.

You aren't leaving them behind they will catch you up.

This will put you in a better position to fight for them.

Giving up is NOT an option as you must rescue them from this sickness. Learn grow and get healthy to get your authentic children's love to shine again.

It's easy to get sucked into the darkness and to hate everything that has happened to you.

Just move a little to your left or a few steps to your right because where there is dark there is also light.

You Cannot Fight For Your Children From A Place Of Panic and Despair.

Elisabeth Kubler Ross introduced the 5 stages of grief following a bereavement and modifying these to fit my experience. I have identified the stages of parental alienation a target parent has to go through, before they are in a mentally healthy space so their children return.

Disbelief, despair and hopelessness leading to anger, grief and acceptance that they are severely alienated.

You cannot fight for your children from a place of disbelief pain despair and hopelessness and must work through grief and towards acceptance if you are to become strong enough to fight for them.

I'm going to deal with the different stages a target parent goes through in some detail beginning with Denial. Most of us with few exceptions have experienced denial and been in the denial stage first hand with an abusive partner so we need to tap into how our children are feeling being stuck in that place where like us they are wanting to believe the disordered parent is telling the truth. We love our children and our children love us right?

Yes but love is no protection against the pathological alienator. Yes our authentic children still have loving feelings for us but we are not dealing with our authentic children right, now, we are dealing with puppets of the disordered parent that they are heavily enmeshed with.

Once you get your head around that bit we can work through the first stage of despair panic hopelessness and denial, but allow yourself time to process this.

## Do not Deny Your Grief

The worst thing you can do is bottle it up or push it down.
You must allow yourself to feel the pain of losing your child or children. During alienation I dreamed of my children. I would go right back to when we were close and at first they were traumatic dreams and I would wake sobbing or panicking about them but as time went on I found these dreams comforting.
I have tears now thinking about them but it actually helps change our mindset as only when we disconnect from hopelessness pain and panic and believe our children will come back that they actually do.

I am reunited with my son after two and a half years of no contact despite me reaching out often.
My daughter is still alienated and I'm right there with you in your pain. Try to move past the panic and trauma by letting yourself feel the grief deeply. If I hadn't I would not be here writing this sitting with my son. I had to do this to move forwards.
I allow myself to routinely grieve for my daughter.
You have to face the pain head on.
Acknowledge it! Feel it deeply and let it go to get mentally stronger.
I know it doesn't feel that way but trust me each tear you shed makes you a warrior.

## Acknowledge it Feel it Deeply and Let it Go

## Dealing With Grief Pain

Accept it as ok then allow yourself to feel it deeply in a part of the day where you choose then let it go. I never believed it was possible to control grief sadness and pain till I went through it and learned to control it, I could literally wait for a good spot to cry. If I was out or had friends round I would say "C'mon hold it together girl, when they've gone I'm going to cry so hard!" After I shut the door I would cry till I was ugly and had panda eyes. It's very important to allow yourself this level of sadness to rinse the pain out your body so it can't consume every waking moment. Then rest and be kind to yourself as crying in itself is exhausting! After a good cry and a lot of self care you will feel emotionally cleansed.

Anyone with me? It's ok to have moments where we feel like this, from months of bottled up negative emotions. Let yourself feel these feelings, cry shout stamp your feet! It's ok to be human. Remember the narc made you minimise your feelings while you were with them as it did not serve them to know you were angry, tearful ill or tired. Now you must re learn how to let those feelings out in a healthy way. Feeling is what makes us human and that is to be celebrated.

Grief is Just Love With No Place to Go

I know how it feels to grieve for children that are still living.
I know how it feels to be utterly bereft and not be able to leave the house.
Everywhere there are loving children and parents reminding us of our pain, there are TV adverts of loving families and children laughing as they run through a cornfield without a care in the world.
I'm going to tell you how I coped after I reached the pits of hell and locked myself away.
I made myself leave the house and I purposefully visited friends with children,
I began to visit my nephews and nieces and every time I went home to my empty house I cried and grieved for my children, but over time
I drew strength from the loving hugs and squeals of delight when my nephew wrapped his arms around me and told me he loved me.
From reading stories to my friends 3 year old, it triggered my pain and sometimes I cried but I smiled too and I giggled at his antics and marvelled at his wide eyed wonder for life.
Sometimes I did lock myself away again and cry but most of the days I threw myself back into life.
If this is you please get out there, hug other children draw strength from the love that is all around us.
Let it touch your pain and let it heal your heart.
For it's only when the pain is lessened and we have worked through our grief that we are in a mentally healthy place and our children will return to our loving arms again.

## Dealing with Anger

## Anger is a Useful Emotion

This is one of the most difficult stages a target parent must progress through after finally admitting to themselves that their child is being alienated.

After leaving the relationship we are shocked and appalled that the very person who professed to love us so much would try and destroy our relationship with our children by hurting not only us but them so deeply. This is when we need to remember we are fighting a pathology not a person.

Anger is a normal and useful emotion to feel when we feel hopeless and powerless but it doesn't feel good because we aren't used to feeling this much overwhelming rage.

We ask ourselves "How dare he or she take our children? How can he or she deliberately hurt our children? Why is he or she doing this? Why is he or she smearing my name and lying about me all over town? Why is he or she trying to destroy me?"

## Coping With Anger

Ways to deal with unprocessed anger.

Go somewhere alone and shout and scream.
Play loud empowering music and sing along.
Take up a sport, I chose kickboxing, swimming and then yoga to calm me down.
Freeze ice and take it outside and smash it against the wall,
Dead head the roses and cut the hedge.
Whatever works for you.

If you can't deal with the anger then get a trained therapist to help you through this stage.

## The Long Term Effects of Anger

Feeling angry for a long period of time can have really negative consequences on both your emotional and physical wellbeing.

It can leave us feeling sick and unable to eat and completely unable to focus on anything so sabotaging our career.

It can cause us to lash out at those around us which can seriously affect our relationships with friends and supporters.

It also leaves us feeling so stuck and so overwhelmed that we end up self harming or turning to alcohol.

It can even cause things like high blood pressure, so addressing our anger is of extreme importance so keep our physical and emotional health topped up through this extremely tough time.

Feel it deeply, acknowledge it and let it go.

For those of you who are also angry at the Nex new OW or the OM as she or he played a large part in alienating your children.

Letters to The Other Woman from my own experiences:

You can switch the gender if you are suffering at the hands of the O.M.

How Dare You!

I wrote this one a few years ago on the eve of Mothers Day and it will resonate with anyone in the angry with the O.W stage.

What kind of woman steals another woman's children?

A modern day Lady Macbeth plotting and lying, working as an accomplice enabling an abuser!

What kind of woman teaches another woman's children to hate the woman who carried them and birthed them?

What kind of woman without a pang of remorse then plays happy families with those children?

What kind of woman sits at the breakfast table opening Mother's Day gifts that are only meant for her because she helped teach those children the distorted truth, the twisted lies and false reality of an abuser so they now have no contact with the mother that raised them, tucked them in bed at night and read them stories, woke them in the morning with a kiss and walked them to school, taught them to use a knife and fork and to use the toilet properly, baked cakes with them and taught them to read, sang songs and danced with them, held them tightly and soothed them when they cried and stroked their forehead when they were sick?

There's a Special Place In Hell Reserved For You!

As the years went on I worked through my feelings and the hate turned to pity.

## You Walk in My Shoes Now

You slipped into them while they were still warm and when I found out he was cheating with you I admit I was jealous. Jealous as I watched you doing all the things he had promised to do for me. Jealous of you stealing my precious time with my children posting pictures of my daughter and my son and my dog and playing happy families. For a while, while I was still trauma bonded with him I was even jealous that you could make him happy when it was clear that I could not.

As the months went by and you alienated my children people told me you had left your house as you suspected he cheated and he had refused to leave but you had gone back and patched things up. I heard he shouted at you and threw things at you in a rage. I heard he made you get out of bed when you were sick to drive him somewhere. The jealousy that you had stolen my life turned to pity. There you are now with my children walking on egg shells every day trying to keep him pleasant, struggling to turn the money wheel as fast as he spends it and I say to myself karma is real. You walk in my shoes now.

## The Nex New Target is a Victim

Don't hate her pity her for she is a victim! Ok I'm going to shed some light on why the new OW behaves the way she does. He likely groomed her while you were in the devalue stage so love bombed her telling her various lies such as my wife doesn't understand me, we aren't intimate anymore she's a bad mother she's abusive etc.

Once in the new relationship the Nex will begin to triangulate you, the ex and try and make the OW jealous saying things like I loved her so much before she changed ( realised he was a narc) so she continues to provide the best narc supply. He will say things like my wife never brought me breakfast in bed, my wife never cleaned the house so the new OW is caught in this treadmill of being the better woman yet at the same time, once he hits the devalue button he begins to compare her unfavourably to you. My wife was so pretty, so slim she always took care of herself till she went crazy or cheated (rumbled him for what he is) so the OW feels the need to clone the ex wife and becomes increasingly insecure that he may leave her and return to his ex. He may say to her if he's stalking his ex wife ( projection) she's obsessed with me! If children are involved sadly the OW has to prove she is the better mother too which is where the alienating behaviour begins.

## Forgive Yourself

Forgive yourself now for what you didn't know then.
How can anyone predict or understand such evil psychopathy unless they are dealing with it?
Always remember you did the best for your children with the knowledge you had at the time.

## Put Your Oxygen Mask On First

Try and let go of the guilt you feel about having to leave your children when you tried to get them out with you. You could not help your children if you had stayed in that toxic relationship.
When I was a student nurse the first thing I was taught before assisting anyone else in an emergency situation was protect yourself first, so even if a patient was gushing blood from a major artery you still go and put gloves on before helping them.
This is the same in all emergency services.
Similarly when travelling on an airplane the advice is if the oxygen masks drop, parents must put their own mask on first and then help their children.
If you are hurt, unconscious or dead you can't help anyone.
If we apply this to getting out of an abusive situation with your children it is the same. Sadly our system creates this scenario where there are services in place where you can escape but then have to leave them. None of this is your fault. Your job now is to get mentally strong so you can help them and find safe ways and the right people to get them out.

## Letting Go of Guilt

Let go of the guilt you feel about moving forwards and living your life. We need to grow and learn so we are mentally healthy when our children come knocking.
Keep putting one foot in front of the other and pushing forward.

Once parental alienation has taken a hold of our children the blame and guilt we feel for losing them is the worst part.

Even when we study the pathology of the Nex and learn it is nothing we have done and there was nothing we could have done or now do to have a better outcome, in our hearts we believe we are a bad Mum or Dad and we believe we failed.

Well I'm here to tell you to put down that huge stick you have been beating yourself with!

I'm here to remind you that in actual fact it's because you are such an awesome parent and it's because you love your children so much that's why the Narc took them.

They cannot hurt or degrade or physically punish you anymore so this is the only way they have left to hurt us and punish us for leaving them and exposing who they really are.

We caused a huge narcissistic injury to their fragile ego. So we must be punished and smeared and have the only thing that matters to us taken away from us.

They observed how we loved our children they watched in envy as the bond developed and now they are a seething mass of revenge.


When my son returned two and a half years later he told me it wasn't anything I did he simply said "Dad told it in a different way and when I was there he made you sound like you were causing trouble!" He said "He understands why his sister still thinks the way she does."

He now reluctantly understands the slow poisoning of his mind.

Anyone in my situation with alienated children you must hang on with your fingertips if you have to.

You must grow mentally strong and fight this pathology with all of your heart and soul.

My son was verbally vile during alienation and told me "If
I told you I loved you the words would stick in my throat!"

If I tried to contact him he would swear and sign his name lots of hate.

Things change and they change fast and that hate that the Narc created in them boomerangs right back at the creator!

My son wrote in my Christmas card last year "You're the best Mum and hope you have a lovely day and I can't wait to spend it with you", with love and kisses.

Your children will one day follow your drips of love home to you, their loving parent.

Keep reaching out despite repeated rejection and keep showing them the door is always open to unconditional love.

## How Do We Build a Happier Brain?

We talked about when you are in an abusive relationship we become addicted to pain peptides. Recovering from this addiction can only take place when we release this by building a happier brain.
Building new positive neural pathways.
How?
By doing anything that makes us soul happy.

## You Need To Find The You That Is Lost

"Who am I? Or rather who was I before this nightmare began?" If you are asking this question or your eyes fill up with tears then there is inner work to be done. Our true selves get lost in this fight as we struggle to remember who we are. "I am a loving Mother or I am a loving Father" I hear you cry!
Yes and no one can take that away from you, that's what our daily pain is about and that is what we are fighting for, to be in our children's lives, but until you let go of the guilt at moving forwards and reconnect with the YOU that you were before this mess nothing can change!
You have to work through the grief despair and brokenness to reach a mentally healthy place to help yourself and help your children.
What are you doing for YOU today to help you achieve that?

You need to reconnect with the 'You' that is lost in all that grief and despair.
Once you rebuild a beautiful toxic free life you will attract your children back.
Remember the Nex is still a flashing red ten toxic narc and your children will have their own issues with him or her. He or she will meddle in their relationships and still display all the controlling behaviour they showed to you. Do whatever you need to do to be mentally healthy to catch your children when they need you to escape the NPD parent! Show them the door is open.
They are going to need you more than they ever have in their lives! Be ready with open loving arms.

Some Days Are Harder Than Others

We feel so thoroughly miserable and we feel so hopeless and powerless we can't get motivated to do anything at all.

The more our family and friends try and jolly us along and involve us in their plans the more angry alone and upset we feel and we push them away because they don't understand.

How can anyone understand the loss of a living child or children unless they've been there?

It's ok on those days to recognise this as a bad day and shut the door on the world.

It's very important to deal with these feelings or risk going to the supermarket and bursting into tears over the bananas because they were your child's favourite fruit. Yes that was me!

So when you have one of these days shut the door get on the sofa sleep eat 'treat' foods and watch mindless things on the TV. Comedy is always good to lift your spirits or get stuck into a boxed set or a good book you've been meaning to read.

You are right no one can possibly understand and you don't have to deal with the rest of the world today!

Tomorrow you will give yourself a huge kick up the butt and start again refreshed.

The Importance of Me Time

During Narc rule you were conditioned to put your needs on hold to pander to his or her every whim. You jumped through hoops with ever changing goal posts that we can never quite reach to ensure he or she remained happy and on a level of pleasant. Once the relationship is over it is not surprising that we continue to put ourselves last.

When the Nex does the unthinkable evil of gradually destroying the close bond we have with our children it's especially important to practice good self care during this time to get mentally strong to fight.

Good self care is a new skill we have to learn and is part and parcel of learning to love ourselves.

I cannot stress the importance of having a little 'me' time during this psychologically challenging time! If you're to fire on all four cylinders and be in full fighting mode you must take regular breaks.

When we become free we must let go of the guilt we feel about leaving our children behind. You know all those things you've been promising yourself for years you will do? It's time to start planning and do them! Get out your bucket list! Do you want to travel? Are there piles of books you keep meaning to read? Do you have unwatched boxed sets? Do you keep putting off college or university? Do you want to teach yourself to cook or improve a particular skill? Have you put off visiting friends? Do these things for you and do these things for your children to show them who you really are! Show them the non dampened down version of you!

What are you going to do today to get in a mentally healthy place?
Go smash new goals at the gym!
Lose that weight you've been meaning to lose!
Go to college or university!
Travel!
Do all those things you have put on hold!
Let your children see you are living your life and have moved on past the drama.
Keep dripping love they will catch you up.

The Wound That Never Heals

This is what the alienator wants.
He or she wants us to be in pain everyday suffering with a big gaping wound that never heals as they hold our child or children captive.
Everyday tinged with sadness and special events like birthdays and Christmas that usually bring us so much joy ruined as our children can't be there. So are you going to let this person that has caused so much pain already in your life continue their control of you? Wreaking havoc through everyday!
Or are you going to show them the greatest revenge of all?
No revenge and being happy despite the fact they have your heart in their hands?
Let us show them we can be at peace and experience joy and love.
This is what the narcissist envies the most, being able to feel joy peace and love.
Close your eyes and imagine not being able to feel the purest of love for your child?

Keep on dripping love alongside the poison and one day soon your children will come.

It's Ok To Feel Numb

When I say I'm over losing contact with my children due to abuse by proxy I mean I don't sob into my pillow at night and rush to tuck them in bed to find them not there, I don't wake to the gut wrenching agony of knowing I don't know where they are and what they're doing right now. Instead after nearly two years of alienation and watching them grow into young adults on snatched updates on Facebook and Twitter and well meaning friends telling me how they bumped into my son and isn't he tall now. Instead there's this numbness. The constant ache that would've killed me is gone.

It can be triggered by songs or visiting places we went together or looking at photographs but the numb feeling keeps me grounded. Keeps me putting one foot in front of the other and helps me to concentrate on what is important. Reuniting with the babies I carried and gave birth to and love so much that it makes my heart physically ache.

I hope they feel my love like an unattached wave of energy from my heart to theirs and they escape from that evil toxic soulless being that they mistakenly believe loves them but in truth keeps them away from me to hurt me as I dared to say "Enough I'm done!"

Tell the Truth Always

Parenting alienated children turns everything we have ever learned about parenting on its head. "Tell the truth always" we tell our children yet we cannot for fear of further alienation.

The softly softly unconditional love approach is the ONLY way that truly works. Over time dripping the truth alongside the poison they are fed and living a virtuous life so they hear in a subtle way through social media and friends and have a reality check of their own.

Do Not Give The Alienator A Loaded Gun To Shoot You With!

Give the alienator NO ammunition! Don't beat yourself up! Find a smaller stick to hit yourself with! It's a natural reaction to want to speak the truth and defend ourselves to our children against lies! However when you are dealing with a pathogenic parent it's like giving them a gun to shoot you with! Validate your child's feelings, show them empathy love and understanding. This is not their mess and they didn't ask for any of this.

We know the Nex is going to lie and exaggerate the truth or twist it or bend it to suit him or her to make you look like a bad parent.
Do not give him or her any fuel to enable them to do this.
Do not engage with them,
Do not badmouth him or her to your children,
Do not accept abuse from your children and correct the lies by encouraging them to think for themselves,
Say to them so "Why do you think I'm crazy?"
Discuss it with them rationally and try to get them to talk beyond the alienators script.
Do not add fuel to the fire, do not give them a loaded gun to fire back at you.
Get help if you need to with your anger and do NOT feed the Narcissist!

I cannot stress this enough!
Do not continuously defend yourself against the lies and make yourself look crazy!
Build a virtuous and beautiful life.
Get yourself mentally in a good place.
Prove you are none of those things the Nex said about you by your behaviour,
Prove to your children through social media through word of mouth you are not who he or she says you are,
They will come.
Show them understanding patience strength and love.

The Softly Softly Approach

With alienated children we have to take a softly softly approach. We cannot orientate them towards the truth. We cannot point out and defend the lies about us and our families. When poison is being dripped into our children's ears the only solution is to drip love alongside it.
To live virtuously so eventually they will see for themselves the truth. It is a horrible realisation for them when they get their light bulb moment as to who their toxic parent really is.. Be ready with open loving arms to

catch them when they fall. They will need you more than they have ever needed you in their lives.

Educate yourself on PA known as Abuse by Proxy now. This is not about loving their children they are incapable of that. This is about using their children their property as pawns in their sick twisted game. Life is a game to a narc about winning and hurting anyone they have discarded or anyone who tries to rip the nice mask off them to reveal the monster to others.

Target parents say to me "It all happened so fast, we were so close and now my child won't speak to me!" I'm going to tell you the truth. It didn't happen fast. The seeds of alienation were slowly and systematically planted a long time ago by the pathogenic parent, most started the brainwashing while you were still together so it's going to take time to counteract it and that's why dripping love slowly alongside the poison is the only method that works.

I cannot give you a 'one size fits all' answer to how to reach out to a specific alienated child as it depends on so many different factors. This is highly specialised very stressful and time consuming work and requires weeks of coaching. We have to look at the child and particularly how long they've been with the alienator how old they are, their role in the new family structure and how deeply entrenched they are, that is how closely aligned to the alienator they are.

However I have successfully used my 'drip love' method that follows in many cases which I describe in many of my articles, so please take your time to read them and study Dr Childress attachment theory which will help you to decide how to reach out without alienating them further.

Remember my son used to say "Go away and leave me alone" anytime he was approached by me during his alienation. Please remember he or she is being bullied and coerced into rejecting you. If they show any positive loving signs towards you they are psychologically hurt by the alienator.

If you could read your alienated child's mind they would be thinking something like this:

Go Away Leave Me Alone!

"Go away leave me alone, if they see me talking to you they will take my laptop and phone away so I can't talk to my friends.

They will not talk to me for hours, they will start saying horrible things about you that I don't want to hear, I've tried defending you when they say nasty things but they are nasty to me and say I'm useless like you.

They told me you spent all the money and you are stealing our house and you are moving on and no longer love me.

I don't understand because I know you love me but I can't see you at the moment because it's too difficult and makes them so angry at me, that makes me upset and angry and I can't be angry at them as they will hurt me and make me feel bad.

They're saying I don't need you because they love me so much and will give me anything I need. They told me if I see you then I can't see them anymore and I can't see my dog ever again.

You stopped trying to contact me.

So do you still love me?

They are telling me that you don't love me and although I don't want to believe it I am starting to see you've forgotten about me.

You don't love me do you?

They're telling me that you never even wanted me!

Is this true?

Well if it is then I don't want you either you are not my Mum or Dad anymore so I'm cutting you out my life!"

How Do I Deal With This?

Unconditional love is the only antidote to Parental Alienation so drip feed it slowly to your children however you can.

Keep Dripping Love Alongside the Poison

Drip 'Love'

If your child was rushed into hospital fighting a disease that was threatening to take over his body what would you do?

You would push for the fastest and best possible emergency care and as a medical team we would quickly assess your child, diagnose the pathogen and act fast!

We would be getting IV antibiotics into your child and probably fluids as well to help your child fight the pathogen.

We would be doing regular observations to assess how your child is responding to the drug regime.

I want you to think of the slow poisoning of your children's mind like this,

We assessed your child is unwell and needs medical intervention fast! So what are we going to do?

Well we can't do this but you can.

We need your help. We are going to ask you to drip feed 'Love' into your child because love is the most powerful antidote to the pathogen that is PA.

We know it's going to be a long haul but we know this is how we are going to overcome this pathogen so your child will be well again.

Would you leave your child or sit by your child's bedside and hold their hand? They need to know you are there.

You can leave for a while take a rest, go for a bite to eat or a walk to clear your head, but ultimately when your child wakes you need to be there dripping love alongside the poison, fighting for them, holding their hand and stroking their forehead.

We know getting your child better is going to take time but that one day when they wake we will notice the flush of their cheeks has returned to pink and they turn to you and smile and say "I love you."

"To reconnect with your authentic child you have to try to create light bulb moments of clarity by dripping love alongside the poison, so over time they begin to question the alienators false reality that they have internalised as the truth."

Drips of Love

When I say to target parents 'drip love' what do I mean?

Ok here's the simple answer and it's not one you or any alienated parent wants to hear.

You can't make him listen to you in the short term and yes he will be seeing you right now as a stalker because that's the negative spin the alienator is putting on it.

Yes he is being lied to and told you no longer care about him.

The whole point is that like my son every time you 'find him' on social media he will block you because that's what he's programmed to do.

So what do you do?

We play the long game.

Imagine your child had a long term illness and he's in the hospital and he's on a drip that is slowly over time making him better, this is what we are doing.

Over time you are dripping love to fight the poison in his system.

Every few months you open a new Twitter or FB and you write as normal a message as you can muster "Hey what a lovely picture looks like you're having loads of fun. Here's a picture of me and kitty I thought you'd like. I hope school is going ok, I love you so much, I'm always here for you." then you press send and wait.

If the message is blocked immediately do not give up wait a few weeks and try again.

However if you aren't instantly blocked then even if there is no response you are winning.

Do NOT reply unless he does or this in itself may be enough pressure to get you blocked again.

If you are still unblocked the next few days like a few of his pictures, stay low you have a channel of communication.

Do not friend request him he can't do that as the alienator is watching.

Now you continue to build your happy social media and show him the opposite of everything the alienator says you are.

1. You are a normal and a nice person and you have friends and family, particularly other children that love you.
2. You miss and love him, so on pictures of a family day out underneath you talk with his aunty "Do you remember when we..."

Mention the alienated child. He would've loved this.

These drips of love over time will lead up to your child's light bulb moment.

Smuggling Love

How do I drip love if I don't see my child and I'm blocked from his life?

It's not easy to smuggle in drips of love through the iron curtain and past the two headed fire breathing dragon but it can be done! You just have to think outside the box!

I want to share with you some of the ways I smuggled my son some love over the two and a half year alienation.

I asked a friend to deliver an Easter Egg.

I worked with family services and arranged to meet him but before each meeting took place he changed his mind.

I took his birthday presents to my daughters workplace.

I opened new social media accounts and wrote short loving positive messages every few months which were always instantly read and blocked.

I took pancakes for pancake day to my daughters workplace.

I sent him messages through his friends which he responded abusively to.

I spoke with and worked with the school counsellor until I got ignored because of the pathogens brainwashing so after a few months I took things in for my son and just left them with reception saying he had forgotten his PE kit or a letter for a trip which contained a card from me and I would laugh with the receptionist how forgetful boys are!

I smuggled a few drips of love every few months using any of these methods.

I want you to think about ways you can smuggle your child some love.

Message to a brainwashed alienated child:

Keep it short and positive,

'Do not says'
Your feelings and how upset you are missing them,
I love you and I miss you more than once as it creates guilt in your child. Do not say "it's been so long when are you going to contact me? How could you do this to me after everything I have done for you?" Your child is already being emotionally bullied by the Nex and won't respond well to pressure from you.

'Do says' to draw the past and the present together and create light bulb moments.

Use a few of these ideas in each message, perhaps one memory trigger, one joke, one meme and one "I love you."

Anymore and you will overwhelm and anger your child and get blocked.

Create memory triggers of better times.

Be chatty "hope you're enjoying school"

"Do you remember when we.."
Use humour and connect with them through memes you used to share.
What did you used to chat about?
Minions? Like "I was watching minions the other day and I thought of you."
Mention other children who love you. You could say, "I looked after your baby cousin at the weekend and we had a sleepover, we had ice cream and he was so funny as he put the bowl on his head. I remember when you used to do that and I had to bath you."
Mention pets that they miss "Your kitty is getting so big now. He was so funny yesterday and caught a mouse and it was running round the house."
Mention things you are doing that you never used to do showing you are not sat around moping. Like "I started learning Japanese cooking, and tie it to a memory trigger "Do you remember when you and me made sushi we stuffed them so full we could hardly roll it!"

Think about it from their perspective.
When light bulbs start popping you will trigger their grief pain and you will likely get what comes over as a hostile angry response perhaps a tirade of swear words or just "Go away leave me alone!" Or "I hated making sushi with you I hate you!" Or they may read the message and ignore it as they are overwhelmed.
If they simply block you they may be overwhelmed and scared so wait a while and try again in a few weeks.
Meanwhile add the picture of his baby cousin with a bowl on his head or his pet in case he peeks on your Facebook through a friend.

Respect Your Alienated Child's Boundaries.

If your child responds angrily to your 'drip of love' then that's ok because you hit a sore spot! Do not respond angrily back. If they do not block you take your cue from them. If it's an angry response or verbal warfare full of swear words and lies then take a step back as you now have an open way of communication.
If they ask you to remove photos of them accusing you of stealing them from their wall do so.
If they ask you to stop contacting them step back a bit, tell them "Okay I respect your wishes, I love you." This is least likely to get you blocked.

If the alienator responds in an angry way to you contacting your child as mine and many do this means you are getting somewhere take a step back! Think of this process like a dance where you take your cue for the next move from your child.

Do Not Accept Abuse From Your Children

You must not accept abuse from your alienated children. I know it's hard but if we do what is the point in leaving our abuser? When we accept mini versions of the same abuse?

You are allowing the alienator to continue abusing you through them.

The opposite of what you are trying to teach them by leaving their abusive parent.

No, you tell your children they must speak to you and treat you with respect when they talk to you badly. You say "Do not speak to me that way! I never raised you to be so disrespectful."

Sometimes taking a stand and distancing yourself by taking a step back from your abusive child is the way we show them we deserve better and do not accept abuse of any form.

Keep showing love and remember when they verbally abuse you it is because they are being poisoned.

Always show them unconditional love and say. "I do not like your behaviour but I love you and when you are ready to be loving and respectful I am here for you."

Your angry partially alienated son or daughter is screaming abuse down the phone!

You are so worried about saying the wrong thing and pushing them further away.

How do I handle this?

You state in a clear and calm voice,

"I do not accept the way you are speaking to me I did not bring you up to be so disrespectful and rude."

Give them a chance to respond then if it continues you can say

"If you continue being rude then I shall end the call."

If they continue you tell them calmly above the shouting,

"I'm ending the call now. Call me back when you can speak to me nicely I love you."

You end the call.

## Clean Up Your Social Media

I know you feel angry and beyond the depths of despair sometimes.
That's normal and ok to feel that way after your children have been ripped out your life.
Clean up your social media right now.
Do not mention brainwashing, alienation or narcissism as your children are not ready to hear that yet. YOU WILL ONLY CONFIRM the alienators lies that you are crazy.
Please do not vent on your own personal page just in case your children are watching or their friends who will tell them.
Or the alienator is watching somehow, as mine does, and anything you write adds fuel to the fire and brings him the drama he wants so badly.
Do not feed narcissists with drama. Do not allow them to point the finger at you and say you are crazy. Starve them.
You have to build a positive happy Facebook and vent on the PA groups on the hard days.
It is only when you reach a stage of peace and acceptance and build a good life for yourself that your children scroll by one day and begin to see that you are not any of the things that the alienator said you are. Do NOT make it easy for them to continue the lies.
Show your children you have got yourself together!

## Build a Happy Social Media

You know I advised you to build a happy social media of authentic loving you? Here's why. Your child is likely to be watching. If your alienated child suddenly unblocks you on social media and friend requests you, you need to handle things really carefully.
I know you want to send him a huge message of how much you've missed him and how you can't wait to see him. Hang fire on that! This alone could get you blocked again as it could totally overwhelm him. Start by liking his pictures. Nothing more. If that is met with a healthy positive response try a little message.
He is slowly awakening. Your job now is to create light bulb moments to reach the authentic child so a funny joke meme on messenger or a "Do you remember when we"... story is enough for now. Wait for your child to reach out to you. Be aware that you will get blocked at any point the alienator finds out. If this happens don't see it as a step back. Try

and understand your child is scared or overwhelmed or not ready at the moment. Keep dripping love and build a happy loving parent on social media. Show him who you really are. He is watching and waiting for a safe time to reach out.

Letting Go

Do you keep your alienated child's room like a shrine?
I even went in and out and opened and drew the curtains and plumped up the pillows.
That was my way of dealing with the grief of losing two living children.
If this is you I'm giving you permission to box that room up if you're ready, you're causing yourself untold pain going in and out of there. Looking through their things as they grow out of their clothes and wondering if they miss their special toys.
Get some very large packing boxes and pack it all beautifully and carefully away, label it with the year and as you sellotape those boxes shut think about your child's joy when he re opens them.
My sons boxes were ripped open in excitement two and a half years later and the joy I experienced watching him rip those boxes open was like three Christmas's combined ( the ones he missed) cries of "Oh Mum you kept everything!" Taking out his toys one by one! Kissing his teddies and laughing as it added up to a huge epiphany moment of my Mum loves me!
My alienated daughters boxes remain unopened and I pray for the day we go together to open them.
If you are causing yourself daily pain by having a shrine for your child please understand if you box it up its because you love them and one day you will experience this joy.
Hang in there everyone!

I Am Damned If I Do and Damned If I Don't

As an alienated Mum you are damned if you do and damned if you don't! If you send gifts and letters the Nex tells your children you are trying to buy them but the minute you stop trying to smuggle things through the iron curtain past the two headed dog that is guarding your children they are told you don't care and have moved on! If you approach your children you are harassing them and they see you at the least as an annoyance and at the worst as stalking them.. You are literally damned if you do and damned if you don't.. That's how Alienation works.. Everything you do and do not do is bastardised.

Do I Still Send Gifts?

To anyone who's children are at this point 'Lost' to Parental Alienation. keep sending love and gifts no matter how futile you think it all is.. The minute we stop, he can say "See she doesn't care" Sadly at the moment the children are lost in a fog of lies and we have to keep reaching out with whatever method or way we can! Sometimes we have to be devious to contact our children. Take photographs of anything you send, in case they do not receive items. Keep a journal for your children to read. One day all these attempts are going to add up in your child's mind as 'love' an epiphany moment that translates suddenly as "My Mum loves me!" At the moment any positive feelings towards us are not allowed, but please don't give up be strong.

Making a Happy Memories Box for Your Alienated Child

Some of the pain when your child is ripped out your life is not being able to share things with him or her.
This is why I suggest making a happy memories box.
Take a good size box and decorate it and write your child a letter when you are feeling sad and post it in the box, it can be a weekly letter or just whenever you have anything to say, encourage alienated family members to do the same, when you go somewhere buy a little gift for him or her like you would usually and pop it in the box, add Christmas and birthday presents into the box..
This will relieve some of the grief you feel being physically apart from your child knowing one day you and him or her will open that box together and fill in those special memories together.

One Sided Love

I'm sure you are all familiar with Harry Potter.
During total alienation from my 15 year old son and my 16 year old daughter I thought of myself like the Mum in the mirror in Harry Potter.

Harry always knows his Mum and Dad is watching over him but he cannot touch or be close to them.

It comforted me to think that both my alienated children felt
I was still there in the mirror, comforting and guiding them.

Sometimes I found out by my sons public self deprecating, suicidal tweets that he was depressed or angry or upset and I was worried he would harm himself and just wanted to make him feel better.

After trying to contact him through his school who was no help because he didn't want to see me therefore there was nothing they could do I opened a new twitter or FB account to send him a positive loving message.

This was met with hostility and he blocked me every time and of course it was like a punch in the gut, but his statuses would become more positive so I did feel he listened and took on board what I was saying.

On reuniting with him he has told me "Mum you're so lovely and I never gave you a chance" and that he had read all those messages and he told me what they meant to him at the time.

So please don't think that one sided love is futile,
Keep reaching out and dripping love alongside the poison.

I Can't Do This Anymore

You can! I know exactly how you feel as I felt like that many times. You gave birth to him and raised him, he is your child and he needs your help escaping a narcissistic parent. I know it's exhausting and I know you can't deal with the pain of the rejection. It's ok to step away for a while and heal yourself but let them know you love them and the door is always open.

I had to send that exact letter to my daughter after she tried to get me charged with harassment for leaving presents at her work place once Dad found out.

I had to then accept that she doesn't want to see me at the moment.

They then know despite the poison they've been fed about you that:
1. you respect her decision and boundaries ( opposite to Nex) and
2. you are there when she needs you ( opposite to what the Nex is telling him about you not loving her and abandoning her)

For Target Parents In Despair

Are you feeling like they can't go on?
The Nex ripped my teens from my life and I know how it feels to want to end my life, I know how it feels to live from bed to chair and not want to go on but I also lived through this and past this and built myself a beautiful life, firstly without my precious children and now I have one back.

I'm telling you this because bad times pass and life is precious. They are going to need you more than ever before. Children work it out and go where they feel safe and loved, hold on for them and work through this pain, these bad times will pass and you will get stronger. I know you will say that's easy for you to say, but brighter days are coming.

What Does My Authentic Child really Think?

I want to share something with you that will help you to understand why you must try and live your life to the best of your ability while your children are lost in the fog of alienation. Think of this from your child's point of view. I know you may see nothing but hostility from your alienated child as I did and you feel they do not care, in fact you feel intense hate from them.

Well I am talking from my own experience when the light bulb went on for my son in his late teens and the hate boomeranged back to the alienator he quickly developed empathy for my situation, and he was clearly pained and very upset hearing what I had been through and hearing that I had thrown myself back into life after all this made him develop a deep admiration for me not just as his Mum but as a person. I remember my son saying to me during alienation that he had lost all respect for me watching his Dad treat me that way and why would he take advice from me when I screwed up my life? so this renewed respect was important to me. He told me "Mum you've changed so much I've seen that on your wall" and that's what I believe made him write that first tentative message.

You are Your Children's Champion and Cheerleader

You may feel beaten down depressed and struggling to put one foot in front of the other but despite this always remember YOU are the mentally healthy parent, YOU are your child or children's champion and cheerleader!

They may be spouting hateful venom at you from the alienators handbook but RIGHT NOW your child or children need you firing on all four cylinders and ready to fight for them! They need YOU to rescue them from their pathogenic parent.

I know that when I give advice to alienated parents it's not what they want to hear. I know it makes them angry and upset and want to shout incredulously "This isn't fair! I'm a good Mum!" Damn straight sisters and brothers!

Nothing about being targeted by a Narc is fair! No one is saying you're not a good Mum or Dad either.

What we are saying though is we are dealing with a pathology and everything we do that doesn't work pushes them further and further away. I learned the hard way with my daughter after trying several times to contact her leaving her gifts over the last few years. But she is so heavily aligned with the alienators that I have had to back right off! I have not had a pleasant word from her now coming up four years. We were extremely close like sisters and I have had to grieve for her.

Since my son now 17 and I have reunited after he escaped to mine she then began to hate him too. I left that relationship to heal while teaching my son about the damage that has been done and the dynamics of golden child ( his sister) and the scapegoat ( him) Now he is understanding this and that she doesn't hate him he has begun reaching out to her on social media telling her little things about his life. He sent her a birthday card saying "I know things are shit but you are still my best friend" and got a abuse back. I have been explaining why she is behaving this way and he's still reaching out to her with messages and she has just sent him the first nice message back since he escaped to mine. It is a long game!

Abuse situations are wounds and like wounds they have to be healed from the inside out.. Layer by layer. Or they will cover over and leave a big necrotic hole there, that will break down again. I am letting my children heal their damaged relationship and once that happens I hope that she will see me in a positive new light.

Abuse Is Not Ok!

For all those mothers or fathers worrying about the effects of their NPD partner on their children.
I have this to say having beaten myself also with that great big guilt stick.
We stood up for ourselves.
We stood up to a manipulative bully and left him or her to show our kids that abuse is not okay.
One day when they see through adult eyes they will understand our journey and why it took so long to leave.
Meanwhile find a smaller stick to beat yourself with.
They will come around to understand and when they do they will go through a similar shock grief anger process you have.
Keep loving them however you can and be ready to catch them when they fall.
They are going to need us more then than any other time in their lives.
It is up to us to stop the circle of abuse repeating itself and educating our children for the sake of theirs and our grandchildren We can do this!

Never Give Up!

You Have To Play The Long Game

I understand and feel your pain and I know your anger your sadness and the feeling of pointlessness and I want to say this to you. Never give up you cannot get into the heads of your children you do not know the pain they are going through from losing you! They are brainwashed right now and it is going to take a trigger moment to wake them. Getting away from the alienator, starting a new relationship or talking to friends about missing the absent parent. You have to play the long game, you have to educate yourself on why they are behaving this way and you must not stop living your life, as hard as that is you must continue to move forwards and get mentally strong and believe in the fact that they will contact you.

You Can Now Teach Your Children The Right Things About Love

Focus on this! You got away!
You've taught your children you do not accept abuse from him, from them, from anyone. Now you have to teach your children the right things

about love. If they are with the abuser you CAN get them out! It will be a process. They have to have their moment of clarity as you did. It will come as they grow up and think for themselves. Remember the word salad and confusion you had to wade through? They are there. You will grow stronger through this experience I absolutely promise you! I know you don't feel it right now but empower yourself with knowledge and get yourself mentally healthy. Learn and grow. Do not feel guilty trying to build a life without them in it. They will catch you up. Believe you can reunite with them and get them out. Being positive is half the battle.

It's Not All Gloom and Doom

We know the parent with NPD cannot love a child or anything for that matter in a normal way. I know how that feels to think your child is doomed and there's no way forward. At this point can we also remember that children who have one dysfunctional parent but one mentally healthy one can do as well as a child with two healthy ones? It's not all doom and gloom.
We have to make up the deficit with unconditional love and understanding as hard as that can be watching our children suffer and picking up the pieces. How? By becoming as mentally strong as we possibly can. We are not only working on our childhood wounds for ourselves we are doing it for our children and their children, our grandchildren of the future. We are breaking a vicious pathological pattern and teaching our families the right things about love.

As this book was going to be published my alienated son contacted me, so I held on through my joy and pain and kept a Reunification diary to help other parents going through their own personal hell.

My son was alienated at 14.
At 14 15 and 16 he used to say go away and leave me alone anytime he was approached by me during his alienation.
He came back at 17 full of questions love and apologies.

Do not feel weak defenceless and powerless your two weapons against the alienator are knowledge and unconditional love. Use them wisely.

# Keep My Love In A Photograph

During the two and a half year alienation from my 14-17 year old son I panicked despaired and couldn't sleep.

That was the hardest part letting go of those little things I had always done. I wasn't there to tuck him in bed and give him a goodnight kiss or chat about his day. I wasn't there to cuddle him when things went wrong in his life or to squeeze him and say well done when things went right. I wasn't there to remind him to wash or brush his teeth and I worried so much because when he left he was a Mummy's boy and we were really close. I wasn't there to ensure he was safely home and tucked up in bed at a decent time or that he ate a healthy diet.

As he got older and I caught glimpses of him on social media out with his friends and girlfriends I continued to worry and panic and lie awake at night hoping and praying that he was ok and only relaxing when I saw a snatched update on a public page.

I cried over his photos and I cried over Ed Sheeran song 'Photograph' and I didn't realise it at the time that I was actively grieving a living child.

On reuniting with him at 17 I realised that he had my strength and resilience and he had a wonderful group of supportive lovely friends. There was a couple of times he had gone down the wrong path but he had found his way back and was in pretty good shape.

He told me that he didn't let his Dad get to him and when he raged he escaped to his room, he told me that he had a lovely group of friends who helped him and I realised that In all my pain and panic and despair the most important thing.

I hadn't been erased, my child is part me, he has my strength and resilience and had learned to cope with the situation he found himself in. I want you guys to hold onto that. We are escaped because we are strong and we said no to the abuse. Never forget your children are part you and they keep your love tucked safely away in a photograph in their hearts.

A Few Weeks Before Matty Made Contact

Several weeks before my son contacted me he began to message his cousins that he had not contacted for several years due to the total alienation of the whole extended family telling them they must not tell

266

me or anyone else that they were talking and stating if they do then he will once again cut off all contact.

My nieces did tell me and their Mum as they were upset and out of their depth how to handle the situation and very worried that they would say the wrong thing and be blocked once again and were briefed by me to just get a relationship going and encourage conversation without mentioning me.

An alienated child will feel their way back only if they feel safe from the alienator to do so.

Like my son they may take tentative steps to test the water before contacting the target parent.

One of my sons former school friends messaged me out of the blue and asked how I was and said how sorry he was that this had happened and told me I didn't deserve to lose my children as I was a good Mum.

He then joked he had several solutions and I should adopt him instead!

He told me he wanted to understand what had happened so I told him very simply how a pathogenic parent achieves parental alienation and sent him a meme to explain. He told me "That's horrible, but I'm happy you've stayed strong" and reminded me I was a lovely person and a great Mum and "Do I remember coaxing him out the bathroom after another boy hit him?" He reminded me of the sleepovers they had and how we always had pancakes.

He began to tell me how he sometimes has a sleepover with my son and how his Dad turns the Internet off but that despite that they have a good time.

He told me my son was okay and he has a girlfriend he adores.

We kept in touch like this for several days discussing how my son is and how tall they both are now which upset me as I had missed so much having not seen my son for two and a half years.

I told his friend the last conversation we had and that after that he wasn't allowed to come again. "Mum I've got to go Dad's staring at me it's really weird."

Then every time I tried to communicate with him after that he told me to go away and leave him alone.

He told me we should focus on the positives "He's doing pretty well in school and loving the sixth form life. He has plenty of friends that respect him and will always be there for him and unknowingly one of the best Mums out there watching over him."

He told me "It just shows you that even while you're not there physically he still takes after you and doesn't get influenced from his Dad. He told me "He's a great friend! and that he will always be there for him and how him and his Mum always talk about me when he comes for tea and says he should see you. He never disagrees, he's just silent. Don't ever doubt yourself, you persuaded me to come out of the bathroom soaked in tears!"

His friend joked with me "Maybe you should come in a disguise, glasses and a moustache with a fake nose and a top hat."

It was to be a few days later on April Fools Day that Matty messaged me.

Matty's Reunification Story

When Matty eventually texted me two and a half years later it was to tell me he was in a bad place and to ask for help.
He told me he understood if I didn't want anything to do with him but he has no one else to turn to.
He apologised for never giving me a chance and as soon as I messaged him back I told him I loved him and would help him.
We continued to text and exchange photos like we had never been apart and it was clear to me that my son hadn't changed much and was still the same loving beautiful boy I remembered.
We arranged to meet for the first time and he brought his girlfriend with him for support.

He told me to promise to keep the fact we were chatting a secret from his Dad and alienated elder sister.

"Now I have my boy back safe I feel emotionally stronger than ever and this will mean I will go from strength to strength as I continue my crusade to get the truth about abuse and PA out there. "

Helping those who need me educating others and getting target parents through this horrific ordeal.

I checked on Matty this morning as I could not sleep. That's why I'm up at 5.20 am. I woke upset and panicking to check his room and he's sound asleep. What a beautiful sight. A lot taller and more hair than I remember but the same angelic baby face. I feel truly blessed. His phone beside him flashing ten missed calls from Dad causes me some anxiety.

Anyway I'm telling you this because I want to share my joy and give every target parent hope and because he is experiencing cognitive dissonance right now talking every single lie he has been told through with me.

I am gaining valuable insight into how his Father achieved this.

He is literally telling me everything, and asking questions now like "So what's wrong with Dad?"

I am learning so much and everything I learn and the way I do things that work for me I will share with you all.

My son has come through this relatively unscathed and now fully switched on and awakened and he and I will help all of you! ( him unknowingly for now) I feel it and know it!


Three Days Out

How to Reconnect With Your Alienated Child.

Build a happy social media. They are watching even if they blocked you. Get mentally healthy and build a life for yourself without guilt.

Keep sending gifts cards and tokens of love as even if you don't think they care when they awaken like my son they remember. He told me "Mum I loved those buttermilk pancakes you sent last year they made loads and were yummy. Chloe loved them too!"

Keep the door open.

Don't be afraid to inbox their friends to check up on them. I had several of his friends chatting to me I educated on PA and Narcissism that Matty is now wanting to meet me.

Do not throw out any of their things. Box them and store them all. Matty went to the attic ripping open boxes exclaiming "Mum I can't believe you kept all my stuff! Look at this Mum!" Every toy has a story he remembered.

He said, "Mum do you remember walking to school and you bought me this? It's better than Christmas opening those boxes."

Photograph all the presents and letters so you can ask "Did you get that?" Jog memories.

Your behaviour they were told was harassment and stalking during alienation will be translated into Mum or Dad loves me once the light bulb goes on.

Get strong keep the faith and be patient.

Four Days Out

Pancakes and the Survival of Childhood Memories.

Everyone loves them, on pancake day or just for a treat right? My son especially loved them throughout his childhood and if he was sad or upset or had a bad day or was recovering from illness he would say "Mummy will you make me a pancake in your biggest pan?" During alienation on both pancake days I managed to send him a box of buttermilk pancakes via my daughters workplace and a card where I drew a flipping pancake and a pan saying "I owed him loads of pancakes."

I cried on that day and then put it out my mind with my happy memories. On reuniting with my son he told me how much he had enjoyed the pancakes last year and how the box made loads saying my daughter loved them too. This was during a time when he was saying "Go away, leave me alone!" I had photographed all the goodies and the card and showed him and we re read the letter I had written now a year later.

After his Dad upset him recently and threatened to throw him out again he asked me at 11pm at night when he had decided to come and live with me "Please will you make me pancakes now?"

Trigger childhood memories year after year and send them things that are personal to them. Money and clothes mean nothing and as my son says "It's just stuff Mum."

It's the little things that cause that light bulb to suddenly flash on.

Create Memory Triggers of Happier Times

I want you all to know and hold the truth in your hearts till they return, every single parent of a reunited child including me will tell you they remember everything and once they escape all their repressed childhood memories comes flooding back.

Create memory triggers of happier times and 'Do you remember when scenarios' of times when you weren't vilified and she or he was allowed to love you.

For example you can say, "Do you remember when we went to stay in that hotel? I bought you that bear and we went on the ride together at the fun park?

Well I still love you like I did then. Wasn't that fun?"

You need to do this to set the memory light bulbs popping to reach your authentic child and tying old and new memories together.

Try it next time you get a chance of contact.

A Week Out

The Step By Step Guide to How the Alienator Alienates Your Child

From talking to my son once we reunited and running alongside the hate campaign against me and my family.

Alienators do this by taking total control.

Moving my son away from anyone that used to know me.

Giving him a phone and never putting credit on it unless he did jobs for him.

Refusing to buy a bus pass so my son had to walk 4 miles to school.

Putting him downstairs in a box room adjoining the main living area where Matty said there was little internet access and he could keep an eye on him.

He told me "Mum I felt uncomfortable sitting on the sofa as Dad would glare at me for sitting down. He would not let me have my friends round and if they came he would make them do jobs for him."

He turned the internet off at night.

At weekends instead of letting him rest from school or catch up with homework and study for his final exams he made him work.

"Dad would barge in my room and drag me out of bed day or night to help him with things. He would get me up and blame me for things that weren't my fault and had been caused by him while I slept.

The dog went missing and it was my fault even though I was sleeping." he complained.

Like Harry Potter who lived under the stairs he was just a pair of hands and a scapegoat to rage at my son is now a much loved member of my family again, has a fully working smart phone contract from his loving grandparents and a beautiful double room that he has organised and arranged to his liking.

He has space to study and is allowed privacy upstairs.

My son is free!

Two Weeks Out

Hating Half of Myself

Over the period of alienation I have read many updates on twitter from my son saying he hates his eyes, his nose and his face.

After we reunited he told me Dad said "You're the spitting image of her and she was a waste of space too!"

Anytime he did anything that displeased Dad he would say "You're just like her f*****g useless!"

He told me "Mum you have the same side profile as me. In all fairness you could rock my nose stud! Just try it Mum" and he puts it in my nose asking his girlfriend and exclaiming "Look shouldn't Mum get one!"

He went on to say "Our features are the same. There was a time I hated my eyes and my lips but I'm happy now with my features and to be fair I'm a lot like you. Remember you used to say "Matty you have a ski slope nose and it's cute the way it turns up at the end? Well yours is like that. I have your big toe and long fingers but look how big my hands are now! Ah your hands are so cute."

The Alienator Makes the Alienated Child Fearful Of The Target Parent

He said "You're so chilled out Mum, how could I be frightened of you? I don't understand how Dad used going to yours as a punishment, saying nasty things about you. He used to threaten me and say "If you don't do what I ask I will drop you off there and you won't come back!"

My entire family was used as a punishment.

He told me that "If I come here You'll get f**k all from me ever again!"

How the Narcissist Divided and Conquers His Golden Child

The Narcs work is complete in an evil display of divide and conquer he has separated his enabler golden child daughter that provides his narc

272

supply and has discarded his scapegoat son after he escaped to mine.

The once close relationship between my two children has been triangulated to the point where my daughter has now said "Who are you anyway?" To my traitor son and blocked him on all social networks. I used to take comfort in the fact they had each other but this is proof that in the world of Narcdom it's all or nothing.

Once you cross into the other camp you become the enemy!

As I tucked him in bed he said to me, "I know you're not trying to turn me against Dad. He already did that when I lived with him." As I shut the light off and got into bed my phone beeped with a text from my once alienated son and it said "You're so lovely, I love you tonnes" and just at that moment and through the tears I realised I would do my life all over. Even the terrible bits just to have my boy in my life.

The Golden Child Blocks the Escaped Scapegoat Child as per Narc Protocol

My alienated daughter is 19 today and has blocked her brother as per narc protocol which really upset and angered Matty.

I explained to him his relationship was damaged and not by him and he used to be so close to her and it would be extremely sad if he were not to send her a birthday card. He chose a lovely one and I had to chase him to write it as she was being verbally abusive to him.

The OW has blocked my son as per narc protocol and he's feeling upset about that as well and he understands that this isn't a normal way to behave.

"Mum why can't I see them and you? Why have they already cleared my room?

All they want me to see me for is my key!"

I am letting him lead with his questions. I have explained the scapegoat/ golden child in a simplistic form and how Dad triangulated their relationship.

The OW is now love bombing and clinging to my daughter today with promises of an amazing birthday weekend.

A sad and pathetic attempt to get my daughter back on board and comply with the Nex.

Despite the fact I know she is also a victim,

I'm struggling not to hate her today as she has my first born in her clutches.

Planting a Seed and Letting it Grow

How to Educate A Re-united Teen About NPD

Remember the shock when you discovered the reasons for his shitty behaviour?
Remember the pain you went through as you stumbled on NPD?
You need to take a softly softly approach when educating your teenager.
Wait for your teen to ask! "Okay Mum so what exactly is a narcissist?"
My son seemed quite upset and had a headache so I cuddled him and gave him paracetamol.
I watched him brooding and then a few hours later he quite randomly asked when he was listening to music and being relaxed and silly "Sooo what is a narcissist?" So I replied "someone who was damaged as a child so they lack empathy so they use people." He said "So that's basically it?"
I said "Yes Matty if you want to know more I will read you something."
He said "Read it Mum! Preach it mother!" In a silly voice. So I said "Alrighty!" In a silly voice back and read out the NPD parents checklist.
His girlfriend pipes up "Yes that's your Dad!"
I said to Matty "It's such a lot to get your head round isn't it?"
Then he carried on singing and being silly.
"I think I get it Mum" I kissed him made him a chocolate spread sandwich and went to bed leaving him with his thoughts and my iPad.

18 Days Out

The Nex lost a pair of hands and I gained a beautiful loving son.
The penny drops.
Matty told me "Mum you know I blocked Dad he's just got his mate to message me and say he needs a hand in the morning. Not that he misses me or cares about me. It's like he just wants me for a pair of hands! He doesn't care about me or respect me Mum he said sadly and went on, "I don't think he's ever cared about me! He doesn't appreciate anything I do to help, He never says thanks. You know Mum he doesn't cuddle me or even greet me he just says give us a hand. That's not normal is it Mum?"
I cuddled him and told him "Your Dad can't love in a normal way Matty he doesn't have the empathy to do that. "
"Your therapist will explain tomorrow" I replied.

My Son Was In Prison

The Nex moved my children a good distance away and had been sabotaging his A levels by refusing to pay bus fare each day to get him to school saying he must work on my old house for a bus pass or he must walk 4 miles to school in the morning and then again after school,
Also he had been refusing to buy credit for his phone so he cannot ring anyone.
Anyway since moving in with me he now has a bus pass and his grandparents have bought him a lovely new iPhone 6 and last night we went to the college open day to discuss the courses my son might actually want to do.
Last night we discussed for the first time what he wanted to do with his life.
My son said to me "Mum this is like starting a new life" I said "Yes because this is your life where you get to choose what you want to do."

Allowing Myself To feel Suppressed Emotions

The last three weeks with my son have passed in a whirlwind following him reuniting and coming to live with me. Two weeks off school where I guess I've had to suppress a lot of my emotions at getting him back.
He's just gone to school and I'm sitting here listening to a list of songs he made for me crying happy uncontrollable tears. I want you all to know in your hearts you can and will get through this and life post narc does just keep getting better and better.
Remember you are getting glimpses of how good life should have been had you not met your insidious evil Nex.
Keep going! Keep putting one foot in front of the other..
Do not let the Nex take your power! Grab your life back with both hands.
It's your life and you can do and be exactly who you choose to be.

One Month out

It is now one month since I rescued my son from living like Harry Potter with the Nex. The awkward scared boy that met with me biting his nails so no white showed and nervously laughing and clinging onto his girlfriend has blossomed into a happy confident laugh a minute young man who no longer bites his nails and no longer springs to his feet when I knock to enter his room. Instead I see before me a happy confident young man who twerks ( yes really) to his favourite music, who sings at the top of his voice and is naturally funny without trying.

At 6ft he is also useful for changing light bulbs and carrying shopping which he does graciously. It's like all the parenting I instilled in him over the years is still there.

He is a true gentleman and I'm so proud of him I could cry.


Re-Bonding With My Re-united Son

I have been extremely busy over the last few weeks re bonding with my son...We are extremely close as we used to be. He texts me all day long and asks my opinion on every aspect of his life. He is very loving and cuddly and his twerking, singing and dancing round the house mean there is never a dull moment!. He now has a lovely job and has finally begun to earn his own money.

Also the good news is that my now reunited son has become very understanding and interested in the book I'm writing about thriving after an NPD relationship.

With him on board with this I am ploughing ahead to finish this book.


3 Months Out

Emotional wreck today! My previously alienated boy is now coming up to 3 months away from his Narc father and yesterday we took a deep breath and went back to the seaside town I brought him up in.( and was chased in the car and stalked in for years) We visited his friends Mums ( people I used to be close to) and I hugged the boy who helped reunite me and my son.

I drank champagne and watched as my friends girl was getting ready for prom ( this triggered me horribly because one of the lasting memories of my still alienated daughter was when her Dad threw her out two weeks before prom)

Me and my son are so close now. He just went through a bad patch with his girlfriend and I was able to comfort him as he cried in my arms. It just deeply saddens me that his once close sister who was always there through everything with her brother now treats him as the enemy because he's with me. I know it will change but dealing with this right now has taken every ounce out of me and I'm totally bereft today that my girl is not in our lives right now. I guess I'm grieving right now.

It's easy to want to continuously over compensate our child or children for a pathological parent. Stop for just a moment and think.
A child doesn't need lots of stuff.
A child doesn't need us to run on a mouse wheel providing for him or her.
A child's needs are simple,
They need you to be a warm loving parent.
A 'go to' person they can confide in and share their life with.
Trust me they will forget the trainers, the ps4 and the expensive clothes.
What they will remember is building memories a loving bond and receiving unconditional love.

What I Have Learned

Narcissistic parents stunt the growth of their children so they are always around to provide supply for them. A previously alienated now reunited child will lack confidence and have poor decision making skills and will likely lack social skills and suffer separation anxiety when you leave them for a while. They may also show signs of depression and lash out in anger. They simply need buckets of love cuddles and reassurance and help re learning these skills from you, their emotionally available parent.

Narcissistic Parents Deliberately Stunt the Growth Of their Teenagers.

Like a cookoo the pathological parent will likely push the non compliant scapegoat child out of the nest as he or she grows. and as traumatic as this is for the child it is their means to escape back to the loving parent.

Narcissistic parents stunt the growth of their teenage children purposefully so they can never leave and remain dependant on them so they are always around to provide supply. They do not teach them independence, to drive, to cook, to fend for themselves for this reason.
They financially control their children by continuously bribing them with material things that normal children have like a working smart phone or travel money, internet access or even basics like food.
These items are attainable in the child's eyes so they work extremely hard for these things thus providing narcissistic supply to the NPD parent.

However the NPD parent continuously moves the goalposts and the games change on a daily basis.

The NPD parent sees the teenage child as an extension of himself and will say things like "I know you better than you know yourself" and never listens to the child's opinion.

As the child matures and begins to think for himself he may rebel by going against the NPD parent in a dramatic way.

Dying his hair blonde or getting piercings or tattoos or taking drugs.

He realises that he needs to break free from the NPD parents view of him, and struggles to remain an individual.

This makes the NPD parent rage as they feel they are losing control.

This is the point where the teenage child's very identity is threatened so much that the child attempts escape.

Distorted Memories and Brain Fog

Over time and through the brainwashing process the alienated child's childhood memories become distorted as the lies are drummed into their brains. The Nex told my son he went to live with him at the age of 11 when in reality it was 14, so it fit with his affair. It's how he convinced my son he hadn't cheated because our marriage had ended. It wasn't till he broke free and escaped to live with me that he told me this and other huge distortions of the truth and over the months as he was going through cognitive dissonance I gently told him the truth that all the family had celebrated his 14th birthday and I reminded him of the presents and cards he received and showed him them.

As it dawned on him that even time had been distorted he was understandably very upset but gradually as he understood this it helped unravel other huge lies and then the smaller ones too. He was made to hate my animals so I showed him pictures of him cuddling them, saying "You love him, I have a photo of you cuddling him. Then he would say "Oh yes look he's so fluffy! I remember now Mum!"

These are their distorted surface memories planted by the alienator but the authentic child deep down remembers everything just as it really was as over the next few months his brain fog began to lift and it was him squealing, "Mum do you remember when we walked home from school and you used to get me these? Do you remember this?"

Each memory unlocks another memory.

This is who we are reaching and trying to constantly trigger, our authentic child.

Wounds Heal From the Inside Out

My reunited son and alienated daughter are meeting for lunch.
It's a wonderfully normal lunch date for two siblings that grew up together loving one another and fiercely protecting one another.
They have come a long way. When my son reunited with me almost a year ago their pathogenic father tried to divide and conquer them so he could lock down and hold onto the narc supply his golden child, my eldest daughter provides for him.
As per narc protocol my daughter was told my son had moved into the enemy camp once he moved in with me. She wrote him vile messages and they argued and she blocked him.
It's taken many months as the enlightened parent to help my son to understand that they were always besties and not to let Mum and Dads mess destroy their loving relationship.
Gradually over the last 11 months my son has begun reaching out to his alienated sister despite her initial anger and hatred towards him.
I have stood back only stepping in to help him nurture this sibling relationship ( which is so painful as I miss her so much and I miss seeing the beautiful relationship they had as children)
I write now with tears in my eyes that she is now cautiously building a relationship with him again.
The Nex has tried to control their last few meetings but this time they are meeting alone. I hug my son and tell him "Hug her for me" and he says "I will Mum."
You see toxic family relationships are like deep wounds that have healed on the outside but once you remove that scab you expose the necrotic rotting flesh and pain.
Wounds have to be healed from the inside out layer by layer and the first layer is healing the sibling relationship without the watchful eye of the alienator.

Keep Dripping Love Alongside the Poison

My son used to say "Go away and leave me alone" anytime he was approached by me during his alienation. Please remember he or she is being bullied and coerced into rejecting you. If they show any positive loving signs they are psychologically hurt by the alienator. Keep dripping love no matter what response you get back.

In the two year alienation on the rare chance I got a message to my son as he blocked me on everything I never accepted abuse. I told him "I do not accept you talking to me that way. I brought you up to be respectful and not to swear." Remember his behaviour is learnt. Never lose your cool. Never swear or badmouth the Nex simply say "I'm going now if you're going to talk that way." My son would say, "I don't swear at anyone and I'm only disrespectful to you because I don't care. You're not even my Mum."

This is classic alienation as everyone I spoke to who knew him then said he was polite and respectful. I would repeat "Well you must not swear at me." Then he would say "Oh go away, leave me alone!" I would say "Night, I love you to the moon and back" and leave and stop messaging. When we reunited he said to me, "I do not deserve your lovely words I never gave you a chance. You never said anything horrible back. You're so lovely."

This is how we have to play the long game everyone.

They have to grow up and wake up.

# Dedicated to my Daughter:

I See Your Face

As I rush through a crowded street I see your long dark hair and I follow you in a trance. I catch you up and my heart quickens as I walk past you and glance back but you're not there.

I'm sitting outside a cafe watching the world go by and I see a flash of you. I leave my coffee and run to catch a glimpse of your beautiful face but you're not there. You're not there but yet you're everywhere.

In the shops as I'm taking a dress off it's hanger I hear the warm tinkle of your laughter and I hear you say "Go on Mum try it on, I saw that and thought of you. "I say to you "Okay but you try this one."

In the coffee shop I hear your bubbly voice asking for more whipped cream on top of your hot chocolate, and "Please could you have marshmallows too." On the beach I see you wading into the sea shouting "C'mon Mum it's not that cold," as your brother playfully splashes you and you say "Mum will you tell him? He's really annoying!"

In the restaurant I glance up from my lunch and I see you chatting a few tables away and I recognise your glossy dark hair piled on top of your head, you're laughing and texting on the phone.

You are not there, but yet I see you my beautiful alienated daughter everywhere.

My Best Friend

I used to have a best friend and we did everything together.

We talked all day on the phone and when we were apart we texted. We shared our lives together, watched our favourite programmes together, we went for a smoothie and to chat about boys and shoes, we shopped for clothes together, we baked cakes together, we laughed everyday about the silliest things!

To a stranger looking in we had a perfect relationship, but they didn't know we shared a dark secret.

We lived with a monster and between us we protected each other and supported each other daily from its psychological and physical attacks.

We escaped but the monster lured her back.

She has my resilience and she has my stubborn determination.
She's a survivor and a warrior trapped in the dragon's lair.
I know she's ok.
You see she's my alienated daughter and I miss her everyday.

# They Remember

Deep down inside they know how much you love them. They miss you too and they remember all the precious times you spent together. They remember holding your hand, skipping to school and chatting about their day ahead. They remember going for lunches and milkshakes with you. They remember having a fit because you refused to buy them those unsuitable shoes for school. They remember baking cakes with you and the time you scolded them for eating them before they cooled and they remember all those special birthdays where you bust a gut to show them how precious they are to you.

They remember your special scent and the warmth of your cuddles when they were sad., They remember your smile as they came home from school to unload their shitty day on you knowing you will understand. They remember you making everything better. They remember your calm voice and they remember your cross voice as you asked them to "Pick those clothes up off the floor."

They miss you deeply and all the good and the bad times you shared together but they know for now to stay safe that they have to pretend to forget, so they push all those positive happy loving feelings for you so far down that they cease to exist, for them for now, but in moments of clarity they remember you as clearly as you remember them.

The Reality of Living with a Toxic Parent

Remember even if you are totally alienated from your child or children's life and you hear nothing. The reality of living with a toxic parent is an ever changing situation as they continue to meddle in their children's lives, trample over their boundaries and triangulate and control all their relationships for their own hidden agenda.
Our children grow older and wiser as their brains mature and as they spend more time away from the pathogenic parent they talk with their friends and their friends parents about what is normal and what is not.
As they begin to work through the cognitive dissonance they will begin to slowly think their own thoughts.

Drips of love at this time are so important to fire those light bulbs into action to help them question the lies they have been programmed with. Keep showing your child the door is always open to unconditional love.

Don't Give Up!

It was an ordinary day shortly after my alienated sons 17th birthday that he messaged me for the first time in two and a half years saying "Mum I'm in a really bad place, I know you probably don't want anything to do with me but I honestly don't know what to do."

Just remember everyday somewhere in the world a light bulb goes on and an alienated child gets the strength to call their estranged parent, or gets the guts to write that first tentative message filled with questions love understanding and hope.
Every ordinary day miracles happen.

For all those mothers or fathers worrying about the effects of their NPD partner on their children. I have this to say having beaten myself also with that great big guilt stick. We stood up for ourselves.. We stood up to a manipulative bully and left him to show our kids that abuse is not okay! One day when they see through adult eyes they will understand our journey and why it took so long to leave.
Meanwhile find a smaller stick to beat yourself with. They will come around to understand and when they do they will go through a similar shock grief anger process you have. Keep loving them and be ready to catch them when they fall. They are going to need us more then than any other time in their lives.
It is up to us to stop the circle of abuse repeating itself and educating our children for the sake of theirs and our grandchildren. We can do this!

To all target parents.
Let go of the guilt you feel about moving forwards and living your life. We need to grow and learn so we are mentally healthy when our children come knocking.

You are his Beacon of Light

Please hold onto the fact your child is part you, he has your strength and resilience and will be learning how to cope to be safe from the alienators wrath. We understand where he is right now because we were there surviving, trying to keep the Narc on a level of pleasant.
Keep reaching out and dripping love alongside the poison.
Your child has to go over jagged rocks and dangerous waters to reach your safe haven.
You are his beacon of light keep shining and showing him the way to unconditional love.

One Year Out

A year ago today me and my 17 year old son were getting to know each other after two and a half long years apart. He was anxiously hiding at mine all week not daring to admit he was living with me. All the memories on Facebook are coming up of me and my family taking him out to places and teaching him to make a cake and secret pictures of him in his new bedroom and reunited with his pets.
He just missed Easter and Mothers Day last year so this year are new firsts and I've bought him a huge chocolate egg.

When he arrived last year people commented he looked unwell and he was pale, he was exhausted and slept a lot but used to spring to his feet if I knocked and went into his room. He was scared of life and highly anxious and he bit his nails and thought he was hopeless and useless and regularly joked "Mum where's the bleach or a noose?" when things went wrong.
He couldn't catch a bus or do anything independently by himself as according to him he was "useless at everything." He was very loving and needed lots of cuddles and reassurance and suffered separation anxiety even if I left him for a few minutes.

It was truly the hardest thing I've ever done being apart from both my children.
It killed me inside which was the Narcs bitter intention after I discarded and divorced him for his abusive behaviour and adultery.
I had PTSD & anger & emotional scars from the abusive relationship I had escaped from. I had to reconnect with who I was and learn to care

about myself again and once again value my future hopes and dreams which I had put on hold for so long.

I could barely tackle the next day let alone my future and after he ripped the children out my life I stumbled through every day living from bed to chair most days unless I had to be at a solicitors appointment, or the police were coming to take a statement to report his daily stalking.

As the weeks went on I found myself feeling better.

There was so much work to be done and my mission kept me occupied and distracted from my pain.

I wrote 'A thousand Joys' at this time.

I walked ahead of my son and daughter and dealt with my baggage and rediscovered joy and love in my life.

Now I walk beside my son and am there to help him deal with his emotional baggage every day.

Fast forward as this book is published and Matty has a rosy happy glow, he's confident funny and capable of most things a teenager should be and this morning I can hear him giggling and singing and talking to his girlfriend about the fun they had at the zoo yesterday.

Tomorrow is his alienated sisters 20th birthday and over the year they have fixed and repaired their relationship after the narc destroyed it after he dared to leave for the enemy camp.

He also has learned how to handle his Dad and I'm teaching him strong boundaries to protect himself from his behaviour.

I'm so proud of the lovely kind empathetic young man he has once again become.

Together we discuss his options for his future and his relationship choices.

He sees a hopeful future.

Teach Your Child Critical Thinking Skills

We now have sufficient evidence to conclude that brainwashed children who have been alienated remain emotionally stunted at the chronological age at which the Parental Alienation took hold. Children who are between 10-13 years are most vulnerable to alienation because this is when they begin to develop critical thinking skills and the alienator has to step up his or her campaign.

What does this mean?

For example my alienated 17 year old son when he first escaped to me was emotionally still around 14 years old. ( the age he was taken) To back up this research my son was very child like and cuddly and wanted to sit beside me and touch me all the time. He also suffered from separation anxiety and needed constant reassurance that I was close by. (As did I. ) My son would jump to his feet when I knocked and went in his room, was self deprecating and lacked confidence in all his abilities telling me he was useless and cracking jokes about "Mum get me a noose" or "Where's the bleach?" when things went wrong. He often could not be coaxed out of his room for days even with plenty of love and reassurance and would be moody and angry.

Research suggests that as the child grows and develops away from the control of the alienator his or her critical thinking skills will kick in allowing them to emerge from the brainwashing.

Once a target parent has even a little contact with their alienated child, they can help their child develop those important critical thinking skills.

With my son I just showed an interest and talked to him about everything that was important to him. I listened without judgement and any time he mentioned an argument with a friend I would help to guide him through it asking him "What do YOU think, How do you think you should deal with that?"
Also most importantly I validated how he felt as while he was living under the narc regime he had been emotionally shut down to the point where he did not recognise his own feelings apart from anger. So I asked "How do YOU feel about that?" Then I listened and tried so hard not to offer my own thoughts, opinions and feelings.

The most important thing for an alienated child is to feel that their opinion matters and to be validated.

Once he begun to master this critical thinking skill, he then began to use it to look closely at all his relationships and successfully weed out his toxic friends which led naturally to other areas of his life including the toxic behaviour of his alienating father. This is when I heard him say "Don't emotionally bully me!" and "Oh here we go he's going for the sympathy vote!"

Suddenly as he sailed past his 18th birthday and without warning my little boy had got it! I struggled then as he began to keep things to himself and wanted to fix his own problems and indeed if I butted in and tried to help he told me "Mum I've got this! I don't need you anymore!"

I realised over the one year of being with me we had crammed in 3 years of life skills at a hugely accelerated rate and although I mourned the loss of my over cuddly 17 year old. My son who had depended on me for everything was now the man he was meant to be, ready to go out into the world fully equipped with the critical thinking skills he needed to survive out there.

With tears in my eyes,
Job done!

Abuse and Parental Alienation Survivor and Thriver
Mum of two teens.. One son who's reunited with me and one daughter who is still stuck in the fog.

# Soul Love

What is Love?

Love is patient and kind; love does not envy or boast; it is not arrogant or rude. It does not insist on its own way; it is not irritable or resentful; it does not rejoice at wrongdoing, but rejoices with the truth. Love bears all things, believes all things, hopes all things, endures all things. Love never ends.
1 Corinthians 13 ESV - Bible

An Amazing Life is Worth Fighting For

I'm not here to tell you it's easy picking yourself up off the floor wiping your tears away and living life as it should be lived post Narc but I will tell you this 'an amazing life is worth fighting for' and is within everyone's grasp.
It's not about material riches it's about a richness in your heart and soul that only comes from experiencing true freedom.
I really want everyone to know that 'soul love' will happen for them too they've just got to do a little work on 'fixing' themselves first working on their self esteem and confidence so they don't succumb to another 'Nark Attack! '

I Will Never Love Again

I smile now when I read the words I will never get over him. I said those words through pain and tears. Washed up at 40 feeling all those things he told me I was an ugly stupid sciatic old bag. Now I have lived through it and many of us with similar experiences know that life just keeps on getting better.
Trust us butterflies when I say the minute you lose their toxicity life will improve day by day.
You will not believe that firstly you can be happy alone in your own company or that you will meet someone who will love you as you should be loved, but hand on heart if you work on your inner wounds you will.

Learning to Trust Love Again

You feel broken and lost and incapable of feeling love for another person like that ever again? How can I invest my heart and soul and risk being broken again? How can I be sure in my vulnerable state I will not attract another toxic person? If this is you spend some time alone read about co-dependency and address those issues. As we work on our 'inner wounds' and where they originated from things become clearer.
Where did you become grateful for drips of love?
As we fix our insecurities, restore our confidence and begin to feel whole again something inside just shifts.
Keep loving yourself and not only will you attract loving partners but also new friends and positive opportunities. You will love again more deeply than ever you thought possible. Only this time you will find someone to love you back with the same intensity.
This is a process and a steep learning curve.
Embrace it all and remember it takes as long as it takes.

You Don't Feel Good Enough or Worthy?

They will treat you like all the rest? Yes it's a self fulfilling prophecy. Expecting to be treated disrespectfully and have your boundaries trampled down means we are drawn to the partners that are emotionally 'potty training' and will provide that. The good looks the charm the fast car, the hard to get cat and mouse attitude. Will they call won't they call gets our hearts racing, but this doesn't lead to anymore than a one sided dalliance with the devil. The good guy seems safe, boring even.
You are programmed to be only attracted to bad boys or girls and resulting dysfunction.
You know the outcome as you expect bad treatment. It's only when you work on your inner wounds and feel worthy that the 'type' of partner you're attracted to changes. and that leads you to a decent respectful partner and true soul love.

Dating Red Flags!

Recognise any of these? I've been unlucky in love. My ex was crazy. She cheated on me. She used to hit me when she was drunk. I loved her but I had to leave her because I could never hit a woman!

This is the bait from a narc trying to reel you in with his 'poor me' and bad luck stories. All his stories will have the underlying thread of him being painted as the victim and nothing is EVER his fault.

Dig a bit deeper and this is a MASSIVE red flag to run!

Getting Your Narc Radar Up and Running

Being cautious when beginning a relationship post narc is a protective mechanism and means your Narc Radar is up and running! Remember 'Anyone can say the words, 'I love you' but does he back it up with actions?'

We are rightly cautious in a new relationship post Narc. We don't want to go down that awful road again so we need lots of reassurance. We need to ask lots of questions.

Has he ever cheated we ask? We test our new partners. We ask ourselves, "Is this the bit where he's going to blow?" We see red flags that aren't there. We assume that he's not going to call then when he does call we relax.

What will happen if we argue? What will happen if he drinks?

Previously abused people respond quickly to face changes so we are on red alert for that contorted rigid set jaw and flashing black eyes. If his face changes or he raises his voice we freak and go into full PTSD meltdown. These hyper sensitive reactions are normal and a mentally healthy man will understand where we are in our heads and why. Joe used to get annoyed that I locked the door so he can't get in from work late at night! The Nex stalked me for two years by staring in my windows from his car with his jeep headlights on full revving his engine, so I am obsessed with locking doors day and night.

We talked about it and I told him I will always lock the door. I don't feel safe otherwise. I cried we hugged and he said "Well you better get used to my grumpy face when I can't get in" and we laughed about it.

So Am I Ready To Date?

Is there a specific time period after which I will feel ready?

I don't think the amount of time away from your Nex is any indicator of whether you are ready for another relationship. You need to go by how healed you feel you are and how whole you feel single and alone.

So if you meet a man six months post Narc or even three years later and he boosts your self esteem and makes you feel confident about yourself it's a good thing but bearing in mind everything we have learned about Narcs and how insidious they are! Be wary as the beginning of any new relationship could also be classed as the love bombing stage. so play your cards close to your chest.

Do not share your finances and do not put all your eggs in one basket as it were. ( British saying) He could be a wonderful guy but just hang fire till you have been together a little longer. Watch out for red flag behaviour and if there's a flicker of a flag abort mission and block him!

If there isn't any relax and try enjoy it. That period post Narc is tough because we even tar the good guys with the same brush. Just proceed with caution but enjoy someone taking care of you. That in itself is a huge learning curve, having someone who cares, someone who is emotionally available when you need them. Wow how amazing is that after a relationship with a Narc where we suppressed all our needs to cater for his. Any doubts read on. It's only by dealing with Narcs with our new knowledge that we fine tune our Narcometer and learn to protect ourselves from them!

Do Not Rush into Dating

It takes time to clear a path from the debris of the last toxic relationships to find a healthy space to meet a decent whole or healed partner. Wait! Do not rush into dating! Do the work on yourself on fixing the inner wounds that the narc was drawn to. Spend time alone getting to know and discover the real you. Learn to enjoy your space, take yourself on dates with yourself and relearn the things that make you tick and fire your passion. Then when he or she comes along it will be a meeting of souls. You'll be on the same page and want the same things.

A lasting connection based on love and trust. Then there is less chance of you getting it wrong and being hurt again.

You've Decided To Dip Your Toe Back Into the Scary World of Dating.

It's the superficial charm I look out for. Is he pleasant to the waiter? Is he listening to you? Is he taking a sneaky peek at that blonde behind you? Does he care how you have your coffee? Is he constantly on his phone? Is he bigging himself up and does he have a cocky attitude..

Does he talk over you? Let's talk about me!
Does he remember details you told him?

Or is it all hey beautiful too full on too much too soon?
Future faking and promising you he will buy you this or that? Take you
here or there in the car, painting a rosy picture of you two together?
Any flicker of you talking about another date or man causing jealousy (
yes test him) Does he want to get to know YOU or are you playing the
game 'How many dates will it take for me to get your kit off?'
Does he seem interested in what you do for a living or do you see $ signs
in his eyes? You can learn a lot on a first date!

'Spot a Narc Schooling'

I do believe after many years of 'Spot a Narc Schooling' I can suss out a
Narc within the first meeting.
Here are my deal breakers! Bearing in mind normal healthy men do some
of these things too but if you tick off a few then you need to start up your
Narcometer!

He is very confidant and self assured when approaching you.
He behaves like the perfect gentleman, he takes your coat and pulls out
your chair.
However he doesn't smile from the eyes.
He is over flattering and tells you that you are amazing,
He uses words like you are so hot, sexy, or babe rather than learning your
name or saying you are beautiful.
He tells you in that first meeting what he will buy you and 'future fakes'
your life with him together.
He over exaggerates everything he owns or has achieved and tells 'big
fish stories' where he is the hero, he shares fantasy 'get rich quick'
schemes with you that never come into fruition and he blames others for
their failure.
He tells you stories where he is charitable and will do anything for anyone.
He preens himself and checks out his reflection in car windows and
appears very vain.
He listens to you talk but does not fully engage and quickly reverts the
topic back to him if you are talking about you.
He treats staff in the room pleasantly then criticises the service as soon as

they're out of earshot,

He tells you stories where he cruelly laughs or makes fun of another person that he knows that you find distasteful.

He puts down another attractive man in the room often marking them as 'Gay' to cover his own homophobia.

He puts down attractive male celebrities that you like.

He flirts openly with the waitress or while chatting to you looks over your shoulder and flirts with the waitress to make you feel this is a one time offer. Suggesting for you to look how in demand he is, so you sign on the dotted line.

If you try to draw him out he refuses to discuss past relationships dismissing exes as crazy or a slut or telling you his ex still loves him and is pursuing him.

If you discuss your past relationships he shows flickers of jealousy that he may try to cover.

He may behave like a gent to begin with but within the date he is touchy feely too soon and he steers you, ignoring your social cues towards seeing you again saying things like 'see how good we are together we both like good food or long walks. Or he is cocky and in your face saying "C'mon how can you resist this", and points at himself.

He ignores and tramples down any boundaries you try to lay down and pushes to come home with you or see you again.

A Decent man-v-Toxic Man

A decent man will back off and be supportive of how you feel if you are not ready to date and want to be friends or wait..

A toxic one will hound you and TRAMPLE YOUR BOUNDARIES so you give in. making out this is a one time offer and he's got other choices to get you to sign on the dotted line

A decent man will call when he says he will and will NOT play cat and mouse.

A decent man will be on time or have a good valid excuse to be late or cancel and apologise and try to make it up to you.

A decent man will behave like a gentleman a toxic one will invade your personal space and be touchy feely too soon.

A decent man on a first or second date will not love bomb you into believing you are the most wonderful woman he's ever clapped eyes on.

He will enjoy the process of getting to know you and not rush your feelings.

Worth reminding you If he says he's going to call and leaves you wondering will he,. won't he? Playing with your emotions he's not decent and or he's got several of you on the go at once.

A decent man will not Future Fake you into believing he will buy you a beach hut and you will live the life of your dreams.

Real decent men do NOT behave this way and let the relationship develop and enjoy the process of taking it at a steady pace and falling in love.

Dating Site Safety

I cannot stress this enough. You are vulnerable and lonely and a 'sitting duck' for predators. Never ever give out your personal details. If you plan on meeting anyone chat for several weeks or months till you get to know them.

Before meeting get them on Facebook check them out and talk on the phone.

Never just meet someone from a dating site and one picture alone.

I had so much fun on the dating sites and I would recommend them to everyone.

It is a great crash course in learning about Narcs because there are Narcs a plenty on there pretending to be decent humans looking for a relationship. When I was single I talked to everyone on there young, middle aged or older men too and I learned a lot about the way men are ( after being stuck in an abusive relationship for 15 years and not being allowed to talk to anyone)

I began to fine tune my Narcometer and see that Narc behaviour really is quite predictable. They basically want to sweet talk you, meet up, love bomb you into a 'relationship' fast so they can have sex!

I weeded these guys out fast using the block button! The men that wanted to actually get to know me I kept to chat to and pass time with when I was lonely with only a cat for company!

I met up with only a small handful over a year. One became my boyfriend and we are still together nearly 4 years on.

## Do I Deserve A Decent Partner?

So you left the Nex and met someone wonderful but you don't feel you deserve them? It doesn't matter what this person says their compliments make you cringe. It doesn't matter how well they treat you as you're always waiting for them to slip up? To cheat to lie to rage? You know it's a self fulfilling prophecy that you're going to push this person away. Until you build your self worth, until you believe in yourself, until you can look in the mirror and say "I'm enough" this won't change.

If like me you feel or felt like this please seek help. My counsellor said when she met me I couldn't look at her I just cried and cried. She kept asking me the question "Who is Tammy?" I could not say anything positive for months. She told me the Nex had conditioned me to be small and true me was trapped inside.

I was then exhausted and enduring his daily stalking and nightmarish behaviour.

As I worked through counselling one day she asked me and I said "Tammy is bubbly, happy kind and loving" and then the words kept coming. It's from this turning point only that I began to like myself and stopped pushing decent men away.

Not long after that I met my soul mate who is seven years my junior. I know without the counselling I wouldn't have him in my life and I would have continued to make poor relationship choices.

If you are or were like me please seek professional help its life changing.

## Looking to the Future

I will never let another man in my life. Oh yes I said that when I was tired and broken. Perhaps this is how you feel right now?

No one can predict the future and as you work on your inner wounds once you feel a little less raw and vulnerable don't you think it might be nice to have someone kiss them better? Someone to encourage you and grow with you? Someone to help you financially and cook the dinner sometimes? Someone to look after you when you are ill? Someone to say "I love you" and mean it. Someone to say "Well done you make me so proud." There are decent partners out there who are attracted to us once we are whole.

Work on YOU and never give up on love and the companionship that a mentally healthy partner can bring to your life.

Looking Back

It's good to sometimes look back on that toxic relationship with your new knowledge and think "Was it me? Maybe it was love?" because we are rational loving beings with a beating heart that feel real love and joy and pain. You now know so much now about what it was and about the love bombing and devaluing process and why our brains are wired to be addicted like a drug to a man or a woman that was no good for us.
You have come such a long way and are FREE and are healing so beautifully.
In moments of weakness don't turn back. Keep going there is light at the end of the tunnel for you too.
There is love peace and beautiful people including a partner in your future who will care for you properly and love you like you can't even imagine. All you have to do is walk away towards the light.

Your Partner Needs to Understand PTSD

I'm sure you are all familiar with Catherine Tate's comedy sketch of the woman screaming because the toast pops up or her husband pours milk on his cereal!
The reality of living like this is however no laughing matter and you need patient kind understanding people around you while you recover from this.
Particularly if you are still being stalked or harassed on a daily basis as I was, living in constant fight or flight off your adrenaline waiting to see which stunt the Nex will pull next.
The next man or woman you allow in your life needs to understand your PTSD and that sometimes you have bad days.
Once you are healed enough you will attract someone like that who will comfort you and understand that and you will be able to laugh at the fact that they just walked in the kitchen and startled you as I learned to.
A huge part of loving someone properly is embracing their inner wounds and loving them through it.

The right one will stay even if you push them away and test their loyalty and love to the limit. They will still be there until you realise one day this person is in it for the long haul,. through the melt downs and tears and panic attacks, through the broken dates because you can't face going out so you stay in instead,. through the Nex stalking and the court battles,. that person will be there, because that is Soul love, and that is what each and every one of us deserves.

Only some of us are too broken to see it yet, but each day we heal piece by piece and one day soon we will get the love we have always deserved. With Valentines Day round the corner I just want to share something with you all.

I spent years with the Nex feeling like okay it's Valentines Day now I can see how much he cares. In the first flush of romance I got the flowers I got the chocolates.

As the years progressed and the love bombing turned to devaluing he used Valentines Day to make up for any aggressive outbursts or wrong doings. Declaring to others "Look at the flowers I got my wife and I'm taking her to dinner!"

It was a great time to send the heartfelt cards and make promises too that now I know meant absolutely nothing to him.

I fast forward to now in a happy loving relationship and I really don't care about this commercial gimmick and exchange of hearts and flowers. Perhaps because I know what true soul love is all about.

Soul love is sharing and soul love is caring.

It is your partner running out to the shop to get medicine because you are sick. It is him making you a sandwich when he's not hungry.

It is him running you a bath when you are tired and have nothing left to give.

It is him watching your favourite chick flick when you are fed up.

It is him thinking of your needs when you have no idea what those are. When you feel so empty and have nothing left to give.

It is him holding you and saying "I'm here for you, I love you" and that has nothing to do with flowers and grand gestures on one day of the year when we are all told to declare our love!

True soul love is the everyday little things that show they care.

# Move on With Your Life
## Like the King or Queen You Are

The Girl You Stole From Me

If you met me now you would fall for me all over again.

I am the girl that makes people laugh with her funny voice, impressions and jokes.

I am the girl that makes people happy.

I am the girl that dances at parties without the need for a drink.

I am the girl who spontaneously in the course of a normal day breaks into song.

I am the girl that is confident in herself the way she looks and what she wears.

I am the girl with a successful business.

I am the girl that doesn't care so much now about what others think.

I am the girl that sees having a kind heart is not a weakness.

I am the girl you stole from me nearly 4 years ago when you tried to break me.

That's why you despise me because I remind you of everything you're not!

Oh and If I mct you today I would weight you up in ten seconds flat and walk the other way.

I'm Not Her Anymore!

Dear Abuser, Im not her anymore. You know the submissive wife! The one that used to cry as you backed her up by the sink spitting 'You're pathetic look at you! as you shouted obscenities in her face.

I'm not her anymore! The wife who never accepted invitations from friends for fear of the narcissistic rage that you would inflict on her. Shouting if you go out we will fall out!

I'm not her anymore, the wife that used to wash her hair put it in a ponytail, never wear make up and dress down to please you!

I'm just not her anymore!

I will tell you who I am though I'm me! I'm the woman who you kept in a box!
I'm the woman that is happy!
I'm the woman who wears lovely clothes and does her hair,
I'm the woman who greets people with a cheery 'Hello' as they walk past and the woman who accepts invitations from friends.

The woman with a life she deserves and a lovely boyfriend that treats me as an equal, laughs with me, spends time with me and supports me!
I'm me and me is pretty awesome!
So abuser you're the loser!

## Move on With Your Life Like the King or Queen You Are

I loved to keep fit and tried everyday to eat healthy nutritious food. I denied myself my favourite chocolates and pastries because he called me 'fat' and criticised my figure as I dressed every morning. I stopped wearing certain clothes because he said you look like a whore. He said "That skirt is too short and those shorts are too tight, and that dress makes you look like a gypsy!". He asked "Why do you have to dress like a teenager?" So I wore baggy t-shirts and loose track suits. "How old are you now?" He sneered.

I got a fringe cut and spent hours doing my hair so I looked pretty for him only to be told "I hate that 1970's haircut on you!" or "You look really old when you wear your hair down!"
I chose my jewellery and shoes to be criticised and asked "Why are you wearing earrings and heels to go shopping?" and accused of "Meeting someone." So I wore trainers and began to tie my hair back in a ponytail and stopped wearing makeup.

I have a golden heart that loved him deeply. I was faithful and wouldn't have dreamt of cheating on him. I'm gentle and sweet and looked after him. I Ran him a bath at the end of the day, made all his favourite foods and pandered to his every whim.

I overlooked his fiery temper and tried throughout the whole relationship to keep him happy and on a level of pleasant. I clung onto the good times and the handfuls of fantastic memories we made together.

I tried everyday to go the extra mile to 'find' glimpses of that man I fell in love with.

Then I found out he was cheating on me and it all made horrible hideous sense! He begged me back on bended knees. He cried and grabbed my sleeve, and proclaimed loudly "I can't live without you!" He promised to buy me an eternity ring and promised he will do all those things he promised in the past, but this time it's different. I'm different! I've heard it all before so many times!
This time I told him "I'm done! We're done!" This time I don't respond anymore to the texts or the voicemails! I delete his number and block him out of my life.

So in the end he loses. I cry and grieve for the false mask of the man I fell in love with. I cry and grieve for the future we had planned.
At the point just as my knees hit the floor and I can't go on anymore I feel my heart stop breaking and I clamber to my feet, wiping the mascara stained tears off my face and move on with my life like the Queen I am.

Moment Of Revelation

Feeling Whole

My Recovery from Narcissistic Abuse.
Yours will be similar..
Where are you now?
Learn about NPD behaviours',
Acceptance,
Take responsibility for making bad choices,
Cut off all contact with your Nex or use the 'grey rock' method if co-parenting,
Work on your inner wounds of insecurity and lack of confidence,
Learn to LOVE YOURSELF,
At a certain point STOP beating yourself up and accept you were duped by a master manipulator.
Know that it's OK to grieve for the person you thought they were,
Tap into your passions again, and learn and grow.
Begin to live your life as it is meant to be lived.
YOU ARE FREE!
YOU ARE AWESOME!

Narcissists search for people who are strong, compassionate, and kind, and who can take care of their demands and childish needs...They don't choose a partner who can't look after them.

YOU are worthy and DESERVE a healthy and loving relationship.

YOUwerechosenbecauseyouhavealltheawesomequalitiesyourNexlacks. They will never change and never experience true love, they will always be an empty void searching for others to 'fill' their black hollow soul.

They try to take it all but they cannot take the thing they envy the most. Our ability to feel empathy and our warmth and compassion and humanness, without which they remain dead inside hunting down other live souls from which to feed.

Twisted Prince Charming

I'm sure that most of you if not all of you have heard of the Law of Attraction

It's Sunday morning here and I want to tell you a short story about a girl who unknowingly was brought up with this law. Who had a Mum and Dad who saw the positives in negative situations. A Mum and Dad that saw good all around them and helped everyone as they brought their children up alongside God and in a friendly village community.
So when that girl went out into the world at 17 she did not know evil people existed amongst us that walked and talked like us. The only evil she knew existed had Devils horns and wielded axes and murdered people. That is when she met the spawn of the devil in the form of a charming man that came disguised as everything she had hoped for. Good looking funny and positive and loved all the things she loved. He needed help after a bad childhood.
Once the love bombing was over and he had reeled her in with his 'poor me stories' he cheated and lied to her and abused her. He went on to rubbish her religion and destroy all the good positive things in her life.
Like a twisted Prince Charming he developed a shield to keep the good and virtuous away from her. She never saw that at the time. It was a fight of good against evil. She kept him out of trouble and tried to straighten her bad boy out.....

We know the story how he destroyed her taking her soul and her children's souls, but she escaped.

Gradually despite all the heartache all the good things that had surrounded her before he met her showed back up in her life. She began unknowingly to practise the law of attraction! This is when her life began to rapidly change for the better. She was bereft after losing her children, who she also brought up with this law unknowingly, but still she saw positives and practised gratitude.

Years later her brush with the devil is over ( yet it still casts a dark stalking shadow over her life and her children are still caught in the turmoil) but everyday she wakes to see positives and practices gratitude.

She unfollows negativity on social media. she censors the evil in the news. She tries not to curse and think in a negative way.

Just as she was brought up and brought her own children up. The beauty and peace and happiness and positive people keep showing up in her life. Yes if you haven't already guessed that girl is me.

Keep positive everyone life just keeps on getting better. We reap what we sow and that goes for the evil creatures too. Their Karma will come.

He Never Took Your Beautiful Soul

"Ordinary riches can be stolen, real riches cannot. In your soul are infinitely precious things that cannot be taken from you."
Oscar Wilde

Reconnecting With Love

We deal everyday with the physiological and psychological fallout but this is for all those suffering financially after being badly stung by a Narc as I was. Let's face it they will take everything they can. Anything they have touched they see as theirs.

'My wife, my children,. my dog, my house, my cars.

They don't like to share. They have to win and to be seen to be winning. They lie to the authorities and manipulate the courts, they play the 'poor me' victim and use the "but sir I left because she was mentally ill' card" They are masters at their game too.

This is a game they've been playing for a long time. They weaken our defences then they punch below the belt before we see what has happened. It's a low blow and we are winded and left reeling from the incredulous pain of it all. Thinking "What just happened?" So for all those who 'lost' to the Nex. Lost their lives,. their children, their pets, their property, their financial assets,. despite telling the truth and the toughest and longest 'fight' in court.

I'm here to tell you something. The Nex never took your most precious most beautiful asset away,. the asset they craved the most. They never took your soul, your warmth and your gentle loving heart.

They never took your capacity to love and to give compassion,. and those assets they took? Well they can be regained. Slowly over time your children will come back and you will love new pets, you will work towards new financial goals, get new jobs,. new properties. You will attract beautiful kind people into your life. and build new loving relationships.

There may not be so many pounds or dollars in the bank anymore but you will be richer than you have ever dreamed because true richness comes from FREEDOM to live your life how it was meant to be lived!

Your Beautiful soul is free!

One amazing revelation comes out of all this evil. We don't feel it at first when we're broken and on our knees but once we start healing and reconnect with love you begin to see that nothing is more powerful than love. That's why Narcs are so jealous.

Imagine not being able to feel or give love? Not being able to love your children? What a senseless existence. If you're like me working towards pitying these evil black souls this is how we get there.

Living with a Narc takes away our focus.

Depletes our energy and sucks out our soul. Now it's time to focus on your hopes and dreams. Think about what you would like to achieve in the future.

Falling Back In Love With Life

When we are healing we can still feel 'stuck.' All your feelings are normal as you are still healing from your Narc experience. Give yourself time. Focus on the future and on happy things. Work through your feelings with a counsellor if you can and only devote a small amount of time to that.

Try and wean yourself off watching narc related material and limit the reading of other people's painful stories on Narcissistic recovery forums. It is so important to refocus your time.

Read the article on our addiction to pain peptides, as in effect, if you continue to read narc related material all day every day you are reinforcing painful brain pathways by going over the same painful stories over and over again. Breathe enjoy and try and fall back in love with your life.

I promise you positive things and people will start showing up when you do this and you can gradually build the life you want.

To the Narcs
"We will live laugh and love while you fester in hate till the end of time."

No More Powerful Emotion Than Love

As we work through our emotions it's okay to feel sad, hurt angry confused, and rejected. You will mourn this loss of your relationship in a similar way to a bereavement.

Coming in and out of the stages of bereavement in a haphazard order.

Denial that you are living through this nightmare, fleeting moments of feelings that if only you could just talk to them and reason with this person,(Bargaining) after all they loved you once. Fear if you are being stalked. Then when it dawns on you that peaceful negotiations are futile then you initiate 'No contact'.

Now there is worsening fear at the narcs imminent narcissistic rage. Anger that you are being treated this way and gradually painful understanding followed by more anger, followed by a realization and pity that your Nex is actually this dysfunctional person. Then eventually acceptance to a point but you will dip back and forwards into the other stages as you heal for quite some time.

Just remember, everything in life is temporary and it takes as long as it takes. Just make a pact with yourself that you won't stay there. Never let anyone rob you of your joy and peace.

One amazing revelation comes out of all this evil. We don't feel it at first when we're broken and on our knees but once we start healing and reconnect with love you begin to see that nothing is more powerful than love.

That's why Narcs are so jealous. Imagine not being able to feel or give love? Not being able to love your children? What a senseless existence. So if you're like me working towards pitying these evil black souls this is how we get there.

"If you are crawling through the 'Shawshank Redemption Tunnel of Shit' that the narc put you in don't quit till you find yourself first crawling then swimming into clear fresh water!"

Shawshank Redemption Tunnel of Shit

You're blindly clambering through his smear campaign everyday trying to put one foot in front of the other.

When will it end? Will it ever end? Will I always be in this deep dark tunnel?

Where's this light that survivors talk about when he's destroying my reputation, taking me to court and bleeding me dry.

Taking my children and teaching them to hate me.

How am I supposed to fight this evil and come out victorious into clear water?

Good always wins right? So why is he looking so smug in another relationship? Like he's fully moved on after I divorced him?

Why does he now have the house I bought, his new girlfriends house and boats and cars while he left me so blacklisted I couldn't even get out a library book?

Why are there family pictures of him grinning with his new girlfriend cuddling my children like I never existed?

Why is he crippling me in court and I'm fighting for everything I own with him?

There's fighting dirty and there's plain evil and this is what it's like.

It's like a fight of good v evil and evil always has the edge!

I don't think I can fight this anymore! What's the point in going on? He has taken everything!

He said he would after I found out he was cheating and told him I wanted a divorce. "You will have nothing! I will take everything from you!" He

had snarled through gritted teeth!
Now he is controlling my babies! The babies I carried and nurtured have been ripped from my life.
So when does the 'good and virtuous begin to win?'
When do I begin to see karma turn things around?

Just as your knees hit the ground and you say I cannot do this anymore.
That's when things begin to slowly change.
At first, there are cracks but they're not detectable on glossy Facebook photos.
The only way now to catch a fleeting glimpse of my children is to stalk them on social media. This is what the Nex has reduced me to.

As you stumble through tears looking at your children's new family pictures, they look so happy right?
Wait, remember your happy family pictures with him in years gone by?.
Were you happy? Or were you in fact playing let's pretend faking the happy family social media for the world to see?
So these cracks how do we spot them?
Well Narcs are cunning creatures that insidiously hide the truth but over time the cracks appear and they begin the only cycle they know.

Love Bomb
Devalue
Discard

You hear snippets from well meaning people as the months and years go by that the Nex and the OW argued because she thinks he cheated and she moved out but then she went back.
You hear your children are now struggling with him too.
You see the signs of the devalue process in your alienated sons twitter updates as he tweets "I hate myself and I wish I could go in the shower and fade away." There is nothing you can do but make another false account and send another positive loving message. Does it reach him? Does he listen? You don't know.
Months go by you feel hopeless and you push the feelings aside that you will never see your children again.

You try to ignore the Nex staring in your windows and flashing his headlights and his daily lies and provocation and your world is just a daily battle of police interviews reporting stalking incidences and writing endless solicitors letters through the brain fog.

Slowly everyone is beginning to come around and see what he has done to you, see the pathogenic person you are dealing with.
You try so hard to move forwards, to step out of the drama.
You come out victorious in court after a long battle of fighting for your assets. The judge saw right through him.
Things begin to turn.
There are more reports of the Nex upsetting your children. Everyday you torture yourself with these updates looking for cracks. You don't see them.

You begin to slowly build a new life. You make new friends and meet a new loving partner and you move house away from the stalking.
Life is good but every day is tinged with sadness as again you are told your children are unhappy.

You hear nothing more until that day now two and a half years later since the beginning of this nightmare when out of the blue your son unblocks you on Facebook and tentatively messages. "I'm in such a bad place, Im so unhappy, I'm so sorry for being so horrible Mum."

As you chat you see the cracks that were there all along. Your scapegoat son is in the discard phase and the Nex is threatening to throw him out. You find out that the once love bombed OW is in the devalue stage as he tells you "He's horrible to her Mum." Your son comes back and finally good begins to win over evil. It's a long game and your daughter is still lost in the fog of lies but hang in there!

The only relationship they know is Love bomb. Devalue. Discard!

.

## 4 Years Out

### Let Go of Old You

For those that have been well and truly narcissized, let go of old you. You are still clinging on because it makes you feel safe and it's all you've known. I too was financially broken with huge legal bills divorcing the Nex.

I previously had my own house ran two cars and had a holiday every year. He broke me destroyed my credit and my business suffered as I could not work after he took the children and I fell apart but I kept trying and moving forwards and it was 2 and a half years ( spent fighting for my children and house) till I was in a happy place. It's 4 now and I have much less but I've never felt happier in my life. Keep going everyone.!

### You Have the Antidotes to This Psychological Cancer

NPD I believe is a silent pathology that creeps up on us and when it finally dawns on us the disease has already taken hold of us and our loved ones. Diseases can be fought and overcome and the knowledge and love we have are the antidotes to them. You see a lifelong mess but I see you all emerging stronger and wiser.

It takes time and great strength to stand up to abusers and your children fight the same battles.

You have the antidotes, there in your hand, and in time you hope and pray our children find their way through the fog as you did, so they can learn as we have as they are the hope and the healers of this sickness in generations to come.

### So Now it's Time

It's time to expose this destructive insidious pathogen that's eating away like a cancer through generations of families, destroying relationships with our loved ones through ignorance alone!

It's time NPD came out of hiding like some dirty secret only searched in panic on the Internet after a Narc attack.

It's time for everyone to understand and to prevent this evil disease from taking our children! It's time for educating every single person who has been affected by this pathogen!

My Splitaversary seems like a life time away now.

Joe and I have been together now just under 4 years. Tonight for no apparent reason I felt my eyes welling up with tears. I was exhausted anyway but something had triggered me. Holding Joe's hand watching TV cuddled up as he tickled my feet was becoming a wonderful normal 'ahhh' moment at the end of every tiring day.

Kind of like the sheer deliciousness of getting into a warm bubbly bath.

The tears came when I thought about my 15 year relationship with the Narc. The revelation that he in fact had never touched me in a non sexual way.

He held my hand and kissed me in public as a sign of ownership. He held my hand after we were married in the car on the way to the reception.

Thereafter he would grope me in public and call me a prude if I stopped him. It was as if my body became his property.

I remember after a hugely stressful day in the hospital begging him to cuddle me just yearning for an emotional connection. Of course there was none, but little did I understand back then he was dead behind those eyes. That behind that self serving mask that only wanted sexual gratification as and when he needed it there was an empty void of nothingness.

Then I dry my eyes and Joe says "What's wrong Hun?" I squeeze his hand and say "Nothing I'm fine."

In that instance warm and snuggled up to Joe and as this book draws to a close I see now that I deserve to be loved.

If I can navigate down the 'Shawshank Redemption Tunnel of Shit' and find clear water then I know there is a beautiful life waiting for each and everyone of you once you distance yourself from negativity.

Pity Their Black Soul

So we are nearing the end of my journey and I want to leave you all with these thoughts. Just Imagine inwardly hating yourself, knowing you were rotten to the core to the extent that you had to develop a false persona.

A charming do anything for anyone mask manufactured for others so you could dupe them to get your needs met.

If your real self was revealed you would have no friends.

You must pretend to the end of your days.

This is a narcissist! Pity their black soul and existence on this earth!

## Until You Reconnect With Love Nothing Changes

It's easy to get sucked into hate. Hate towards the Nex for taking your babies, hate at the corrupt archaic court system that has failed so many of us, and hate towards the world.

Until we reconnect with love nothing changes, so work through your hate and your pain because ultimately love is the only thing that matters and the only way to change the world is to love one another.

## Acknowledging the Box Full of Darkness as a Gift

I know recovery is really hard. I know that empty lost feeling is indescribably painful, almost like we don't belong anymore, anywhere.

I know how it feels when we wake and realise yes the rumours were true all the good I saw in the Nex was a fiction. A huge fat lie so they could rinse me financially and emotionally while hiding their true nature and hidden agenda behind our good reputation. In my case as a wife, mother and nurse while duping others into the belief he is a good person.

I know he used me as a smokescreen of his vile lies and cheating.

We must now acknowledge this 'box full of darkness' this life experience gave us as a gift. Let us not think of the things the Nex took from us.

Let us consider the things this experience gave us that we don't fully see yet.

It gave us knowledge and the clarity to see each and every person on this earth in a different light.

It gave us a guarded sense of ensuring that anyone who comes into our life now is a good person. It taught us who is toxic and needs to be kept at arms length so they cannot harm us.

We learned that we were too trusting and must now be more cautious.

It taught us also we are important and worthy of love.

It taught us to fix our inner wounds and to learn to love ourselves.

It taught us to stop putting ourselves last.

Look around you and see the most important thing that is happening.

Little by little day by day as you distance yourself from the toxic Nex and you block them from your life.

Look at the new positive good people and opportunities that can now reach you.

It won't happen overnight. There will be so much pain and brokenness to work through and many lonely nights and days.

Days where you feel so empty and lost there is no point in anything, but work through that pain and gather that knowledge.

An amazing beautiful life will come right at that point where you become a butterfly. That is what you are working towards, the day when you look back and smile and say "Thank you for this knowledge I would never go back!"

That is when you can spread your wings and fly.

You are FREE!

# Testimonials

Lisa
Tammy was born to love and help people. She is an angelic gift to those who need her. She changes lives and helps the hurt to heal. She was there for me at my darkest of days, when living was harder than beating the narcissist at their sick games. There are no better words than simply thank you.

Susan
I believe I was one of the first members for this group and a complete basket case! I have posted off and on here and have watched others progress in healing. I still have healing to do as I have not been able to find a therapist in my area who is knowledgeable in victims of narc abuse enough to help me. I felt like I was educating those whom were suppose to educate me! I have learned so much from this group that I can tell you has been life saving for me! After suffering 35 yrs of Narculas abuse and suffering from spinal stenosis with mylopathy and fibromyalgia on top of major reoccurring depression that I was diagnosed with 5 yrs into my relationship with Narcula, I had no will to live! This group has helped change it around and Tamsin is an angel! I now have a care coordinator from my medical group looking for a therapist versed enough to counsel me. I pray they do as when my insurance company tried, they failed. I want to thank you Tammy for the guidance and support you have given me! Hugs to you and prayers too!

Ed
Get this woman a degree in counselling based on life experience.

Donna
I am quite new to this site also. I feel like I was going insane and like some others said did not even identify what narc behaviour was . I just always blamed myself. Although I'm still dealing with My Nex and he is still trying to destroy my soul this site and Tammy has been a god send. Thank you so much to everyone I feel like everyone is holding my hand as I try and heal.

Silver

I'm still at the beginning of accepting what has happened to me for 20 yrs. I've never been able to identify the behaviour and genuinely kept seeing my GP and asking if I was going mad. I am very grateful to Tammy for this group. I don't feel alone or quite so stupid

Elizabeth

I haven't been here very long, but I have had the opportunity to talk to Tammy and she shed some light on things I just couldn't grasp. I truly appreciate what you have done for me, but what speaks volumes of her character is what I saw yesterday. There was a post yesterday morning from a woman whose name I don't remember that felt ready to start out on her own because of the help she got here during the last two years. That says it all.

Lea

You know with our chats how much more I understand of what my teenager is going through. Thank you so much for your time & understanding.

Carrie

This group has been pivotal in my healing! I don't know what I would have done without it and I am so extremely grateful for Tammy!!

Louise

Tammy found me, I was real wary at first because some other sites I was on and was "stalked their, she has created a fantastic safe haven for all of us I have made a few friends from here too without her creating this I would have never met everyone and never had the opportunity to talk with her and help me move on, and for this I am grateful. Thank you Tammy.

Misty

Thank you Tammy for helping me get off the Narc merry go round. Without you & my butterfly friends I would be in a straight jacket by now!

April
Your an answer to prayer. I don't feel alone or doubt my gut, which I have been doing. Thank you

Chrissie
Thank you for recognizing my fragility and 'Snatching', Me up and out of a group that I wasn't quite ready for - I've never had a tough skin and your group is kinder and gentler and geared towards us newbie's...I'll be forever grateful

Corrine
.'I remember going through this process very well and gave chance after chance my boss at work said to me you will get to a point where you will just say enough is enough and I got there, each time he was abusive to me I found myself distancing me self a little more each time until I just used to look at him in disgust like Tammy says there are no wrongs or rights and you will know when you are ready I spend 7 years with everyone I knew telling me to leave him but it's harder than they know and only people who have experienced it can understand but you will get there and then wonder why it took you so long. You deserve happiness and it is out there I never believed it and never knew how sad I was before its just the unknown on the other side that's scary after all the controlling, Tammy was my rock through my escape and she helped me so much when she was going through the same if not worst than me. I was lucky not to have children with mine when I finally saw the light. I blocked him totally out of my life and anyone who had anything to do with him.
Myriah

She is the reason I am alive today. She pulled me out of deep depression, made me get out of bed, take a shower, and live life again. I am forever grateful.

Christin
The ladies and gents on this page (and tonnes of pain and prayer) I was able to walk away FINALLY and have been free over one year now! I don't even look the same. My parents have me back and my friends slowly are getting me back. I feel amazing!
Jenny

Tammy has been there for my journey, too! I come from a very small town and my Narcopath had turned everyone he could against me. Life long friends that are no more, his whole family and even my own family for a time....but I got them back! Tammy came into my life at the perfect time and helped me realize that it wasn't me and that the road to freedom is a difficult one but we can do it one day at a time. Seek out positive energy in your transition but also be aware that negative energy is still everywhere and we must learn to protect ourselves from it!

Hayley
You won't believe anyone when they tell you that as soon as he is truly gone every day you will feel yourself return and you will be amazed. Because you are lost right now. Only because you forgot yourself for a bit. You will be back and you will paint your nails and massage your feet and remember your worth and the broken bits will melt softly back together. I was at your stage a couple of weeks ago and with my total commitment to staying away I feel better every day.
I had to hit the bottom first. Love n light to you.

Barbara
Your story gives me hope to cling to and I'm clinging to it. I realize how lucky I am to have been found and brought to this group. I was out there in outer space spiralling around not knowing what next step to take and then I was accepted into this group and in the short time I've been here is where real healing has begun.. I now know there is a way to freedom. It's within my reach. I just need to keep going forward. Everyone here are wonderful people that got caught in the same craziness as I. Being in this group has helped in many ways but one Important thing is that I don't feel as alone anymore. Isn't that the worst feeling being around trusted friends and family and not being able to convince them of the severity of the situation. This group offers everything that goes towards healing. It offers hope, love, beauty, advice and other tools to be used for healing, and friendship. I know I will never take this group for granted. I believe a higher power led me to it. Thanks Tammy for all the work and time you take to manage this group. Are you sure you're not an angel in disguise?

71504471R00189

Made in the USA
Middletown, DE
25 April 2018